高职高专旅游与酒店管理类教学改革系列规划教材

酒店服务英语

杨珍 齐超 主编

ENGLISH FOR HOTEL SERVICES

化学工业出版社
·北京·

本书是高职高专旅游与酒店管理类教学改革系列规划教材之一,共分为八章,基本涵盖了酒店管理和服务的所有领域,如礼貌用语、前台服务、客房服务、西餐服务、中餐服务、酒吧服务、酒店服务以及其他服务等,每章包括阅读短文、对话、情景模拟和课后练习等内容。本教材所有内容均与酒店服务的实际有紧密的联系,学生在学习酒店各岗位实用英语的同时,也能了解酒店对客服务的全过程。本书可作为高等院校酒店管理和旅游类专业教材,也可作为相关从业者自学参考用书。

图书在版编目(CIP)数据

酒店服务英语 / 杨珍,齐超主编 . —北京:化学工业
出版社,2018.12(2024.8 重印)
ISBN 978-7-122-33342-1

Ⅰ.①酒… Ⅱ.①杨…②齐… Ⅲ.①饭店 - 商业
服务 - 英语 - 高等职业教育 - 教材 Ⅳ.①F719.2

中国版本图书馆CIP数据核字(2018)第270389号

责任编辑:王 可 蔡洪伟 于 卉 装帧设计:张 辉
责任校对:宋 玮

出版发行:化学工业出版社(北京市东城区青年湖南街 13 号 邮政编码 100011)
印 装:北京盛通数码印刷有限公司
787mm×1092mm 1/16 印张 19 字数 480 千字 2024 年 8 月北京第 1 版第 2 次印刷

购书咨询:010-64518888 售后服务:010-64518899
网 址:http://www.cip.com.cn
凡购买本书,如有缺损质量问题,本社销售中心负责调换。

定 价:48.00 元

编写人员名单

主　编：杨　珍　齐　超

副主编：姚　倩　侯　铂　胡慧敏

参　编：崔怀荣　崔　健　胡顺利　杨凤岐　王　丹

前 言

日益发展的中国经济和大量境外商务旅客、休闲游客的涌入，以及大量外资跨国酒店管理集团在华投资的增加，对我国高端酒店的服务提出了新的要求，对我国酒店行业从业人员的专业技能、管理能力和外语沟通能力也提出了更高的要求。高素质酒店英语专业服务与管理人才供不应求已成为我国大力发展旅游业急需解决的问题之一。在全球一体化的今天，英语在世界文化交流和经济交往中扮演着重要的角色，在酒店行业发挥着举足轻重的作用，许多酒店更以"具备较高的酒店英语服务技能"作为选择人才的一个重要考核指标。

《酒店服务英语》教材是以酒店管理专业教学标准为基础，以学生就业为导向、以职业岗位需求为核心、以工作任务为主线、以操作过程为载体的应用型课程体系。《酒店服务英语》是在深入酒店企业实践、调研和认真听取酒店行业专家建议的基础上，依托酒店服务核心岗位的职责、操作流程和技能，结合编写者多年探索、实践、积淀的酒店管理专业实用英语的教学与培训经验，策划编写而成。本书具有以下特点。

内容完善。本书涵盖了星级酒店的前厅服务（Front Desk Service）、客房服务（Housekeeping Service）、西餐服务（Western Food Service）、中餐服务（Chinese Food Service）、酒吧服务（Bar Service）、综合服务（Comprehensive service）、其他服务（Other Service）等全部核心部门的服务环节，重点突出，范围广泛。

形式新颖。每课内容从主要解决的任务出发，包括学习目标（Objectives）、课前导入（Warming Up）、情景对话（Dialogues）、词汇（Vocabulary）、重点句型（Useful Expressions）、角色扮演（Practices）、精选练习（Exercises）、挑战与应对（Challenges and Solutions）、知识拓展（Knowledge Link），形式丰富多样，融教、学、思、练、做为一体。正文内容中穿插练习与拓展阅读，以二维码形式呈现，学生可以扫码拓展学习，调动学生学习的积极性。

简单实用。本书立足于高职学生酒店管理专业，以星级酒店各岗位工作职能为出发点，本着实用为主、够用为度的原则，以为高职酒店管理专业培养适应酒店岗位需求的人才为目标，为学生提供切合实际的语言学习、培训和提高的素材，具有很强的实用性。

形象生动。结合星级酒店实际情况，紧密联系工作岗位要求和时代发展节奏，书中设置的情景对话真实具体，并具有代表性和创新性。

详略得当。章节安排上，各部分内容紧密结合，环环相扣，既有一定的逻辑关系，又有相对的独立性。主要采用对话的形式，让学生掌握日常服务英语，练习环节简单易懂，便于学生自主学习。

《酒店服务英语》由天津海运职业学院杨珍、黑龙江旅游职业技术学院齐超担任主编。天津海运职业学院姚茜、天津城市职业学院侯铂、天津海运职业学院胡慧敏担任副主编。天津海运职业学院崔怀荣、崔建、胡顺利，天津外国语大学杨凤岐，延安职业技术学院王丹参与编写。具体编写分工如下：杨珍进行总体方案策划、具体组织、内容校对和统稿。Chapter 1、Chapter 2由崔怀荣、齐超、侯铂编写，Chapter 3由崔怀荣、胡顺利编写，Chapter 4、Chapter 7由胡慧敏、姚茜、齐超编写，Chapter 5、Chapter 8由崔建、侯铂、王丹编写，Chapter 6、Appendix由杨珍、杨凤岐编写。

在编写过程中，我们参考了部分酒店服务英语方面的最新书刊资料及网络资料，并得到了酒店行业专家教授的具体指导，在此特别致以衷心的感谢。编者衷心希望这本书能够帮助高职学生学习酒店管理专业打下良好的英语基础，提高英语服务技能，做高技能、高素质的酒店从业人才。由于编写时间紧，书中难免存在不足之处，敬请酒店专业的专家学者、高等职业教育界的同仁和广大学子、读者给予批评指正。

编　者

2018年6月

目　录

Chapter 1

Courtesy English

Objectives

➤ To help the students master useful expressions and sentences about courtesy English.
➤ To help the students familiar with the departments and positions of hotel.
➤ To help the students make some dialogues about courtesy English.

Warming Up

1. Look at the following pictures and fill in the blanksaccording to the corresponding description.

_____ is known as the general service counter or called the reception desk and responsible for selling hotel product and service, organizing reception and business scheduling, which is a comprehensive service department.

The _____ Department is the performing of necessary housework, including making or changing beds, dusting furniture, sweeping or cleaning floors and carpets, washing bathrooms, replacing towels and washcloths, and supplying the rooms with the necessary items, etc.

The _____ Department is usually equipped with proper size of small hall, Chinese and western restaurants, coffee shops and bars, is one of the most important department in hotel and provide breakfast, lunch and dinner for guests.

The _____ Department is responsible for the regular operation of the hotel and the safety of the hotel staff and guests and their properties.

The _____ Department maintains the property's structure and grounds as well as electrical and mechanical equipment.

The _____ Department is a general department to satisfy the guests needs of recreation and fitness, which has swimming pools, gym, ballroom, night club, spa, etc.

M1-1 Warming Up

Dialogues

Key sentences:

> Good afternoon. Long Ding Hotel May I help you?
> Could you give me your passport and fill in this form?
> Is there anything breakable or valuable in your bag?
> May I put your luggage here?
> If you need any help, please call up front desk.

Pre-questions:

1. Do you know which department in hotel is responsible for help guest book a room?
2. Do you know who in hotel is responsible for handling luggage for guests?
3. What should the hotel staff say to guests when they help guest check-in?

Dialogue 1

Operator:	Good afternoon. Long Ding Hotel May I help you?
Guest:	Good afternoon. I'd like to reserve a room in your hotel.
Operator:	Wait a moment, please, madam. I'll put you through.
Guest:	Okay, thank you.
Receptionist:	Room reservation. May I help you?
Guest:	Yes, I want to book a single room in your hotel.
Receptionist:	For which date, please?
Guest:	From April 1st to 3rd.

Receptionist:	For how many people? For which date, please?
Guest:	Just me.
Receptionist:	Could you please hold the line? I'll check our room availability for those days... Thank you for your waiting. We have a single room and it is 300yuan per night.
Guest:	Well, I'll take it.
Receptionist:	May I have your name and telephone number, sir?
Guest:	Yes, it's John Smith. Then number is 06-342-3344.
Receptionist:	Okay, Mr. Smith. You have booked a single room form April 1st to 3rd. Is that right?
Guest:	That's right.
Receptionist:	Thank you. We look forward to your coming.

Dialogue 2

Receptionist:	Good afternoon, Madam. Welcome to our hotel.
Guest:	Good afternoon. I have book a family suite in your hotel.
Receptionist:	Okay, madam. What's your name, please?
Guest:	It's Mrs. Black.
Receptionist:	Let me check. Oh, it's here. Your room number is 321. Here is your room card and breakfast coupon.
Guest:	Thank you.
Receptionist:	Could you give me your passport and fill in this form?
Guest:	Ok... Here you are.
Receptionist:	Okay, let me check, your passport number, signature. It's right. The bellman will take your luggage and show you to your room.
Guest:	Thank you.
Receptionist:	You are welcome. I hope you enjoy your stay with us.

Dialogue 3

Bellman:	Good afternoon, sir. Welcome to our hotel. I'll show you to your room. You have one luggage, right?
Guest:	Yes, that's right.
Repairman:	Is there anything breakable or valuable in your bag?
Guest:	No, just some clothes.
Repairman:	Okay. This way, please.
Repairman:	This is your room, sir. May I have your key?
Guest:	Okay, here you are.
Repairman:	After you, sir. May I put your luggage here?
Guest:	Of course.
Repairman:	If you need any help, please call up front desk. The extension number for front desk is 8.
Guest:	Okay. Thank you for yourinformation.

Vocabulary

reserve[rɪˈzɜːv]   v. 预定

put through   v. 接通

single room   n.单人间

hold   v. 持有，持续

availability[ə,veɪləˈbɪləti]   n.可用性

telephone number   n. 电话号码

family suite   n. 家庭套房

room card   n. 房卡

coupon[ˈkuːpɒn]   n. 赠券

passport   n. 护照

fill in   v. 填写

signature[ˈsɪɡnətʃə]   n. 签名

luggage[ˈlʌɡɪdʒ]   n. 行李

breakable[ˈbreɪkəb(ə)l]   adj. 易碎的

valuable[ˈvæljʊəb(ə)l]   adj.有价值的

extension number   n. 分机号码

information   n. 信息

Useful Expressions

Welcome and greeting

1. Good morning/noon/afternoon/evening, Sir/Madam! May/Can I help you?

早上好/中午好/下午好/晚上好，请问我能为您服务吗？

2. How do you do? (— How do you do?)

您好！

3. Nice/Glad to meet (see) you!

很高兴见到您！

4. It's nice to meet you again, Mr.××.

太好了，××先生,再次见到您。

5. Welcome to our hotel!

欢迎光临我们酒店！

6. Have a good time!

祝您在酒店过得愉快！

7. We wish you a pleasant stay in our hotel.

愿您在我们饭店过得愉快。

8. Have a good rest.

祝您休息好。

9. Thank you for staying in our hotel.

感谢您在我们饭店下榻。

10. Please enjoy your stay.

祝您住宿愉快。

Telephone Etiquette

1. Wait a moment, please.

对不起，请稍等。

2. Sorry, he is not in at the moment.

对不起，他暂时不在。

3. I beg your pardon?

对不起（我听不大清楚）。

4. Could you speak a little slower, please?

请稍微讲慢一点。

5. I'll switch you to Room 1120.

我马上给您接1120房间。

6. Who is speaking/that, please?

请问您是哪位？（电话用语）

7. Wait a moment, please.

对不起，请稍等。

Congratulation

1. Congratulations!

祝贺您！

2. Happy birthday!

生日快乐！

3. Happy New Year!

新年快乐！

4. Merry Christmas!

圣诞快乐！

5. Have a nice holiday!

节日快乐！

6. Wish you every success!

祝您成功！

Appreciation

1. Thank you!

谢谢！

2. It is very kind of you! It doesn't matter.

谢谢，您真客气！

3. You are welcome! /Not at all.

不用谢！

4. It is my pleasure!

非常高兴为您服务！

5. I am at your service!

我随时愿为您服务！

6. That is all right.

没关系。

Guide

1. This way, please.

这边请。

2. Go ahead,and turn left/right.

向前走，然后往左 / 右边拐。

3. It is on the second floor.

在二楼。

4. It is next to...

它紧靠着……

5. It is opposite the...

它在……对面

6. I will take you there.

我带您去。

7. Go upstairs/downstairs to the third floor.

请上楼，走到三楼。

8. You first, please.

您先，请。

9. I will take you there.

我带您去。

10. Take the lift to the third floor.

乘电梯到三楼。

Apology

1. I'm awfully/very sorry, sir.

非常对不起，先生。

2. Sorry to keep you waiting.

对不起，让您久等了。

3. I'm awfully/very sorry for my carelessness.

对于我的粗心大意我非常抱歉。

4. I am very sorry for the inconvenience.

很抱歉造成您的不便。

5. I would like to apologize for the mistake.

为这个错误我深致歉意。

6. I'm terribly sorry. It's my fault.

非常抱歉，那是我的过错。

7. Sorry to interrupt you.

对不起，打扰了。

Goodbye

1. Goodbye/See you later.

再见。

2. Good night/dream.

晚安。

3. Thank you for staying in our hotel.

感谢您在我们饭店下榻。

4. Have a good/nice trip. /time. / Wish you a pleasant journey.

旅途愉快。

5. Goodbye and thanks for coming.

再见，多谢光临。

6. Goodbye and hope to see you again.

再见，欢迎下次光临。

M1-2　Practice

Exercises

1. Questions and Answers

(1) What departments of hotel do you know?

(2) What positions in hotel do you know?

(3) What qualities should a hotel staff have?

2. Match the words or expressions in Column A with their Chinese equivalents in Column B.

A	B
(1) reserve	a. 接通
(2) put through	b. 可用性
(3) ID card	c. 护照
(4) availability	d. 签名
(5) passport	e. 预定
(6) extension number	f. 身份证
(7) signature	g. 易碎的
(8) luggage	h. 分机号码
(9) breakable	i. 有价值的
(10) valuable	j. 行李

3. Match the sentences in Column A with their corresponding answers in Column B.

1. Excuse me, where is the washroom?	a. You are welcome.
2. Thank you for your help.	b. Sure, wait a moment, please.
3. You are so kind.	c. Not at all. I just do my part.
4. Could you bring me a cup, please?	d. Have a nice day.
5. Goodbye.	e. Follow me, please.

4. Read the passage and decide if the statements are true (T) or false (F).

A general manager typically assumes the top spot in the organizational structure of a hotel. For smaller establishments, this could be the owner. This is the person ultimately responsible when things go well and when they go wrong.

Under the top managers are a few or a group of departmental managers, depending on the size and success of the establishment. One may handle the overnight shift, another may be a chef in charge of the kitchen and room service. A trusted maid may be placed in charge of the housekeeping operations, and the front desk attendant with the most experience may manage other similar employees.

Under all of the managers in the organizational structure of a hotel are the rest of the employees, who deal on a more direct basis with the customers and their needs. These are the cashiers, waiters, cooks, busboys, housekeepers, valets, pool attendants, maintenance workers, activities directors and gophers. Each of these employees is tasked with helping to create an environment of memorable service at the hotel. If organized correctly, this should gain these employees respect and recognition from all the managers stationed above them.

Exercises:

(1) A general manager typically holds the highest position in in the organizational structure of a hotel. (   )

(2) For smaller hotels, a general manager could be the owner. (   )

(3) Under the top managers are directly cashiers, waiters, cooks, busboys, housekeepers,

valets, etc. (　　)

(4) Generally, a trusted maid may be placed in charge of the housekeeping operations. (　　)

(5) All the managers should gain respect and recognition from the employee below them. (　　)

Challenges and Solutions

1. If you were a bellman, you saw a guest just arrive, what should you do?

Solutions:

2. If you were a bellman and helped guests handle luggage, when the guests said thank you, what should you say?

Solutions:

3. If a guest got lost in your hotel, what should you do?

Solutions:

4. If a guest lost his wallet in the hotel, what should you do?

Solutions:

5. If a guest made a call to you, but he spoke too fast, what should you do?

Solutions:

6. If a guest complained that the room's air conditioner did not work, what should you do?

Solution:

7. If a guest was angry with you, what should you do?

Solutions:

M1-3　Knowledge Link

M1-4　Key to Exercises

Chapter 2

Front Desk Service

Lesson One   Reservation

Objectives

➢ To help the students master useful expressions and sentences about room reservation.
➢ To help the students familiar with procedure of room reservation.
➢ To help the students make some dialogues about room reservation.

Warming Up

1. Look at the following pictures and fill in the blanks according to the corresponding description.

_____ is the first department which has the first contact with the guests and helps guests reserve rooms.

_____ arethe staff who help guests make room reservation.

_____ is usually the tool people use to make room reservation.

_____ is a kind of form which front desk staff need to fill in carefully when guests make room reservations.

M2-1   Warming Up

Dialogues

Key sentences:

➢ For which date, please?

➢ How many nights will you be staying with us, please?

➢ What kind of room would you prefer?

➢ What time do you expect to arrive?

➢ Would you like me to put you on our waiting list and call you when we have a cancellation?

Pre-questions:

1. Have you ever reserved a room in a hotel? How?

2. When you reserve a room in a hotel, what information should you provide for the hotel?

3. If the hotel doesn't have your room type, what will you do?

Dialogue 1

Reservationist:	Good morning. Long Yuan hotel. May I help you?
Guest:	Yes, I' d like to reserve a room at your hotel.
Reservationist:	Okay, madam. For which date, please?
Guest:	From April 5th.
Reservationist:	How many nights will you be staying with us, please?
Guest:	For four nights.
Reservationist:	How many guests will be there be in your party?
Guest:	Three, my parents and myself.
Reservationist:	All right, madam. What kind of room would you prefer?
Guest:	One single room and a double room, please.
Reservationist:	Please wait a moment as I check our room availability for those days... Sorry to have kept you waiting, madam. We have a double room at 1200 yuan and a single room at 800 yuan per night. Shall I make the reservation for you?
Guest:	Yes, that will be fine. Thank you.
Reservationist:	May I have your name and telephone number?
Guest:	Of course. My name is Mary Brown and my telephone number is 0037-3254678.
Reservationist:	Your name is Mary brown and your telephone number is 0037-3254678. Is that right?
Guest:	Yes, it is.
Reservationist:	What time do you expect to arrive?
Guest:	Oh, about 5 p.m.
Reservationist:	Okay, madam. Let me confirm your reservation. A double room at 1200 yuan and a single room at 800 yuan per night for four nights from April 5th to April 9th. My name is Alice and we look forward to seeing you in April.

Dialogue 2

Reservationist:	Good morning. Great Wall hotel. How may I help you today?

Guest:	Yes. I'm a guide from Hongxiang Travel Agency. I want to book some room at your hotel from October 1st to October 7th.
Reservationist:	Could you tell me how many people in your group?
Guest:	Twenty-five persons.
Reservationist:	What kind of room would you like?
Guest:	One single room and twelve twin rooms, please.
Reservationist:	Please give me a moment. Let me check if we have enough rooms for those days... Thank you for waiting. I can make the reservation for you and we offer you 10% discount for group reservation.
Guest:	That will be fine. Thank you.
Reservationist:	Would you like to guarantee the rooms?
Guest:	Yes. How can I do that?
Reservationist:	You may prepay, use a credit card or traveler's check.
Guest:	I will send you a traveler's check soon.
Reservationist:	May I have your name and telephone number?
Guest:	Li Ming, 2867456.
Reservationist:	Okay, Li Ming, 2867456. One single room and ten twin rooms for seven nights from October 1st to October 7th. My name is Janie and we look forward to seeing you.

Dialogue 3

Reservationist:	Good morning. Room reservation. Can I help you?
Guest:	Yes, I'd like to reserve a Honeymoon Roomat your hotel in July 7th.
Reservationist:	Okay, sir. Wait a moment, please. Sorry, sir. Our Honeymoon Rooms have been fully reserved on that date. Would you mind changing a room?
Guest:	Oh, it is our wedding anniversary on that day. I want to give a surprise to my wife. Could you recommend another hotel that won't be full for me?
Reservationist:	Sorry, sir. We don't have any information about other hotel's room availability. Would you like me to put you on our waiting list and call you when we have a cancellation?
Guest:	Yes, please.
Reservationist:	May I have your name?
Guest:	My name is William Jefferson.
Reservationist:	And your telephone number?
Guest:	It is 08-67823645
Reservationist:	Okay, William Jefferson, 08-67823645. We will call you as soon as we have a Honeymoon Room. Good-bye.
Guest:	Good-bye.

Vocabulary

reserve[rɪ'zɜːv] *v.* 预订
book *v.* 预定

single room *n.* 单人间
double room *n.* 双人间

availability [ə,velə'bɪləti]   *n.* 可用性，可得性

confirm [kən'fɜ:m]   *vt.* 确认；确定

discount[dɪs'kaʊnt]   *n.* 折扣，贴现率 *vt.* 打折扣；将……贴现

guarantee[,gærən'ti]   *n.* 保证；担保   *vt.* 保证；担保

prepay[pri'pe]   *vt.* 预付；提前缴纳

credit card   *n.* 信用卡

traveler's check   *n.* 旅行支票

twin room   *n.* 双床房

Honeymoon Room   *n.* 蜜月房

wedding anniversary [,ænɪ'vɜ:səri]   *n.* 结婚纪念日

recommend ['rɛkə'mɛnd]   *vi.* 推荐；建议

waiting list   *n.* 等候名单

cancellation [,kænsə'leʃən]   *n.* 取消；删除

cancel   *vt.* 取消；删去

Useful Expressions

1. Good morning. Long Yuan hotel. May I help you?

您好，龙苑酒店，请问有什么可以帮您吗？

2. For which date, please?

请问哪天？

3. How many nights will you be staying with us, please?

请问您要住几天？

4. How many guests will be there be in your party?

你们一行有多少人？

5. What kind of room would you prefer?

您想要什么房型？

6. Please wait a moment as I check our room availability for those days.

请稍等，我要查查那几天有没有空房间。

7. Sorry to have kept you waiting, madam.

很抱歉，女士，让您久等了。

8. Shall I make the reservation for you?

我可以为你预订吗？

9. May I have your name and telephone number?

请问您的姓名和电话号码？

10. What time do you expect to arrive?

您什么时候到？

11. Let me confirm your reservation. A double room at 1200 yuan and a single room at 800 yuan per night for four nights from April 5th to April 9th.

跟您确认一下，一间双人房，每晚1200元，一间单人房，每晚800元，4月5日到4月9日共4晚。

12. We look forward to seeing you.

我们期待您的光临。

13. Let me check if we have enough rooms for those days.

让我来检查一下那几天是否有足够的房间。

14. We offer you 10% discount for group reservation.

团体预定可以享受10%的优惠。

15. Would you like to guarantee the rooms?

您想保证订房吗？

M2-2　Practice

Exercises

1. Questions and Answers

(1) Which department in hotel is responsible for room reservation?

(2) Do you think this department is important? Why?

(3) What information should reservationist know about guests when they make room reservation for guests?

2. Match the words or expressions in Column A with their Chinese equivalents in Column B.

A	B
(1) recommend	a. 等候名单
(2) credit card	b. 账单
(3) coupon	c. 预付
(4) prepay	d. 打折
(5) confirm	e. 信用卡
(6) bill	f. 取消
(7) cancel	g. 优惠券
(8) waiting list	h. 推荐
(9) traveler's check	i. 确认
(10) discount	j. 旅行支票

3. Choose the best English translation for each sentence.

(1) 您哪天入住？（　　）

A. Would you like to live in?　　B. Which day would you like to live in?

C. Which day will you arrive?　　D. What time will you arrive?

(2) 您想住几晚？（　　）

A. Do you want to live in our hotel?　　B. How many nights will you be staying with us, please?

C. You live here for how many days!　　D. When do you want to check in?

(3) 您一行几人？（　　）

A. How many guests will be there in your party?

B. Do you have other partners?

C. How many people do you want to bring?.

D. How many people, one, two, three?

(4) 您想住什么房型？（　　）

A. What kind of room do you have?　　B. What kind of room would you prefer?

C. What kind of room in your hotel?　　D. Do you want to live in single room?

(5) 您什么时候到？（　　）

A. What time do you expect to arrive?　　B. When will you come here?

C. Which day do you come here?　　D. Do you come here today?

4. Read the passage and decide if the statements are true (T) or false (F).

Hotel is an important part in the whole process of business and leisure travel, while the room reservation is usually the first connection between guests and the hotel. Room reservations can be made face to face over the phone, by guests themselves or a third party. Letters, which used to be a popular way to make reservations, are now out of date, and are being gradually replaced by some prompter ways, like e-mails or faxes, which are considered much more secure. Room reservations are usually operated by the Front Desk (the reception), the Room Reservation Department or Sales Department. Guests can choose what they need or favor, and should be informed of the price, standard, the floor, the window view, etc. Price is relatively higher in the peak season and discount is usually found in the slack season. Once a room reservation is requested, the clerk should first check the room availability for the required days; if available, a reservation form is made, with all relevant information taken down. Confirmation is necessary and required. Room reservations can be changed or cancelled with advanced notification. With the development of the internet, there is a tendency to build a network connecting hotels, airlines as well as some travel agencies, so that guests can arrange their travel well at one place of the whole net.

Exercises:

(1) Room reservation is usually the first connection between guests and the hotel. (　　)

(2) Room reservation can only be made face to face over the phone. (　　)

(3) Room reservations are usually operated by the Front Desk. (　　)

(4) Price is relatively lower in the peak season. (　　)

(5) After the room reservation is made, it cannot be changed or cancelled. (　　)

Challenges and Solutions

1. What steps are there in accepting room reservation?

Solutions:

2. What kind of guests can be offered a discount from the hotel?

Solutions:

3. If your hotel doesn't have the rooms guests like, what will you do?

Solutions:

4. If a guest wants to book a room in your hotel, but your hotel is fully booked, what will you do?

Solutions:

5. How do you receive a group reservation?

Solutions:

6. What is the difference between room reservation and restaurant reservation?

Solution:

7. What do you think reservationists should be like?

Solutions:

M2-3　Knowledge Link

M2-4　Key to Exercises

Lesson Two   Check-in Service

Objectives

> To help the students master useful expressions and sentences about check-in service.
> To help the students familiar with procedure of check-in service.
> To help the students make some dialogues about check-in service.

Warming Up

1. Look at the following pictures and fill in the blanks according to the corresponding description.

_____ have the first face-to face contact with the guests and help guests register and check in.

_____ is a card which guests use to open the door.

_____ is an important document used by guests when they check in.

_____ is a kind of form which front desk staff need to fill in carefully when guests check in.

M2-5   Warming Up

Dialogues

Key sentences:

➢ Have you made a reservation before?

➢ Would you please fill out this registration form?

➢ You forget to fill in the date of departure. May I fill it in for you?

➢ May I see your passport, please?

➢ Is there any change in your schedule?

Pre-questions:

1. Have you ever checked-in a hotel? How?

2. What kind of document does a guest need to check in a hotel?

3. If a guest doesn't make a reservation in advance, can he check in a hotel?

Dialogue 1

Receptionist:	Good morning, madam. Can I help you?
Guest:	Good morning, I want a standard single room, please.
Receptionist:	Have you made a reservation before?
Guest:	No, I haven't.
Receptionist:	How long do you want to stay?
Guest:	Three days.
Receptionist:	Let me check. Oh, yes. I can offeryou a standard single room. It is 100yuan per night.
Guest:	Okay, thank you.
Receptionist:	May I see your ID card?
Guest:	Of course. Here you are.
Receptionist:	Thank you. Madam. Could you fill inthis form, please?
Guest:	Yes. Here it is.
Receptionist:	Thank you. Here is your key. It's Room 808 on the third floor.
Guest:	Thank you very much.
Receptionist:	You are welcome. Have a nice day.

Dialogue 2

Receptionist:	Good afternoon, sir. Welcome to our hotel. May I help you?
Guest:	Yes. I booked a room two weeks ago.
Receptionist:	May I have your name please, sir?
Guest:	John Smith.
Receptionist:	Just a moment, sir. I need to look through our list. Yes, we do have a reservation for you, Mr. Smith. A balcony room with 500 Yuan RMB as a deposit. Is that correct?
Guest:	Yes, it is.
Receptionist:	Would you please fill out this registration form?
Guest:	What should I fill in under Room Number?
Receptionist:	You can skip it. I' ll put in the room number for you later.

Guest:	Okay. Here you are. I think I've filled in everything.
Receptionist:	Let me see... name, address, nationality, passport number, signature and date of departure. Oh, here, sir. You forget to fill in the date of departure. May I fill it in for you? You are leaving on...
Guest:	September 14th.
Receptionist:	May I see your passport, please?
Guest:	Yes, here you are.
Receptionist:	Thank you. Your room number is 1201 on the twelfth floor. Here is your key. Please make sure that you have it with you all the time. You need to show it when you sign for your meals and drinks in the restaurants and the bars.
Guest:	Okay. I'll keep it with care, thank you.
Receptionist:	If you are ready, I will call the bellboy to take you to your room.
Guest:	Yes, I'm ready. Thank you.
Receptionist:	I hope you enjoy yours stay with us.

Dialogue 3

Receptionist:	Good evening. Welcome to Rose Hotel. May I help you?
Guest:	Yes, I'd like to check in. I'm the tour leader. I have made a reservation a week ago.
Receptionist:	May I have your name?
Guest:	Of course. My name is Wang Ping.
Receptionist:	Yes, madam. You have made a reservation of 10 double rooms and 5 single rooms. Is there any change in the number of your group?
Guest:	No.
Receptionist:	Here is the room list. Do you have a group visa?
Guest:	Yes, here you are.
Receptionist:	All right. I'll make a copy of your group visa. Please wait a moment. Here are the room cards and meal coupons. Are you going to divide them by yourself?
Guest:	Yes.
Receptionist:	I'd like to reconfirm the schedule of your stay here. Is there any change in your schedule?
Guest:	Yes, we would like to change our check-out time to 9:00p.m.
Receptionist:	No problem, sir. Would you please place your luggage in front of your room door by 8:30 a.m.? We will have your luggage picked up. Anything else?
Guest:	No. Thank you.
Receptionist:	If there is any change, please informthe Front Desk.
Guest:	Ok. Thank you.

Vocabulary

standard single room　*n.* 标准单人间　　deposit [dɪ'pɒzɪt]　*n.* 押金

balcony room　*n.* 阳台房　　fill in/out　*v.* 填写

offer　*v.* 提供　　skip [skɪp]　*vt.* 略过

registration form ['rɛdʒɛɪ'streʃən]　　*n.* 登记表
nationality[,næʃə'næləti]　　*n.* 国籍
passport　　*n.* 护照
signature['sɪgnətʃə]　　*n.* 署名；签名
departure[dɪ'pɑrtʃə]　　*n.* 离开
bellboy　　*n.* 行李员
tour leader　　*n.* 导游

visa ['vizə]　　*n.* 签证
coupon['kupɑn]　　*n.* 赠券；优惠券
reconfirm　　*vt.* 再确认
schedule['skedʒʊl]　　*n.* 时间表；计划表
luggage ['lʌgɪdʒ]　　*n.* 行李
inform　　*vt.* 通知；告诉

Useful Expressions

1. Welcome to our hotel. May I help you?
欢迎光临我们酒店，请问有什么可以帮您吗？

2. Have you made a reservation before?
请问您之前预定过房间吗？

3. How long do you want to stay?
请问您要住多久？

4. Let me check. Oh, yes. I can offer you a standard single room. It is 100yuan per night.
让我查一下。是的，我可以给您提供一间标准单人房，每晚100元。

5. May I see your ID card?
我可以看一下您的身份证吗？

6. Would you please fill out this registration form?
请您填一下这张登记表。

7. May I have your name please, sir?
先生，请问您贵姓？

8. I need to look through our list. Yes, we do have a reservation for you, Mr. Smith. A balcony room with 500 Yuan RMB as a deposit. Is that correct?
我需要看看我们的名单。是的，我们有您的预订，史密斯先生。您预定了一间阳台房，预付了500元押金。请问对吗？

9. You forget to fill in the date of departure. May I fill it in for you?
您忘记填写离开日期了。我可以为您填写吗？

10. May I see your passport, please?
我可以看一下您的护照吗？

11. Here is your key. Please make sure that you have it with you all the time.
这是您的房门钥匙，请一定随身携带。

12. You need to show it when you sign for your meals and drinks in the restaurants and the bars.
当您在餐厅用餐和酒吧喝酒签账单时，您需要出示一下房卡。

13. If you are ready, I will call the bellboy to take you to your room.
如果您准备好了，我会叫行李员带您去您的房间。

14. I hope you enjoy yours stay with us.
我希望您在我们酒店住的愉快。

15. Is there any change in the number of your group?
你们团队人数有变化吗？

M2-6 Practice

Exercises

1. Questions and Answers

(1) Which place in hotel is responsible for receiving guests?

(2) What are the procedures of check-in service?

(3) What important items should be filled in the registration form?

2. Match the words or expressions in Column A with their Chinese equivalents in Column B.

A	B
(1) balcony room	a. 国籍
(2) offer	b. 阳台房
(3) deposit	c. 提供
(4) registration form	d. 护照
(5) skip	e. 签名
(6) nationality	f. 门童
(7) passport	g. 押金
(8) signature	h. 登记表
(9) bellboy	i. 阳台房
(10) tour leader	j. 导游

3. Fill in the blanks

(1) May I know your _____（离开日期）?

(2) Would you mind _____（填写）this registration form?

(3) Could you arrange a king-size bed room _____（带浴室）us?

(4) I want to stay here _____ the April 15th _____ 17th.

(5) Have you made any reservation?

= Do you have a _____ with us?

(6) Wait a moment please. = _____

(7) Please show me your passport. = _____ I see your _____?

May I (看一看)_____ your (身份证)_____?

(8) How are you going to pay, _____ cash or _____ credit card?

=How would you like to make your payment?

(9) Here are the _____（钥匙）to room 1108.

(10) The _____ will show you up with your baggage.

=Our _____ will _____ you to your room.

4. Read the passage and decide if the statements are true (T) or false (F).

The front desk of a hotel is called Reception, and this is where you will officially check-in.

Have your identification, reservation confirmation, and form of payment (preferably a credit card with lots of room on it) at hand. This can include your Driver License, Passport, and one or more credit cards.If you are staying abroad, the concierge will usually either copy the front page of your passport, or keep your passport for the duration of your stay. A print out of your reservation confirmation can be useful, particularly if you secured a special rate or promotion.If you do not have a reservation, be prepared to be turned away if the hotel has no vacancies. Ask the concierge for suggestions for alternate hotels.Most hotels will place a hold of the full amount of your stay plus a percentage as incidentals per day, so it's best to not give them your debit card.

Exercises:

(1) The front desk of a hotel is where you will officially check-in. (   )

(2) Your identification includes driver license. (   )

(3) If you are straying abroad, you must give your passport to the hotel. (   )

(4) If you don't have a reservation, you may be refused by the hotel if the hotel has no room available. (   )

(5) You can ask the concierge for other hotels' information. (   )

Challenges and Solutions

1. What's the difference between a single guest checking in and a tour group checking in?
Solutions:

2. If a guest checks in your hotel, but there is no room available, what should you do?
Solutions:

3. If you are on the phone, a guest arrives and wants to check in, what should you do?
Solutions:

4. How would you receive a disabled guest at the front desk?
Solutions:

5. If you know it is the guest's birthday during his/her stay in the hotel, what should you do?
Solutions:

6. If a guest's reserved room is occupied by other guest, what should you do?
Solution:

7. What do you think is the most important quality for a receptionist in a hotel?
Solutions:

M2-7   Knowledge Link

M2-8   Key to Exercises

Lesson Three　Concierge Service

Objectives

➢ To help the students master useful expressions and sentences about Concierge Service.
➢ To help the students familiar with duties of Concierge.
➢ To help the students make some dialogues about Concierge Service.

Warming Up

1. Look at the following pictures and fill in the blanks according to the corresponding description.

_____ are stationed at the hotel and help guests or other visitors in and out of cars and taxis and do other work.

During their work, they usually need to handle _____ for hotel guests.

They also need to _____ guests at the airport or train station or summon _____ or other type of transportation for guests.

They may also need to give _____ for the place guests want to go in hotel or local places that guests wish to visit.

They also need to helpguests make _____ _____ in dining room.

They will escort guest and his luggage to the room and introduce the _____ in the room.

M2-9　Warming Up

Dialogues

Key sentences:

➢ Is there anything valuable or breakable in your bag?

➢ This is your room. May I have your key, madam?...May I put your bag here?

➢ How are you enjoying your stay here so far?

➢ Here is a map and timetable of our tour. Do you have any places in mind to visit?

➢ One more thing, could you get us a taxi?

Pre-questions:

1. Do you who usually help guest handle luggage in hotel?

2. If a guest wants to make a reservation of the dining room, who can help him?

3. Who often introduce hotel to guests and give guests directions of local spots?

Dialogue 1

Concierge:	Good morning, madam. Welcome to our hotel.
Guest:	Thanks, good morning. I want to check in.
Concierge:	Please come in andcontact the reception desk.
Guest:	Where is it?
Concierge:	It's straight ahead. May I take your luggage for you?
Guest:	Thank you.
Concierge:	Is there anything valuable or breakable in your bag?
Guest:	No.
...	
Concierge:	This way please. I will show you to your room.
Guest:	Thank you.
Concierge:	This is your room. May I have your key, madam?... May I put your bag here?
Guest:	Okay. Just put them anywhere.
Concierge:	Here are the light switchesand air conditioner switch. This is the remote control. Just press here and you can turn on the television.
Guest:	Thank you very much.
Concierge:	This is the bathroom. The towelsare the shelf. If you have some dirty clothes, just put them in the laundry bag which is behind the bathroom door. The maid will pick it up when she comes to clean the room.
Guest:	All right. Could you tell me something about your hotel?
Concierge:	Certainly. Dining room is on the thirteenth floor. Cafe and bar are on the first floor.
Guest:	Okay. Thank you.

Concierge:	You are welcome. If there is anything we can do for you, just let us know. The extension for our department is "232".
Guest:	Okay. Thanks.

Dialogue 2

Concierge:	Good morning, sir. How may I help you?
Guest:	Yes. My friend and I want to take a tour of the city.
Concierge:	Okay. May I have your name, sir?
Guest:	Steve Smith.
Concierge:	Nice to meet you, Mr. Smith. Please have a seat. How are you enjoying your stay here so far?
Guest:	Everything is good, thank you.
Concierge:	When would you like to leave, sir?
Guest:	We plan to leave the day after tomorrow.
Concierge:	That should not be a problem. Our hotel provides one-day tour of the city. The bus leaves at 9:00 in the morning and returns at 5:00 in the afternoon. Would you like to have a try?
Guest:	Yes, that would be a big help. You know this is our first time to Xian.
Concierge:	Here is a map and timetable of our tour. Do you have any places in mind to visit?
Guest:	We want to visit Qin Shi Huang Terracotta Warriors and Horses Museum. Does your tour include it?
Concierge:	Yes, of course. As you can see in the map, we also have trips to Giant Wild Goose Pagoda, Huaqing Hot Spring and Ming Great Wall except Qin Shi Huang Terracotta Warriors and Horses Museum. What's more, our guide will also take you to try our local food. A lot of guests think highly of our tours.
Guest:	Very good. We want to join your one-day tour tomorrow. Do we need to book it now?
Concierge:	Yes. And please go downstairs before 9:00 tomorrow morning.
Guest:	Okay, thank you.
Concierge:	You are welcome. If there is any other way I can help you just let me know.

Dialogue 3

Guest:	Hello. Is this the Concierge's desk?
Concierge:	Yes, speaking. May I help you?
Guest:	My wife and I want to check out tomorrow. Could you arrange to have our luggage brought down while we are out?
Concierge:	Certainly, sir. May I have your room number, please?
Guest:	1220.
Concierge:	1220. When do you want to check out?
Guest:	Around 11:30 a.m.
Concierge:	Okay, sir. How many pieces of luggage do you have?
Guest:	Two suitcases and one bag.
Concierge:	Okay. Could you make sure that your luggage is packed before you leave?

Guest:	Sure. One more thing, could you get us a taxi?
Concierge:	Certainly. Where do you want to go, sir?
Guest:	Pudong Airport.
Concierge:	Yes, sir. According to the mileage, it is 15yuan one kilometer.
Guest:	Okay, I see. Thank you.
Concierge:	You are welcome. I hope you enjoyed your stay here.

Vocabulary

towel ['tauəl]   *n.* 毛巾

shelf [ʃɛlf]   *n.* 架子

laundry bag   *n.* 洗衣袋

Cafe' [kæ'fe]   *n.* 咖啡馆

extension[ɪk'stɛnʃən]   *n.* 电话分机

tour [tʊr]   *n.* 旅行

timetable   *n.* 时间表

terracotta warriors   *n.* 兵马俑

pagoda[pə'godə]   *n.* 宝塔

arrange[ə'reɪn(d)ʒ]   *v.* 安排

suitcase['sutkes]   *n.* 手提箱

pack   *v.* 打包

contact['kɑntækt]   *v.* 使接触、联系

reception desk   *n.* 接待处

luggage['lʌgɪdʒ]   *n.* 行李

switch[swɪtʃ]   *n.* 开关

air conditioner   *n.* 空调

remote control   *n.* 遥控

Useful Expressions

1. Good morning, madam. Welcome to our hotel.

早上好，女士。欢迎光临我们酒店。

2. Please come in and contact the reception desk.

请进来与接待处联系。

3. May I take your luggage for you?

我可以帮您拿行李吗？

4. Is there anything valuable or breakable in your bag?

您的包里有贵重或易碎物品吗？

5. This way please. I will show you to your room.

这边请。我带您到您的房间去。

6. This is your room. May I have your key, madam?... May I put your bag here?

这是你的房间。夫人，请把您的钥匙给我好吗？我可以把你的包放在这儿吗？

7. Here are the light switches and air conditioner switch.

这是电灯开关和空调开关。

8. This is the remote control. Just press here and you can turn on the television.

这是遥控器。只要按这儿，你就可以打开电视了。

9. If you have some dirty clothes, just put them in the laundry bag which is behind the bathroom door.

如果你有脏衣服，就把它们放在浴室门后的洗衣袋里。

10. Could you tell me something about your hotel?

你能跟我介绍一下你们酒店吗？

11. Dining room is on the thirteenth floor. Café and bar are on the first floor.

餐厅在十三层，咖啡厅和酒吧在一层。

12. If there is anything we can do for you, just let us know.

如果有什么需要我们帮忙的，尽管告诉我们。

13. How are you enjoying your stay here so far?

您在这里住的怎么样？

14. When would you like to leave, sir?

先生，您什么时候想离开酒店？

15. That should not be a problem. Our hotel provides one-day tour of the city.

这不是个问题。我们的酒店提供市内一日游。

M2-10　Practice

Exercises

1. Questions and Answers.

(1) Who usually receive guests at the door of the hotel?

(2) What are daily work of concierges in hotel?

(3) If a guest wants to store his luggage for a moment, what should he do?

2. Match the words or expressions in Column A with their Chinese equivalents in Column B.

A	B
(1) contact	a. 接待处
(2) luggage	b. 联系
(3) reception desk	c. 架子
(4) switch	d. 行李
(5) remote control	e. 咖啡馆
(6) towel	f. 空调
(7) air conditioner	g. 开关
(8) laundry bag	h. 洗衣袋
(9) shelf	i. 毛巾
(10) cafe	j. 遥控

3. Fill in the blanks.

(1) Would you mind me taking your _____（行李）？

(2) Is there anything _____（贵重的）or _____（易碎的）in your bag?

(3) These are the _____ _____（电灯开关）and _____ _____ _____（空调开关）.

(4) If you have some dirty clothes, just put them in the _____ _____（洗衣袋）.

(5) Could you tell me something about your hotel?

= Would you like to _____ your hotel to me?

(6) If there is anything we can do for you, just let us know.

= _____

(7) 您在这住的怎么样？

_____?

(8) 先生您有几件行李？

_____?

(9) 我们酒店提供市内一日游。

_____?

(10) 我们离店的时候，你能安排把我们的行李拿下来吗？

_____?

4. Read the passage and decide if the statements are true (T) or false (F).

In the service industry, the word "concierge" was first used by Mr. Ferdinand Gillet, who founded Les Clef d'Or in Paris, France in 1929. Les Clef d'Or (pronounced: "lay clay door"), is the oldest surviving personal, professional, international network service-industry organization in the world. It has no religious or political affiliation, but is solely focused on a genuine desire to serve hotel guests around the world.

Les Clefs d'Or boasts more than 5,000 concierge members located in more than 40 countries worldwide. Their motto, "There will be, in every country, Clefs d'Or members who are able to continue with our mission: to be of service to our profession, and the hotel and tourist industry," speaks of their commitment to guest-service and satisfaction. Yearly, Les Clefs d'Or organizes and sponsors a global congress whose goal is to their brand and service-oriented network development through friendship, cooperation, education, and training.

Exercises:

(1) Ferdinand Gillet founded Les Clef d'Or in Paris, France in 1930. (   )

(2) Les Clef d'Or has no religious or political affiliation. (   )

(3) Les Clef d'Or is solely focused on a genuine desire to serve hotel guests around the world. (   )

(4) Les Clefs d'Or boasts more than 6,000 concierge members located in more than 40 countries worldwide. (   )

(5) Les Clef d'Or's mission is to be of service to our profession, and the hotel and tourist industry. (   )

Challenges and Solutions

1. If you were a concierge, what would you say when you open the car door for the guest?
Solutions:

2. If you were a concierge, a guest lost his luggage in hotel, what would you do?
Solutions:

3. If you were a concierge, a guest comes to ask directions of local scenic spots, what will you do?
Solutions:

4. If you were a concierge, how would you direct the guests to park their car?
Solutions:

5. If you were a concierge, what would you say to guests who have checked out?
Solutions:

6. If you were a concierge, how should you help guests store their luggage?
Solution:

7. If you were a concierge, how would you receive a guest at the airport?
Solutions:

8. If you were a concierge, how would you book flight ticket for guests?
Solutions:

M2-11　Knowledge Link

M2-12　Key to Exercises

Lesson Four　Switchboard Service

Objectives

➢ To help the students master useful expressions and sentences aboutSwitchboard Service.
➢ To help the students familiar with duties of Switchboard Service.
➢ To help the students make some dialogues about Switchboard Service.

Warming Up

1. Look at the following pictures and fill in the blanksaccording to the corresponding description.

_____ is an important service in hotel which is based on computerized telephone systems or conventional multi-line telephone systems to complete connections for incoming calls and calls to places outside the hotel.

_____ serves an important part of the proper functioning of any successful hotel. They usually take calls from guests or others and deal with urgent matter on behalf of the hotel or guests.

M2-13　Warming Up

Dialogues

Key sentences:

➤ Good morning, this is the operator. What can I do for you?

➤ Could you transfer my call to him?

➤ Domestic or international call?

➤ Please call me again if you need any help.

➤ Wake-up service by operator, computer or knocking at the door?

Pre-questions:

1. Have you ever used the switchboard service in hotel?

2. What are the daily jobs of telephone operator?

3. What should the operator pay attention to when receiving a call?

Dialogue 1

Operator:	Good morning, this is the operator. What can I do for you?
Guest:	Good morning. I want to reach another guest in your hotel. He is in room 1301.
Operator:	Sure, sir. For room-to-room calls you may dial the room number directly.
Guest:	I have tried it. But I can't get through. Could you transfer my call to him?
Operator:	Okay. May I know the guest's name, please?
Guest:	John Black.
Operator:	Please wait for a moment. I will transfer your call to room1301.
Guest:	Ok.
...	(A few seconds later)
Operator:	Thank you for waiting. But I'm afraid Mr. Black is not in his room at this moment. Would you like to leave a message for him?
Guest:	All right.
Operator	May I have your name?
Guest:	Peter White.
Operator:	And your message, please.
Guest:	Please tell Mr. Black I will wait him in the dining room at 5:00 p.m.
Operator:	I see. Mr. White, you will wait Mr. Black in dining room at 5:00 p.m. Is that right?
Guest:	That's right. Thank you.
Operator:	You are welcome, sir. Thank you for calling. Good-bye.

Dialogue 2

Operator:	Operator. May I help you?

Guest:	Yes. I'd like to make a call outside.
Operator:	Okay. Domestic or international call?
Guest:	I'd like to reach a friend in the city. How should I do?
Operator:	Just dial "6" and then the number directly.
Guest:	Thank you for your help. But if I want to make a call to my family who live outside of the city?
Operator:	For all calls outside of the city, you need to dial "0" first and then the area code followed by the number you are trying to reach.
Guest:	Thank you very much. If by chance I need to make an international call to my business partner?
Operator:	You can make a call directly from your room. That's cheaper than going through the *General Switchboard*. As for international calls, press "3-0-0" before the country code and then press the area code and the telephone number. You can find the country code list on your table.
Guest:	You have been a big help. I will have a try.
Operator:	Please call me again if you need any help.
Guest:	Thank you very much.
Operator:	You're welcome. Have a nice evening!

Dialogue 3

Operator:	Good evening, operator Alice speaking. May I help you?
Guest:	Mr. Black speaking. I'd like to have a wake-up call tomorrow morning.
Operator:	Certainly, sir. At what time?
Guest:	At around 6:30 p.m.
Operator:	All right, sir. Wake-up service by operator, computer or knocking at the door?
Guest:	By operator. Thanks.
Operator:	Okay. May I have your room number, sir?
Guest:	Room 2123.
Operator:	All right. You will receive a morning call at 6:30 by operator tomorrow morning, Mr. Black. Wish you have a good dream.
	(The next morning)
Operator:	Good morning, Mr. Black. This is your 6:30 morning wake-up call. I wish you have a nice day.
Guest:	Thank you very much.
Operator:	It is my pleasure. The outside temperature is 20℃. It is very warm and comfortable.
Guest:	Okay, I see. Thank you. By the way, I want to check out today. Can you send a bellman to help me carry the luggage down?
Operator:	No problem.
Guest:	Thanks a lot.
Operator:	I'm always at your service.

Vocabulary

message   *n.* 信息

dining room   *n.* 餐厅

domestic [dəˈmɛstɪk]   *adj.* 国内的

area code   *n.* 区域号码

country code   *n.* 国家号码

General Switchboard   *n.* 电话总机

press   *v.* 按，压

wake-up call   *n.* 叫醒服务

knock   *v.* 敲打

receive[rɪˈsiv]   *v.* 接待，收到

temperature[temprətʃə(r)]   *n.* 温度

operator[ˈɑpəretə]   *n.* 话务员

room-to-room calls   *n.* 酒店内房间通话

dial[ˈdaɪəl]   *v.* 拨号

directly   *adv.* 直接地

get through   *v.* 接通

transfer [trænsˈfɜ:(r)]   *v.* 转移，传递

Useful Expressions

1. Good morning, this is the operator. What can I do for you?

早上好，接线员。我能为您做些什么？

2. I want to reach another guest in your hotel.

我想联系一下你们酒店的另一位客人。

3. For room-to-room calls you may dial the room number directly.

打酒店各房间之间的电话，请直接拨房间号。

4. Could you transfer my call to him?

您能帮我跟他转一下电话吗？

5. May I know the guest's name, please?

请问客人姓名？

6. Thank you for waiting. But I'm afraid Mr. Black is not in his room at this moment.

谢谢你的等待。但是，恐怕布莱克先生此刻不在他的房间里。

7. Would you like to leave a message for him?

你要给他留言吗？

8. Mr. White, you will wait Mr. Black in dining room at 5:00 p.m. Is that right?

怀特先生您下午五点在餐厅等布莱克先生对吗？

9. You are welcome, sir. Thank you for calling. Good-bye.

您客气了。谢谢您的来电，再见。

10. I'd like to make a call outside.

我想往外面打个电话。

11. Domestic or international call?

国内电话还是国际电话？

12. I'd like to reach a friend in the city. How should I do?

我想联系一个市内的朋友。我该怎么办？

13. Just dial "6" and then the number directly.

先拨6，然后直接拨号码。

14. But if I want to make a call to my family who live outside of the city?

但如果我想给家人打个电话呢？

15. For all calls outside of the city, you need to dial "0" first and then the area code followed by the number you are trying to reach.

打国内长途电话，请先拨0，再拨区号和电话号码。

M2-14 Practice

Exercises

1. Questions and Answers

(1) Who usually receive guests' telephone calls in hotel?

(2) What should the operator pay attention to when receiving calls in hotel?

(3) Do you know something about telephone language? List some.

2. Match the words or expressions in Column A with their Chinese equivalents in Column B.

A	B
(1) operator	a. 转接
(2) dial	b. 信息
(3) get through	c. 话务员
(4) transfer	d. 拨打
(5) message	e. 区号
(6) dining room	f. 接通
(7) area code	g. 敲打
(8) wake-up call	h. 国内的
(9) knock	i. 叫醒服务
(10) domestic	j. 餐厅

3. Choose the right answer.

1. This is _____ speaking, what can I do for you?

A. Operator   B. Operation   C. Waiter   D. Waitress

2. Please wait for a moment; I will _____ your call to room 1228.

A. give   B. transfer   C. send   D. bring

3. Please _____ the line and leave your message when you hear the beep.

A. on   B. hold   C. take   D. wait

4. How can I make an _____ direct dial call from my room?

A. domestic   B. foreign   C. long-distance   D. international

5. I'd like to have a _____ at 6:30 tomorrow morning by operator.

A. reservation   B. wake-up call   C. bath   D. dinner

6. An operator should be patient, friendly and _____.

A. helpful   B. helpless   C. careless   D. rude

7. The outside _____ is 10℃, and the weather forecast says a _____ is coming.

A. temperatures ... story   B. wind ... story

C. degrees ... rain D. temperature ... storm

8. Please _____ an umbrella and _____ warm when you are going out.

A. take... keep B. twitch... have

C. bring... have D. hold... keep

9. You can make a call _____ from your room.

A. direct B. directly C. indirect D. indirectly

10. _____ will relax your facial muscles and you sound more sweet and friendly.

A. Smiles B. Smile C. Have smile D. Keep smiling

4. Read the passage and decide if the statements are true (T) or false (F).

The switchboard service is an important service in hotel which is based on computerized telephone systems or conventional multi-line telephone systems to complete connections for incoming calls and calls to places outside the hotel. The hotel operators are responsible for this service, though he or she may never be seen. They handle all in-house calls, local calls, long-distance calls and even international calls. They provide also wake-up calls, Do Not Disturb calls for many guests, especially business travelers. In addition, if the guests are not in room, they also help guest leave message for another guest. Their voices, tones and demeanors can greatly influence the new guests' image of the hotel and staff. They must be ready at all times to deal with urgent matters on behalf of the hotel or the guest.

With the development of globalization, today most of the operators must speak fluent English. In fact, well-spoken English is a requirement for operators in most large, modern hotels. They also should be well informed about everything of the hotel and their city. So they can help guests solve problems in hotel stay and plan their trip. Operators must be ready to answer any questions regarding hotels, restaurants, sightseeing, hotspots, shopping, entertainment, transportation, and upcoming events.

Exercises:

(1) The hotel operators are responsible for switchboard service. (   )

(2) The operator cannot provide also wake-up calls. (   )

(3) If the guests are not in room, the operators can help guest leave message for another guest. (   )

(4) The voices, tones and demeanors of the operators are very important. (   )

(5) Today well-spoken English is a requirement for operators in most large, modern hotels. (   )

Challenges and Solutions

1. If you were an operator, what telephone etiquette should you know?

Solutions:

2. If you were an operator, how to leave telephone message for guests?

Solutions:

3. If you were an operator, how to deal with guest's complaints?

Solutions:

4. If you were an operator, what should you say to the caller when the guest is not in?

Solutions:

5. If you were an operator, what would you say to guests when you finish the call?

Solutions:

6. If you were an operator, how should you help guests when guests want to make an international call?

Solution:

7. What qualities should a telephone operator have?

Solutions:

M2-15　Knowledge Link

M2-16　Key to Exercises

Lesson Five　Check-out Service

Objectives

➢ To help the students master useful expressions and sentences aboutcheck-out service.

➢ To help the students familiar with duties of check-out service.

➢ To help the students make some dialogues about check-out service.

Warming Up

1. Look at the following pictures and fill in the blanks according to the corresponding descriptions.

_____is an important service in hotel which is conducted at the front desk when the guests finish their stay in hotel.

When guests want to leave hotel, they will go to the front desk and need to settle their _____.

Dialogues

Key sentences:

➢ You have paid an advance deposit of RMB500, haven't you?

➢ How do you wish to settle your account, sir? In cash or credit card?

➢ Could I have my bill settled, please?

➢ Mr. Smith, do you have any charges during your stay here?

➢ What card do you have?

Pre-questions:

1. Do you know how to check out in a hotel?

2. How do you usually pay for a bill?

3. If there are some mistakes on you bill, what will you do?

Dialogue 1

Cashier:	Good morning. May I help you?
Guest:	Good morning. I want to check-out. May I have my bill?
Cashier:	Certainly, sir. Can I get your name and room number, please?
Guest:	My name is John Walker. I was in room 2002.
Cashier:	Yes, Mr. John Walker. You checked in a week ago in the morning of April19, didn't you?
Guest:	Yes.
Cashier:	And when are you leaving?
Guest:	Around 11:00 a.m.
Cashier:	Okay. One moment, please. I' ll print the bill for you. Sorry to have kept you waiting. Here you are. The total for your stay comes to RMB 1540. All the charges are itemized.Please take a look and check it.
Guest:	All right. That's correct.
Cashier:	You have paid an advance deposit of RMB500, haven't you?
Guest:	Yes, here is the receipt.
Cashier:	Thank you. How do you wish to settle your account, sir? In cash or credit card?
Guest:	In cash.
Cashier:	This is your invoice and your change RMB60.Count it, please.
Guest:	That's quite all right. Thank you.
Cashier:	We hope you'll enjoy your trip, Mr. Walker. Goodbye.

Dialogue 2

Cashier:	Good afternoon, sir. May I help you?

Guest:	Yes. Could I have my bill settled, please?
Cashier:	Certainly, sir. Which room, please?
Guest:	1203. Mr. Smith.
Cashier:	Just a moment, please. Mr. Smith, do you have any charges during your stay here?
Guest:	I had breakfast every day, but I used your coupons and paid for it.
Cashier:	Have you used any hotel services?
Guest:	Yes, I used wake-up service this morning.
Cashier:	All right. Here is the bill, sir. Please check it.
Guest:	OK. Let me see. What is the 5 dollars for?
Cashier:	It is for the mini-bar. Let me check. You drink a bottle of beer.
Guest:	No, I don't drink anything. You can send a staff to have a check.
Cashier:	I'll check it with the department concerned. Please wait a moment.
	(*Several minutes later*)
Cashier:	I'm terribly sorry. We make a mistake. You really don't drink the beer.
Guest:	Okay. You should be careful.
Cashier:	Yes. I correct the bill for you right now. And how would you like to pay the bill, sir?
Guest:	I want to pay with traveler's check.
Cashier:	All right. The total is 800 dollars.
Guest:	All right, here you are.
Cashier:	Mr. Smith, could you please sign your name here?
Guest:	Oaky.
Cashier:	Thank you and here is your receipt. Do you need bellman to help you carry luggage?
Guest:	Yes, I have packed them.
Cashier:	I will call the Bell Captain to send it down for you.
Guest:	Thank you.
Cashier:	You are welcome. Have a nice trip.

Dialogue 3

Guest:	Good morning. Is this desk open?
Cashier:	Yes, it is. May I help you?
Guest:	I am leaving today. May I have my bill?
Cashier:	Your name and room number, please?
Guest:	Mr. Singh. Room 2016.
Cashier:	Mr. Singh. Have you used the mini-bar or other services?
Guest:	No.
Cashier:	OK. Mr. Singh. One moment, please. Your bill totals 880 Yuan RMB. Here you are. Have a check, please.
Guest:	Correct. Can I pay by my credit card?
Cashier:	Of course. What card do you have?
Guest:	Master Card.

Cashier:	Fine. Let me take an imprint of it.
Guest:	Here you are.
Cashier:	Thank you. Just a moment. Please sign your name on the print, Mr. Singh.
Guest:	OK... Here you are.
Cashier:	Thank you. Please take your credit card and keep the receipt. I hope you had a nice stay here.
Guest:	Thank you. One more thing. I'd like to change some US dollars.
Cashier:	According to today's exchange rate, every US dollar in cash is equivalent to 6.8 Yuan, RMB. How much would you like to change, sir?
Guest:	Well, I'll change two hundred and here's the money.
Cashier:	Please fill in this exchange memo, your passport number and the total sum, and please sign your name here.
Guest:	All right. Thank you.
Cashier:	You are welcome. Here is the money. Please have a check and keep the exchange memo.You can go to the Bank of China or the airport exchange office to change the left money back into dollars by showing the memo.
Guest:	Oh, that's right. Thanks a lot.
Cashier:	You are welcome. Have a nice day.

Vocabulary

count[kaʊnt]　v. 计算

coupon ['ku:pɒn]　n. 赠券

mini-bar　n. 小冰柜

concerned [kən'sɜ:nd]　adj. 有关的

traveler's check　n. 旅行支票

sign[saɪn]　v. 签名

Bell Captain　n. 礼宾部领班

Master Card　n. 万事达信用卡

imprint[ɪm'prɪnt]　n. 印记

exchange rate　n. 汇率

equivalent[ɪ'kwɪv(ə)l(ə)nt]　adj. 等价的，相等的

exchange memo　n. 外汇兑换水单

Bank of China　n. 中国银行

check-out　n. 结账退房

total ['təʊt(ə)l]　n. 总数，合计

charge　v/n.收费，费用

itemize['aɪtəmaɪz]　v. 逐条列记

advance deposit　n. 定金

receipt[rɪ'si:t]　n. 收据

account[ə'kaʊnt]　n. 账户，账目

cash　n. 现金

credit card　n. 信用卡

invoice['ɪnvɔɪs]　n. 发票

change　n. 零钱

Useful Expressions

1. Good morning. I want to check-out. May I have my bill?

早上好。我想退房。可以结账吗？

2. Can I get your name and room number, please?

请问您的姓名和房间号是什么？

3. And when are you leaving?

请问您什么时候离开？

4. One moment, please. I'll print the bill for you.

请稍等，我给您打印一下账单。

5. The total for your stay comes to RMB 1540, including10% service charge.

您的住宿费用为人民币1540元，包括10%的服务费。

6. All the charges are itemized. Please take a look and check it.

所有的费用都是分项的。请检查一下。

7. You have paid an advance deposit of RMB500, haven't you?

您已经预付了500元人民币的定金，对吗？

8. How do you wish to settle your account, sir? In cash or credit card?

先生您想怎么结账？现金还是信用卡？

9. This is your invoice and your change RMB60.Count it, please.

这是你的发票和60员零钱。请数一下。

10. We hope you'll enjoy your trip.

希望您旅途愉快。

11. Could I have my bill settled, please?

请问现在我可以结账吗？

12. Do you have any charges during your stay here?

你在这里居住期间有任何费用吗？

13. Have you used any hotel services?

您使用酒店服务了吗？

14. I had breakfast every day, but I used your coupons and paid for it.

我每天都吃早餐，但我用了你的优惠券并付了钱。

15. I'll check it with the department concerned. Would you mind waiting for a moment?

我将和有关部门核对一下。您能等一会儿吗？

M2-18　Practice

Exercises

1. Questions and Answers

(1) Who usually help guests checkout in hotel?

(2) What is the procedure of check-out service in hotel?

(3) What are guests' common ways used to settle the account?

2. Match the words or expressions in Column A with their Chinese equivalents in Column B.

A	B
(1) count	a. 结账退房
(2) check-out	b. 有关的
(3) coupon	c. 旅行支票
(4) total	d. 费用
(5) charge	e. 收据

(6) concerned   f. 定金

(7) itemize   g. 总数

(8) traveler's check   h. 赠券

(9) advance deposit   i. 计算

(10) receipt   j. 逐条列记

3. Translate the following abbreviations on the bills into Chinese.

RC = Room Charge   TR.CR = Transfer Credit

T = Telephone Call Charge   PD.OUT = Paid Out

L.DIST = Long Distance Call   PAID = Paid

RESTR = Restaurant   C.I.A (Cash In Advance)

L = Laundry   P.I.A. (Paid In Advance)

MISC = Miscellaneous   B.N.P. (Bill Not Paid)

TR.CH = Transfer Charge

4. Read the passage and decide if the statements are true (T) or false (F).

The duties of cashier are a lot, such as settling guests' accounts, making changes, cashing, traveler's checks, exchanging foreign currencies. balancing accounts at the close of each shift, and so on. Check-out service means settling the account for the guests. Like the check-in procedure, check-out procedure takes only a few minutes when the system works efficiently. The cashier usually asks departing guests if they have any last-minute charges for the minibar or for food and beverage service in the hotel restaurants. If the answer is "yes", the cashier must ask the departments concerned how much the guest has to be charged for that before presenting the final bill. The cashiers are often required to ask if the guest has turned in his key. Lost keys are an expense for the hotel; more seriously, they might be a threat to security if they fall into the wrong hands.

Usually the hotel has an accounting system to maintain guests' consumption items within the hotel and keep them up-to-date. All charges must be entered or posted on their accounts as soon as possible. In addition to the charges for the guests' rooms, there may also be charges resulting from the use of telephone, the laundry service, the restaurants, and room service. All the financial transportation not only must be posted, but also be checked for accuracy. This is usually the job of a night auditor, who goes through this mass of figures on the night shift, when there is little activity in hotel.

Exercises:

(1) Check-out service means settling the account for the guests. ( )

(2) The cashiers need to ask if the guest has turned in his key when guest check out. ( )

(3) Exchanging foreign currencies is not a job of the cashiers. ( )

(4) Hotels often have an accounting system to maintain guests'consumption items within the hotel and keep them up-to-date. ( )

(5) When guests check out, they need to pay all fees in hotel including the fees of telephone, the laundry service, the restaurants, and room service. ( )

Challenges and Solutions

1. If a guest wants to check out, what will you do?

Solutions:

2. If a guest wants to pay the bill by credit card, how do you deal with it?

Solutions:

3. If a guest pays the bill by traveler's check, how do you deal with it?

Solutions:

4. How do you deal with the miscalculation of a bill?

Solutions:

5. If a guest wants to exchange some money, how do you deal with it?

Solutions:

6. If a guest leaves the hotel, what will you say?

Solution:

7. If a guest comes to the front desk to check out, but the housekeeping staff reports a hanger is missing in the guest's room, what will you do?

Solutions:

M2-19　Knowledge Link

M2-20　Key to Exercises

Lesson Six　Handling Complaints

Objectives

➤ To help the students master useful expressions and sentences about complaints in front desk.

➤ To help the students familiar with the common complaints in front desk.

➤ To help the students analyze the reasons of complaints and handle complaints in front desk.

Preamble

Thursday night July 4, 2018

Dear Mr. Green,

Thank you for writing to us here at the Heng Yun Hotel. We are sorry to hear that your stay at our hotel did not meet your expectations.

In your letter, you state that your room was not ready when you arrived even though it was after the established check-in time. We are sorry to have inconvenienced you on your visit to Heng Yun. Your complaint has inspired us to re-train the front desk staff. Now, all employees have been reminded that the appropriate procedure in this situation is to hold the guests' luggage and offer vouchers to the hotel restaurant.

You also stated that your room was excessively noisy due to the construction next door. You say that you called the front desk but you were not given a new room. We have checked our records, and it seems there was no other room available to give you. Even so, we apologize for the noise and wish we could have done more to make your night more comfortable.

Please accept our most sincere apologies. Given the unfortunate experience you had here at the Heng Yun Hotel, we would like to extend to you this $100 voucher for your next stay at our hotel. We hope that your next stay with us will better meet our standard of excellence.

Sincerely yours,

(Signature) Bob Smith

Dialogues

Key sentences:

> I'm very sorry, sir. As you arrived too late, we thought you didn't come. So we've let the room to someone else.
> I'm sorry to hear the news, sir. We do apologize for the inconvenience. We will send a room attendant to clean the room at once.
> Thank you for your understanding. Now let me help you check in.

Pre-questions:

1. What are the common complaints about the front office service?
2. How to deal with these complaints about the front office service?
3. Do you think it's an important to handle complaints of the front office service? Why?

Dialogue 1

Receptionist:	Good evening. May I help you?
Guest:	Good evening. My name is Mr. White. I have booked double room in your hotel.
Receptionist:	I'm very sorry, sir. As you arrived too late, we thought you didn't come. So we've let the room to someone else.
Guest:	What? You've let the room? But I never call you I don't come!
Receptionist:	I'm sorry. We only hold rooms for our guests till 6:00 p.m. on the expected time. It was in the letter of confirmation.
Guest:	That's interesting. My train was four hours late. And now you tell me that you've let my room.
Receptionist:	I'm terribly sorry, but that is the situation. We can upgrade your room to a family suite. Are you satisfied with it?
Guest:	All right. My wife and I are really tired now. We want to have a rest.
Receptionist:	Thank you for your understanding. Now let me help you check in.

Dialogue 2

Guest:	Front desk, I'd like to make a complaint.

Receptionist:	What's the trouble sir?
Guest:	First, I wait almost one hour for the bellman to send my luggage to my room. Then when I open my luggage, I find my glasses is broken.
Receptionist:	I'm terribly sorry. There are a lot of guests checking in today. Maybe we are a little busy. But next time we will send your luggage as soon possible.
Guest:	Even if there are a lot of guests, you should guarantee that the luggage is sent to guest's room timely. You can employ more bellmen.
Receptionist:	Yes. As our hotel has just opened, we are short of help. I promise when you come next time, everything will be all right. As for you glasses, we will compensate for it. Do you have receipt of your glasses?
Guest:	But I bought the glasses last year, I have lost the receipt.
Receptionist:	Okay, you can but a new one of this style and give us the receipt. Then we will refund money to you.
Guest:	All right, thank you.
Receptionist:	You are welcome. Thank you for calling us. If you need any help, please let us know.

Dialogue 3

Receptionist:	Good afternoon, sir. How may I help you?
Guest:	Good afternoon. I am from room 356. People in next room are singing all this afternoon. It's too noisy. Can you change a room for me?
Receptionist:	I'm so sorry, sir. I'll look into the matterimmediately.
	(Several minutes later)
Receptionist:	Sir, I have called to them and ask them to stop singing. Do you still want to change the room?
Guest:	Yes, I'm afraid they are too young and active. Tomorrow I have am important meeting. I want to have a quiet room.
Receptionist:	Okay. There is a room in the corner of this floor. It's very quiet, but it is not facing the sun. Is it okay?
Guest:	Are you sure it is quiet?
Receptionist:	Yes, because the room beside it is vacant.
Guest:	Okay. I'll take it. Thank you.
Receptionist:	You are welcome. I'll send a porter to help you carry the luggage.

Vocabulary

confirmation[kɒnfə'meɪʃ(ə)n]　n. 确认
expected　adj. 期待的
situation[sɪtjʊ'eɪʃ(ə)n]　n. 情况
upgrade　v. 升级
satisfied['sætɪsfaɪd]　adj. 满意的
understanding [ʌndə'stændɪŋ]　n. 理解
complaint[kəm'pleɪnt]　n. 抱怨
guarantee[gær(ə)n'ti:]　v. 保证

timely　adj. 及时的
employ[ɪm'plɒɪ]　v. 雇佣
increase　v. 增加
promise['prɒmɪs]　v. 允诺
compensate['kɒmpenseɪt]　v. 赔偿
receipt[rɪ'si:t]　n. 收据
refund['ri:fʌnd]　v. 偿还
active　adj. 积极的

vacant [ˈveɪk(ə)nt]   *adj.* 空的   porter[ˈpɔːtə]   *n.* 行李搬运工

Useful Expressions

1. Good evening. May I help you?

晚上好。我可以帮你吗？

2. I'm very sorry, sir. As you arrived too late, we thought you didn't come. So we've let the room to someone else.

很抱歉，先生。你来得太迟了，我们以为你不来了。所以我们把房间让给别人了。

3. I'm sorry. We only hold rooms for our guests till 6:00 p.m. on the expected time. It was in the letter of confirmation.

我很抱歉。我们只在预定的时间内为客人保留房间，直到下午6:00。这在确认信提到过。

4. I'm terribly sorry, but that is the situation. We can upgrade your room to a family suite. Are you satisfied with it?

我非常抱歉，但情况就是这样。我们可以把你的房间升级为家庭套房。你对此满意吗？

5. Thank you for your understanding. Now let me help you check in.

谢谢你的理解。现在让我帮你办理入住手续。

6. Front desk, I'd like to make a complaint.

前台，我想投诉一下。

7. What's the trouble sir?

先生，有什么问题吗？

8. I promise when you come next time, everything will be all right.

我保证下次你来的时候，一切都会好起来的。

9. I'm terribly sorry. I'll attend to it at once.

我很抱歉。我马上去处理。

10. As for you glasses, we will compensate for it. Do you have receipt of your glasses?

至于你的眼镜，我们会赔偿的。你有没有收到你的眼镜？

11. Thank you for calling us. If you need any help, please let us know.

谢谢你打电话给我们。如果你需要帮助，请告诉我们。

12. We are terribly sorry for all this mess. As our hotel has just opened, we are short of help.

我们对这一切的混乱感到非常抱歉。当我们的酒店刚刚开业时，我们缺少帮助。

13. So if you would please get your luggage ready, we'll move you to another room.

所以，如果你能把行李准备好，我们会把你送到另一个房间。

14. Please wait a moment. I promise to get everything done.

请稍等。我保证一切会好的。

15. It's too noisy. Can you change a room for me?

太吵了。你能帮我换一个房间吗？

Exercises

1. Match each word or phrase in the column on the left with its meaning in the column on the right.

(1) confirmation   a. give better travel conditions to.

(2) situation   b. statement in which you express your dissatisfaction with a situation.

(3) upgrade   c. make payment to.

(4) complaint   d. say sorry to some one.

(5) compensate   e. not being used by anyone.

(6) stain   f. information that confirms or verifies.

(7) employ   g. the general state of things.

(8) vacant   h. a mark on something that is difficult to remove.

(9) satisfied   i. engage or hire for work.

(10) apologize   j. to make someone feel pleased by doing what they want.

2. Complete the following dialogue according to the Chinese in brackets and read it in roles.

R=Receptionist   B=Guest

R: Good evening. Front Desk. Can I help you?

B: This is Miss Li from Room 1503. _____ （我刚入住但是我对房间并不满意。）

    R: _____（请问有什么问题吗？）

B: The room is smelly and there is someone's hair on my bed!

R: I'm sorry to hear the news. Miss Li. _____（我立马派一个客房服务生去您的房间。）She will bring air fresher and change the bed sheet for you. （很抱歉给您带来不便。）

    B: All right. Thank you.

    R: It's my pleasure, Miss Li. _____（如果有任何需要我帮忙的请给我打电话。）

3. Choose the correct steps for replying guest's complaints letter.

a. Confirm the customer complaint item responsibility and undertake the lose cost.

b. Affirm customer complaint item and analyze carefully its root cause.

c. Relative technical or supervisor people should affirm the corrective and prevent action result.

d. Need customer to assistant purpose.

e. Take corrective and protective action.

4. Choose the best English translation for each sentence.

(1) 听到这样的事情，我真的非常遗憾！（   ）

A. I'm sorry for that.   B. I'm sorry for see that.

C. I'm terribly sorry to hear that.   D. I'm very sorry about it.

(2) 我马上去查清这件事情。（   ）

A. I'll see to it.   B. I'll deal with it now.

C. I'll look to it.   D. I'll look into this matter at once.

(3) 我们为给您带来不便深表歉意。（   ）

A. We do apologize for the inconvenience.   B. We are sorry for it.

C. We are sorry for the inconvenience.   D. Sorry for causing you trouble.

(4) 我派个行李员来帮您搬行李。（   ）

A. I'll send a receptionist to help you with the luggage.

B. I'll send a waiter to help you with the luggage.

C. I will send a porter to help you with the luggage.

D. I'll send a porter to help you.

(5) 请允许我派一位服务员来帮您再仔细找找。（   ）

A. Allow me to send a room attendant to look for you.

B. I will send a man to help you look for it.

C. Please let me look for it.

D. Please allow me to send a chambermaid to your room to help you look for it again.

5. Read the passage and choose the best answers to the following questions.

Dealing with complaints

When the customer pays for a product or service, it is assumed that the product will work correctly or that the service received is as promised. Ideally, the customer will be satisfied, and there will be no complaints.

If there is a problem and the customer complains about it, your company should quickly answer the complaint and solve the customer's problem. This is often done through your company's customer service activity. But also, you need to follow up and improve your business processes to rectify the problem.

Solve the problem

You need to immediately answer the complaint and solve the problem. It may be to give money back, exchange a product or do some repair.

Special bonus

To make sure the customer is completely satisfied, some companies will provide some special service or a reduced price on another product. This is done to assure the customer will come back for more business. Many retail stores have a generous return policy to satisfy dissatisfied customers.

Dishonest customers

Unfortunately, there are dishonest customers who will make false claims to get some bonus. Some people will use a product or piece of clothing and then return it, saying they weren't satisfied.

High-end women's clothing stores often will have expensive gowns returned after some important event. The clothes have obviously been worn, but the customer says she is not satisfied or has changed her mind. Usually, the store will refund the money.

Since it is often difficult to tell if the complaint is valid or not, the company will follow the adage, "The customer is always right." But since some dishonest people repeat their crimes, a better adage is, "The customer is always right... once."

Price in customer service

When a company sells a product or a provides a service, part of the pricing should include the cost of servicing a certain percentage of defective products or complaints.

Rectify problem

The second thing a company should do upon receiving a complaint is to seek to rectify the problem.

Although a company hopes not to get complaints, they often can be blessing in disguise. Sometimes problems can be caught and fixed before they cause serious negative feedback or even legal problems.

It is in the company's best interest to solve any problems and try to make sure that they don't happen again. It is foolish for a company not to use customer complaints to initiate a corrective action.

Quickly and properly solving customer complaints can help your business grow and prosper.

Ignoring complaints or dealing with them in a dishonest manner can result in loss of business or even lawsuits.

(1) When will compliant happen? (   )

A. Product will work correctly.   B. Service received is good.

C. The customer is not satisfied with the products.   D. The products are too popular.

(2) Which department usually deal with the complaints in company? (   )

A. Sale department.   B. Customer service.

C. Marketing department.   D. Accountant.

(3) Why company provide special bonus for customers when dealing with complaint? (   )

A. Assure the customer will come back for more business.

B. This is the company's sale promotion.

C. Because customers are not easy to deal with.

D. To attract more customers.

(4) Which of the following statements is TRUE according to the passage? (   )

A. Quickly and properly solving customer complaints can help your business grow and prosper.

B. It is no need to immediately answer the complaint and solve the problem.

C. All problems can be caught and fixed before they cause serious negative feedback or even legal problems.

D. When a company sells a product or service, it does not include the cost of servicing.

Challenges and Solutions

1. If the guest was not satisfied with the room, what should you do?
Solutions:

2. If the guest complained the next room was too noisy, what should you do?
Solutions:

3. If the guests complained you spoke too fast, what should you do?
Solutions:

4. If the guest complained the bathroom was too wet and dirty, what should do you?
Solutions:

5. If the guests complained the bellman was impolite, what should you do?
Solutions:

6. If the guest complained that the bellman lost his luggage, what should you do?
Solution:

7. If the guest complained that your service was not good, what should you do?
Solutions:

M2-21　Knowledge Link

M2-22　Key to Exercises

Chapter 3

Housekeeping Service

Lesson One   Hotel Rooms and Facilities

Objectives

➢ To help the students master useful expressions and sentences about hotel rooms.
➢ To help the students familiar with room types and room facilities.
➢ To help the students make some dialogues about room introduction.

Warming Up

1. Look at the following pictures and fill in the blanks according to the corresponding descriptions.

_____ is an important document used by guests when they check in.

_____ is a kind of form which front desk staff need to fill in carefully when guests check in.

_____ is a room with three beds that can accommodate three persons.

_____ is a room with a king-sized bed, which can be occupied by one or more people.

_____ is a room located on the 'executive floor' which enables convenient access to the executive lounge.

_____ is a room with one or more bedrooms and a separate living space.

M3-1　Warming Up

Dialogues

Key sentences:

➢ Could you show me how to use the telephone?

➢ After you, sir. May I put your bags here?

➢ Shall I open the curtains for you?

➢ Here is the laundry bag. You just need to put your clothes in it. And the housekeeper will pick it up when she comes to do the room in the morning.

➢ If you need any help, you can give a call to the front desk.

Pre-questions:

1. Have you ever lived in a hotel? What kind of room do you live in?

2. Have you ever used the guest supplies in the hotel. Can you name some of them?

3. What service can hotel provide for guest?

Dialogue 1

Bellman:	Is this everything,sir?
Guest:	Yes,that's everything.
Bellman:	Follow me,please.
Guest:	Thank you.
Bellman:	Here we are,sir. Here's the lightswitch and air conditioner switch.
Guest:	Fine.
Bellman:	Here's the closet and you can hang your clothes in it. If you need more hangers, please tell me. This is the bathroom. Here are towels, bath gel, shampoo, comb, shaving kit, etc.
Guest:	Great!I just want to wash up.
Bellman:	Will there be anything else,sir?
Guest:	Yes. Could you show me how to use the telephone? Because I want to make a call to my friend who leaves in the city.
Bellman:	Yes, of course. First dial " 2 " and then the telephone number.
Guest:	Ok, I get it. Thank you.
Bellman:	You are welcome. If you need any help, you can give a call to the front desk. Its extension number is 290674.
Guest:	All right. Thank you very much.
Bellman:	It's my pleasure. Have a nice day.

Dialogue 2

Receptionist:	Sir,how do you like this room? It's just facing the Tiananmen Square and you can see the flag-rising ceremony tomorrow morning. It's also quite spacious.

Guest:	I'm afraid it is a little noisy. Because tomorrow I will attend a meeting and I want to have a good rest.
Receptionist:	Okay, let me find a quiet room for you. How about this one. It's at the back of the hotel and very cool and quiet at night. And this is a Business Room. It's very convenient for you to do some work.
Guest:	Excellent. I want this one.
Receptionist:	All right. Please wait a moment. I will arrange a bellman to take you to your room.
Guest:	Okay.
	(Serval minutes later)
Bellman:	Good afternoon, sir. I'm the bellman here. Let me help you with your luggage.
Guest:	It's very kind of you to do so.
Bellman:	This is your room. After you, sir. May I put your bags here?
Guest:	Sure, just put them anywhere.
Bellman:	Shall I open the curtains for you?
Guest:	Yes, that's a good idea.
Bellman:	This is the mini-bar and it is fully stocked. You can choose what you like.
Guest:	Okay. Thank you very much.
Bellman:	The bathroom is over there. Maybe you can take a shower as I see you are a little tired.
Guest:	Okay. And I have some clothes to be washed. Do you provide laundry service?
Bellman:	Yes. Here is the laundry bag. You just need to put your clothes in it. And the housekeeper will pick it up when she comes to do the room in the morning.
Guest:	Oh, I see. Thanks a lot.
Bellman:	Sir, if you need something, just call me over the phone or press the button over there.

Dialogue 3

Bellman:	Sir and madam. This is your room. I hope you like it.
Guest:	It looks nice.
Bellman:	May I put your luggage here?
Guest:	Yes, of course. By the way, could you tell me about your hotel service?
Bellman:	Yes. Our hotel has Chinese, Japanese and Western food restaurants. Usually we provide buffet breakfast in the morning. In addition, we also have a complete set of service facilities including ballroom, physical fitness center, squash,billiard room, beauty salon, sauna,swimming pool, bar, shopping arcade and taxi service,etc.
Guest:	It sounds great. I'd like to have a brochure of your hotel.Where could I get one?
Bellman:	You can get it from the Reception Desk.If you don't mind, I'll come up again and offer you one.
Guest:	That's very kind of you.By the way,what about the daily service hour of the restaurant?

Bellman:	From 7:00 a.m.till 10: 30 p.m., nearly serving all day long.
Guest:	When will the bar and cafe open?
Bellman:	From 3:00 p.m.till midnight.And then,you might keep your valuables at the hotel's vault.
Guest:	You give very good service in your hotel.Thank youa lot.

Vocabulary

bath gel *n.* 沐浴露

shampoo[ʃæm'pu:] *n.* 洗发露

shaving kit *n.* 剃须套装

extension number *n.* 分机号码

Tiananmen Square *n.* 天安门广场

flag-rising ceremony *n.* 升旗仪式

spacious['speiʃəs] *adj.* 宽敞的

attend[ə'tend] *v.* 出席

convenient [kən'vi:niənt] *adj.* 方便的

Business Room *n.* 商务房

stock[stɒk] *v.* 贮存

laundry bag *n.* 洗衣袋

button['bʌtn] *n.* 按钮

ballroom *n.* 舞厅

physical fitness center *n.* 健身中心

switch [swɪtʃ] *n.* 开关

closet ['klɒzɪt] *n.* 壁橱

hanger ['hæŋə] *n.* 衣架

squash[skwɒʃ] *n.* 壁球

billiard room *n.* 台球房

beauty salon *n.* 美容院

arcade[ɑ:'keɪd] *n.* 拱廊

brochure['brəʊʃə] *n.* 手册

vault[vɔ:lt] *n.* 保险柜

Useful Expressions

1. Is this everything, sir?

这是全部东西吗，先生？

2. Here we are, sir. Here's the light switch and air conditioner switch.

我们到了，先生。这是电灯开关和空调开关。

3. Here's the closet and you can hang your clothes in it. If you need more hangers, please tell me.

这是衣橱，你可以把衣服挂在里面。如果你需要更多的衣架，请告诉我。

4. This is the bathroom. Here are towels, bath gel, shampoo, comb, shaving kit, etc.

这是浴室。这里有毛巾、沐浴露、洗发水、梳子、剃须用具等。

5. This room is facing south, and it has a nice view.

这个房间朝南，而且能看到很美的风景。

6. First dial "2" and then the telephone number.

先拨2再拨电话号码。

7. If you need any help, you can give a call to the front desk. Its extension number is 290674.

如果你需要帮助，你可以打电话到前台。它的分机号码是290674。

8. Sir, how do you like this room? It's quite spacious.

先生，你觉得这个房间怎么样？房间也很宽敞。

9. And this is a Business Room. It's very convenient for you to do some work.

这是一个商务房。你做一些工作很方便。

10. Please wait a moment. I will arrange a bellman to take you to your room.

请稍等。我将安排一个行李员带你去你的房间。

11. May I put your bags here?

可以把你的行李放在这里

12. Shall I open the curtains for you?

我帮你把窗帘拉开好吗?

13. This is the mini-bar and it is fully stocked. You can choose what you like.

这是迷你吧,里面装满了各种饮料。你可以选择你喜欢的。

14. The bathroom is over there. Maybe you can take a shower as I see you are a little tired.

洗手间在那边。也许你可以洗个澡,因为我看到你有点累了。

15. Special laundry bags with price lists are placed in the closet.

洗衣袋和洗衣单放在壁橱里。

M3-2　Practice

Exercises

1. Questions and Answers

(1) What kind of rooms does hotel usually provide?

(2) What facilities are usually in hotels?

(3) If a guest doesn't like his room, can he change a room? How?

2. Match the words or expressions in Column A with their Chinese equivalents in Column B.

A	B
(1) closet	a. 衣架
(2) hanger	b. 洗发露
(3) bath gel	c. 分机号码
(4) shampoo	d. 宽敞的
(5) shaving kit	e. 沐浴露
(6) extension number	f. 出席
(7) flag-rising ceremony	g. 壁橱
(8) spacious	h. 方便的
(9) attend	i. 剃须套装
(10) convenient	j. 升旗仪式

3. Fill in the blanks

(1) Could you tell me where is the _____ (电灯开关)?

(2) There are _____ (毛巾) _____ (沐浴露) _____ (牙膏) _____ (梳子) in bath room.

(3) Could you tell me if your hotel has _____ (健身中心) because I want to do some exercise?

(4) Do you need me to _____ (设置洗浴温度)?

(5) Will there be anything else?

= _____

(6) You may keep your _____ (贵重物品) in our hotel's safe deposit box.

(7) You can use the _____ （遥控器）to choose the channel you like.

(8) There are all kind of drinks in your room's _____（小冰柜）.

(9) On the 3rd floor of our hotel, there are _____（酒吧）_____（咖啡厅）_____（台球馆）_____（桑拿），etc.

(10) _____（您觉得这个房间怎么样）

The room _____（面向超市）. I think it is a little noisy.

4. Read the passage and decide if the statements are true (T) or false (F).

A hotel is an establishment that provides paid lodging on a short-term basis. Facilities provided may range from a modest-quality mattress in a small room to large suites with bigger, higher-quality beds, a dresser, a refrigerator and other kitchen facilities, upholstered chairs, a flat screen television and en-suite bathrooms. Small, lower-priced hotels may offer only the most basic guest services and facilities. Larger, higher-priced hotels may provide additional guest facilities such as a swimming pool, business center (with computers, printers and other office equipment), childcare, conference and event facilities, tennis or basketball courts, gymnasium, restaurants, day spa and social function services. Hotel rooms are usually numbered (or named in some smaller hotels and B&Bs) to allow guests to identify their room. Some boutique, high-end hotels have custom decorated rooms. Some hotels offer meals as part of a room and board arrangement. In the United Kingdom, a hotel is required by law to serve food and drinks to all guests within certain stated hours. In Japan, capsule hotels provide a tiny room suitable only for sleeping and shared bathroom facilities.

Exercises:

(1) Hotel usually provides a short-term accommodation for guests. (   )

(2) Larger hotels provides more services and facilities than small hotels. (   )

(3) To help guests find their rooms, hotel rooms are usually numbered. (   )

(4) In Japan, a hotel is required by law to serve food and drinks to all guests within certain stated hours. (   )

(5) In Japan, capsule hotels provide a tiny room only for sleeping without bathroom facilities.(   )

Challenges and Solutions

1. What are the different forms of pricing in hotels?

Solutions:

2. What are the difference ways to offer guests room rates?

Solutions:

3. What are the basic premises for room upgrading?

Solutions:

4. If a guest doesn't like his room, what will you do?

Solutions:

5. If a guest wants to have an extra bed, can wo offer to them?

Solutions:

6. If a guest feels too cold in his room, what will you do?

Solution:

7. If the guests complain the bathroom doesn't have hot water, what will you do?

Solutions:

M3-3 Knowledge Link

M3-4 Key to Exercises

Lesson Two   Chamber Service

Objectives

➢ To help the students master useful expressions and sentences about chamber service and making bed.

➢ To help the students familiar with the procedure of chamber service and making bed.

➢ To help the students make some dialogues about chamber service and making bed.

Warming Up

1. Look at the following pictures and fill in the blanks according to the corresponding descriptions.

_____ is one of the busiest and the most important components in a hotel, which mainly deals with the room-related affairs, and provides room-related services to guests.

_____ of this department are critical to the success of the hotel because they are on the frontline. They see and interact with the guests daily, and when in the hotel, the guests spend the majority of their time in their rooms.

M3-5   Warming Up

Dialogues

Key sentences:

➢ I'm sorry to disturb you, madam. But I would like to clean the room. May I do it now?

➢ Do you mind my opening the window?

➢ May I make your bed now?

➢ Would you like me to set the bed up for you now, or leave it folded in the corner till nighttime?

➢ I will place the "Do Not Disturb" sign on your door when I leave today.

Pre-questions:

1. Do you think keeping room clean and tidy is important in hotel?

2. Do you know how the room attendant clean rooms in hotel?

3. How should the room attendants deal with do not disturb room when they clean rooms?

Dialogue 1

Chambermaid:	Housekeeping. May I come in?
Guest:	Yes, please.
Chambermaid:	I'm sorry to disturb you, madam. But I would like to clean the room. May I do it now?
Guest:	No, not now. I don't feel well at the moment.
Chambermaid:	Sorry to hear that. Shall I send a doctor for you.
Guest:	No, thanks. I've bought some medicine myself.
Chambermaid:	What can I do for you?
Guest:	That's very kind of you. Can you get me a thermos of hot water?
Chambermaid:	Yes, I'll fill it right away. If you need any help, just dial 3 or press the button over there. I hope you will recover as soon as possible.
Guest:	Thank you vey much. And please hang the Do Not Disturb sign after bringing the water.
Chambermaid:	Okay. I'll be back soon.

Dialogue 2

Chambermaid:	Good morning, sir. I am here to clean your room. May I come through, please?
Guest:	Yes, come right in.
Chambermaid:	Do you mind my opening the window?
Guest:	Of course not. Could you tidy up the bathroom first? I've just had a bath, and it's quite a mess now.
Chambermaid:	Certainly, sir. I'll tidy it up at once.
Guest:	Thank you.
Chambermaid:	It's my pleasure. May I make your bed now?
Guest:	Yes. By the way, could the change the bed sheet and get me a blanket?
Chambermaid:	Certainly, sir. Is there anything else I can do for you, sir?
Guest:	Yes. I would like to request an early wake-up call. Can you make it at 7:00 a.m.?

Chambermaid:	Certainly, sir.
Guest:	Thank you very much.
Chambermaid:	That's right. Have a good rest. Goodbye.
Guest:	Goodbye.

Dialogue 3

Chambermaid:	Good morning! Housekeeping!
Guest:	Yes, what is it?
Chambermaid:	I'm sorry to disturb you, madam. Would you like me to clean your room now?
Guest:	Yes, please.
Chambermaid:	I'll be done shortly, madam. Is there anything else you will need or that I can do for you?
Guest:	Well, yes. My daughter will be coming here today. I am going to pick her up now? Would it be possible to get an extra rollaway bed for her?
Chambermaid:	Absolutely, I will call on the radio now and have it brought to your room. Would you like me to set the bed up for you now, or leave it folded in the corner till nighttime?
Guest:	It would be wonderful if you set it up for us.
Chambermaid:	No problem, madam. I will also leave you extra towels in the bathroom for her.
Guest:	That's so kind of you.
Chambermaid:	Is there anything else, madam?
Guest:	She will probably be exhausted when she arrives. She may want to sleep late in the morning. Could you clean the room later tomorrow?
Chambermaid:	Certainly, madam. I will place the "Do Not Disturb" sign on your door when I leave today. And tomorrow I will clean your room after lunchtime.
Guest:	That will be perfect. Thank you so much for the kind service.
Chambermaid:	You are welcome, madam. It is definitely my pleasure. Have a great day.

Vocabulary

disturb[dɪ'stɜ:b]　v. 打扰
moment['məʊm(ə)nt]　n. 片刻，瞬间
tidy up　v. 整理
mess　n. 混乱
thermos ['θɜ:mɒs]　n. 热水瓶
button['bʌtn]　n. 按钮
recover[rɪ'kʌvə]　v. 恢复
Hang[hæŋ]　v. 悬挂
sign[saɪn]　n.标记，牌

bed sheet　n. 床单
blanket['blæŋkɪt]　n. 毛毯
request[rɪ'kwest]　v. 请求
wake-up call　n. 叫醒服务
rollaway bed　n. 折叠床
fold [fəʊld]　v. 折叠
towel ['taʊəl]　n. 毛巾
exhausted [ɪg'zɔ:stɪd]　adj. 疲惫的
definitely ['defɪnɪtlɪ]　adv. 清楚地

Useful Expressions

1. Housekeeping. May I come in?
客房部，我可以进来吗？
2. I'm sorry to disturb you, madam. But I would like to clean the room. May I do it now?

很抱歉打扰您，夫人。但我想打扫房间。现在可以吗？

3. Sorry to hear that. Shall I send a doctor for you.
很抱歉听到这个消息。我可以为你派一个医生吗？

4. Can you get me a thermos of hot water?
你能给我拿一壶热水吗？

5. If you need any help, just dial 3 or press the button over there.
如果你需要帮助，只需拨3或按下按钮。

6. I hope you will recover as soon as possible.
我希望你能尽快恢复。

7. And please hang the Do Not Disturb sign after bringing the water.
您送水后请把请勿打扰的牌子挂在门上。

8. Do you mind my opening the window?
你介意我打开窗户吗？

9. Could you tidy up the bathroom first? I've just had a bath, and it's quite a mess now.
你能先把浴室收拾好吗？我刚洗了个澡，现在很乱。

10. Could the change the bed sheet and get me a blanket?
您能把床单换一下，给我一条毯子？

11. I would like to request an early wake-up call. Can you make it at 7:00 a.m.?
我想要求提前叫醒服务。你能在早上7点前给我打电话吗？

12. I'll be done shortly, madam. Is there anything else you will need or that I can do for you?
我很快就会完成的，夫人。你还有什么需要我帮你做的吗？

13. Would it be possible to get an extra rollaway bed for her?
是否有可能为她多弄一张折叠床？

14. Absolutely, I will call on the radio now and have it brought to your room.
当然，我现在就打电话把它带到你的房间。

15. Would you like me to set the bed up for you now, or leave it folded in the corner till nighttime?
你想让我现在为你铺床，或者把它放在角落里直到晚上？

M3-6 Practice

Exercises

1. Questions and Answers

(1) What are the duties of housekeeping department?

(2) What is the procedure of cleaning guest's rooms?

(3) What qualities should room attendants have?

2. Match the words or expressions in Column A with their Chinese equivalents in Column B.

A	B
(1) disturb	a. 整理

(2) moment   b. 打扰

(3) tidy up   c. 热水瓶

(4) mess   d. 标记

(5) thermos   e. 恢复

(6) hang   f. 床单

(7) recover   g. 毛毯

(8) sign   h. 悬挂

(9) bed sheet   i. 片刻

(10) blanket   j. 混乱

3. Choose the right answer for each question.

(1) Hotels and restaurants are also known as the _____ Industry.

A. tourism   B. banquet   C. hospitality   D. food service

(2) To be _____ , a company must make more money than it needs for expenses.

A. profitable   B. accommodating   C. hospitable   D. properly run

(3) Hotel _____ are the people who work for the hotel.

A. hosts   B. salaries   C. employees   D. travelers

(4) The _____ take care of the cleaning, reparing and laundering of guests' clothing.

A. valet service   B. laundry   C. room attendant   D. room service

(5) The housekeeping is responsible for _____ of all guestrooms in a hotel.

A. profit   B. accommodating

C. neatness and cleanness   D. management

(6) The room being "out of order" means the room is _____.

A. is occupied   B. is very dirty   C. is untidy   D. needs repairing

(7) In hotels the 'DND' sign stands for _____.

A. Do Not Disturb   B. Being Occupied   C. Out of Order   D. Vacant

(8) A room maid is sent to clean the room by the _____.

A. front office   B. food and beverage   C. housekeeping   D. laundry

(9) It is impolite to _____ guests when they are sleeping in room.

A. talk   B. eat   C. argue   D. disturb

(10) The room is in a _____ because the children are playing now.

A. mess   B. clean   C. tidy   D. order

4. Read the passage and decide if the statements are true (T) or false (F).

The Housekeeping Department is the backbone of a hotel. In a sense, it is possible to say that a clean and attractive guestroom is the product that a hotel sells. The main duty of the housekeeping staff is to see to the cleanliness and good order of all rooms and public areas in the hotel. The laundry and valet service and many personal services are also parts of their jobs. And they must coordinate the work closely with the Front Office. Housekeeping in a hotel is a very physically demanding job that includes many, varied tasks. The actual amount of work depends on the size of a room and the number of beds. A housekeeper needs between fifteen and thirty minutes to do one room. In their work, there are main risk factors for repetitive motion injuries: heavy physical workload and excessive bodily motions which are a high risk for back injuries and forceful upper limb motions in awkward positions which are a high risk for neck or shoulder and arm injuries.

Exercises:

(1) A clean and attractive guestroom is the product that hotel sells. (　　)

(2) Housekeeping is to see to the cleanliness and good order of all rooms and public areas in the hotel. (　　)

(3) Housekeeping department cannot provide laundry and valet service. (　　)

(4) Housekeeping staff may have some injuries during their work. (　　)

(5) The actual amount of work depends on the size of a room and the number of beds. (　　)

Challenges and Solutions

1. How should room attendant knock at the guest's door?

Solutions:

2. What is the procedure for room attendants to clean guest't room?

Solutions:

3. What will you do if the guest asks for an extra bed?

Solutions:

4. What should you do if you find some lost property of a guest when you clean guest's room?

Solutions:

5. If a guest wants to have an extra bed, can wo offer to them?

Solutions:

6. What should you do if you find the air-conditioner does not work when you clean guest's room?

Solution:

7. What will you do when you clean guest's room and find the guest's telephone is ringing?

Solutions:

M3-7　Knowledge Link

M3-8　Key to Exercises

Lesson Three　Laundry Service

Objectives

➢ To help the students master useful expressions and sentences about laundry service.

➢ To help the students familiar with the types and procedure of laundry service.

➢ To help the students make some dialogues about laundry service.

Warming Up

1. Look at the following pictures and fill in the blanks according to the corresponding description.

_____ service is very important and necessary in hotel because all hotels should provide clean linen for its guests and many upscale hotels also help clean guests' clothes.

Usually the _____ pick up the guests'clothes, send the clothes to laundry and deliver them back to guests. Some hotels especially set up laundry department responsible for laundry service.

M3-9   Warming Up

Dialogues

Key sentences:

➢ Housekeeping. Have you got any laundry?

➢ Have you filled out the laundry list?

➢ Is there anything special you need to do for any of these items?

➢ We usually collect laundry before 9:00 a.m. and deliver it back by 8:00 p.m. But now it's already 1:00 p.m. I'm afraid it's too late for today's laundry.

➢ Would you tell me how much your dress?

Pre-questions:

1. Have you ever used the laundry service in hotel?

2. Do you know which department is responsible for laundry service?

3. Do you know how to provide laundry service for guests?

Dialogue 1

Room Attendant: Housekeeping. Have you got any laundry?

Guest: Yes. Here are my dress and my husband's shirt. I have put them in the laundry bag.

Room Attendant: Great. Have you filled out the laundry list?

Guest: Yes. Here it is.

Room Attendant:	Perfect. Is there anything special you need to do for any of these items?
Guest:	Please dry clean and iron the dress and shirt. There are a few stains on the dress's collar. Please clean them up.
Room Attendant:	Oaky, I noticed them. We will try our best to remove the stain, but we can't guarantee the result.
Guest:	By the way, a button came off my husband's shirt. Could you have a new one sewn for me?
Room Attendant:	Yes. But I'm afraid the new one is not exactly the same as the others.
Guest:	Never mind. It doesn't matter.
Room Attendant:	Is that all, madam?
Guest:	Yes. That's all.
Room Attendant:	Okay, please sign the laundry list here. Excellent, here is your copy. I will have this cleaned, pressed and delivered by tomorrow evening.
Guest:	Great. Thank you.
Room Attendant:	You are welcome. Good-bye. Have a nice day.

Dialogue 2

Front Desk Staff:	Good afternoon, Madam. How may I help you?
Guest:	Good afternoon. I want to have my coat and scarf washed right now.
Front Desk Staff:	We usually collect laundry before 11:00 a.m. and deliver it back by 6:00 p.m. But now it's already 1:00 p.m. I'm afraid it's too late for today's laundry.
Guest:	But I need it this evening.
Front Desk Staff:	Don't worry. We provide three-hour express service, but there is an extra charge of 50%.
Guest:	Great. I will have the express service.
Front Desk Staff:	All right. I will send a valet to your room to pick up your laundry soon.
Guest:	Okay. By the way, my scarf is silk. Please wash it by hand in cold water. It might shrink otherwise.
Front Desk Staff:	Please write your request in the laundry list. We will be careful with it. Anything else?
Guest:	No, thank you vey much.
Front Desk Staff:	It's my pleasure. We are always at your service.

Dialogue 3

Room Attendant:	Laundry service. May I come in?
Guest:	Yes, please.
Room Attendant:	Here is your laundry, Mrs. Black. Please have a check.
Guest:	Ok. Look at my dress. It's badly shrunk. You see there is a hole.
Room Attendant:	I'm awfully sorry, Mr. Black. I'll bring it back to the laundry department right away. The laundry will pay for the damage. Would you tell me how much your dress?
Guest:	About 400$.
Room Attendant:	Could you give us the receipt? We will refund the cost of the laundry and the new dress.

Guest: I bought it last year. I can't find the receipt.

Room Attendant: Could you buy a new one here and give us the receipt?

Guest: Okay.

Room Attendant: Would you please fill in this form? I do apologize for causing you so much inconvenience.

Vocabulary

laundry['lɔ:ndrɪ]　*n.* 洗衣房，要洗的衣服

laundry bag　*n.* 洗衣袋

laundry list　*n.* 洗衣单

item['aɪtəm]　*n.* 条目，物品

dry clean　*v.* 干洗

iron　*v.* 熨烫

stain[sten]　*n.* 污点

collar['kɒlə]　*n.* 衣领

notice['nəʊtɪs]　*v.* 通知；注意到

guarantee[gær(ə)n'ti:]　*v.* 保证

sew[səʊ]　*v.* 缝补

deliver[dɪ'lɪvə]　*v.* 递送

scarf [skɑ:f]　*n.* 围巾

collect　*v.* 收集

express service　*n.* 快洗服务

extra['ekstrə]　*adj.* 额外的

valet['væleɪ]　*n.* 服务员

shrink[ʃrɪŋk]　*v.* 缩水

otherwise['ʌðəwaɪz]　*adv.* 否则

request[rɪ'kwest]　*v.* 请求

damage['dæmɪdʒ]　*n.* 损害

receipt[rɪ'si:t]　*n.* 收据

refund['ri:fʌnd]　*v.* 退还，退款

apologize[ə'pɒlədʒaɪz]　*v.* 道歉

inconvenience[ɪnkən'vi:nɪəns]　*n.* 不便；麻烦

Useful Expressions

1. Housekeeping. Have you got any laundry?

客房部，你有衣服要洗吗？

2. Have you filled out the laundry list?

你填好了洗衣单？

3. Is there anything special you need to do for any of these items?

这些衣服有什么需要特别处理的吗？

4. Please dry clean and iron the dress and shirt.

请干洗并熨烫大衣和衬衫。

5. There are a few spots on the dress's collar. Please clean them up.

在礼服的领子上有几个斑点。请清理。

6. By the way, a button came off my husband's shirt. Could you have a new one sewn for me?

顺便说一下，我丈夫的衬衫上有一个扣子掉了。你能帮我缝一枚新的吗？

7. But I'm afraid the new one is not exactly the same as the others.

但我恐怕新的与原来的并不完全一样。

8. I will have this cleaned, pressed and delivered by tomorrow evening.

我会清洁、熨烫，并于明晚送到您的房间。

9. We usually collect laundry before 9:00 a.m. and deliver it back by 8:00 p.m.

我们通常在9:00之前收洗衣服。然后在晚上8点前把它送回客人房间。

10. We provide three-hour express service, but there is an extra charge of 50%.

我们提供三个小时的快洗服务，但额外收费是50%。

11. Please write your request in the laundry list. We will be careful with it.

请把你的要求写在洗衣单上。我们会小心的。

12. By the way, my scarf is silk. Please wash it by hand in cold water. It might shrink otherwise.

顺便说一下，我的围巾是丝绸。请用冷水手洗。否则，它可能会缩水。

13. It's my pleasure. We are always at your service.

这是我的荣幸。我们随时为您服务。

14. Here is your laundry, Mrs. Black. Please have a check.

这是你的衣服，布莱克夫人。请检查。

15. I'll bring it back to the laundry department right away. The laundry will pay for the damage.

我马上把它送回洗衣部。洗衣部会赔偿损失。

M3-10 Practice

Exercises

1. Questions and Answers

(1) What types of laundry service do you know?

(2) Whose job is to collect laundry in a hotel?

(3) When a guest lost some laundry, what should you do?

2. Match the words or expressions in Column A with their Chinese equivalents in Column B.

A	B
(1) item	a. 洗衣单
(2) laundry list	b. 污渍
(3) stain	c. 保证
(4) collar	d. 缝补
(5) notice	e. 条目，物品
(6) guarantee	f. 注意
(7) sew	g. 快洗服务
(8) deliver	h. 递送
(9) express service	i. 衣领
(10) refund	j. 退款

3. Complete the following dialogue according to the Chinese in brackets.

(RA: Room attendant G: Guest)

RA: ＿＿＿＿＿＿＿＿＿＿＿＿＿（客房部）. Can I help you?

G: ＿＿＿＿＿＿＿＿＿＿＿＿＿（我有一件衣服要洗）. I split some coffee on it and I need to wear it this evening.

RA: It's afternoon now. I suggest you to use express service. We can have it dry cleaned and ＿＿＿＿＿＿＿＿＿＿＿＿＿（三小时后给您送回）.

G: Okay, we will not leave until 6:00 p.m. ＿＿＿＿＿＿＿＿＿＿＿＿＿（快洗费是多少）?

RA: We charge 40% more. There is a price list in your drawer and you can have a look.

G: Thank you. By the way, ＿＿＿＿＿＿＿＿＿＿＿＿＿＿＿＿（你们有熨烫服务吗）?

RA: Yes, we have. Is there anything else I can do for you?

G: No, thanks.

RA: ＿＿＿＿＿＿＿＿＿＿＿＿＿＿（请填一下您抽屉里的洗衣单）. I will send a room attendant to pick up your clothes.

G: All right. Thank you

RA: You are welcome. Goodbye.

4. Read the passage and decide if the statements are true (T) or false (F).

Most hotel laundries that provide personal service will offer three categories of service:"next-day""same-day"and"express"service. Next-day service means the guest's laundry or mending request will be completed by the following day. With same-day service, the guest's order will be completed the same day it is received by the Laundry Service department. Both of these services usually require the guest to turn-in their order by a specific time to ensure prompt delivery. The last category, express service, is required when the guest is in a hurry. Express service means the guest will receive his garments within a couple hours. The laundry attendant should be able to give the guest a firm time for delivery, and it will vary depending on how busy the laundry is that particular day. The charge for all three of these categories of service will vary, with express service being the most costly.

Exercises:

(1) Most hotel laundries offer only offer next day and same day service. (　　)

(2) Same-day service means the guest's laundry or mending request will be completed by the same day. (　　)

(3) When the guest is in a hurry, he/she can use the express service. (　　)

(4) Same-day service is more expensive than express service. (　　)

(5) Express service is the fastest among these three services. (　　)

Challenges and Solutions

1. How do you provide laundry service to guests?

Solutions:

2. What should attendants confirm when they collect clothes?

Solutions:

3. When you collect guest's clothes, how to deal with DND room?

Solutions:

4. When you collect guest's clothes, if the guest is not in the room,what should you do?

Solutions:

5. What should you do if the guest gets the wrong clean laundry delivered to his room?

Solutions:

6. What should you do when you find a guest's clothes is damaged?

Solution:

7. What should you say if a guest asks the attendant to remove stain on his clothes?

Solutions:

Lesson Four   Room Service

Objectives

➢ To help the students master useful expressions and sentences about room service.

➢ To help the students familiar with procedure of room service.

➢ To help the students make some dialogues about room service.

Warming Up

1. Look at the following pictures and fill in the blanksaccording to the corresponding description.

_____ is also known as in-room dining. It is a service provided by hotels generally hotels of 4-5 star standards as a convenience and choice of dinging option for their guests.

Room service is organized as a subdivision within the _____ Department of high-end hotel and resort properties.

M3-13   Warming Up

Dialogues

Key sentences:

➢ You can use the doorknob menu if you'd like. Please check the items you would like to have for breakfast. Mark down the time and hang it outside your door before you go to bed.

➢ You may just leave them in your room or put them outside your door. We will take them away.

> And would you like croissant or toast?

> I've brought you your supper ordered. Where shall I put them?

> Thank you for using room service. Please enjoy your supper and have a nice day.

Pre-questions:

1. Have you ever used the room service in hotel?

2. What do you order when you use the room service?

3. Do you think this service is good? Why?

Dialogue 1

Waiter:	Good morning, this is front desk. What can I do for you?
Guest:	Good morning. It's Mr. Green in Room 307. I want to have breakfast in my room tomorrow morning. Do you have room service?
Waiter:	Sure, sir. Our hotel has very good room service. You can use the doorknob menu if you'd like. Please check the items you would like to have for breakfast. Mark down the time and hang it outside your door before you go to bed.
Guest:	Okay. Is there any other way to order room service?
Waiter:	Yes, Mr. Green. You may order breakfast by the phone. The extension number for room service is 4.
Guest:	All right. I get it. By the way, what should I do with the plates when I finish the breakfast.
Waiter:	You may just leave them in your room or put them outside your door. We will take them away.
Guest:	Thank you for your information.
Waiter:	It's my pleasure. Have a good night.

Dialogue 2

Waiter:	Good morning, room service. May I help you?
Guest:	Good morning. It's Miss Wang from 1302. I'd like to have an English breakfast in my room.
Waiter:	Okay, madam. What kind of drink would you like?
Guest:	I'd like to have a cup of Latte.
Waiter:	And would you like croissant or toast?
Guest:	Toast for me, please.
Waiter:	How would you like the egg?
Guest:	Fired, sunny-side up. Thank you.
Waiter:	And you can have either sausage or bacon.
Guest:	Sausage, I think, and some tomatoes.
Waiter:	Anything else, Madam?
Guest:	No, thank you. By the way, how long will it take?
Waiter:	It will take about 30 minutes. Okay, Miss Wang, you have ordered a cup of Latte, toast, sunny-side up egg, sausage. Is that right?
Guest:	Yes, that's right.
Waiter:	Please wait a moment. We will send them to your room as soon as possible.

Dialogue 3

Operator:	Room Service. May I come in?
Guest:	Yes, come in, please.
Operator:	Good evening. Mr. Smith. I've brought you your supper ordered. Where shall I put them?
Guest:	Oh, thank you. Could you put them on the desk over there?
Operator:	Okay. Here is the green salad, one mushroom soup, one salmon, one sirloin steak, one ice cream and one souffle, a bottle of red wine. Here is the bill.
Guest:	Thank you. Can I have it charged to myaccount, please?
Operator:	Certainly, sir. Would you sign here?
Guest:	Yes, of course.
Operator:	Shall I open the wine for you?
Guest:	Oh, thank you.
Operator:	Mr. and Mrs. Smith, if you need anything else, please dial 5 or press the button over there. We're always at your service.
Guest:	Okay, I see. Thank you.
Operator:	Thank you for using room service. Please enjoy your supper and have a nice day.

Vocabulary

doorknob menu　*n.* 门把菜单

mark down　*v.* 记下

hang[hæŋ]　*v.* 悬挂

extension number　*n.* 分机号码

English breakfast　*n.* 英式早餐

Latte ['lɑ:teɪ]　*n.* 拿铁咖啡

croissant [krwɑ:sɒŋ]　*n.* 羊角面包

toast　*n.* 吐司

sunny-side up　*adj.* 单煎一面的

bacon　*n.* 培根

green salad　*n.* 蔬菜沙拉

mushroom soup　*n.* 蘑菇汤

salmon['sæmən]　*n.* 三文鱼

sirloin steak　*n.* 沙朗牛排

souffle['su:f(ə)l]　*n.* 奶蛋酥

account[ə'kaʊnt]　*n.* 账户

Useful Expressions

1. Good morning, room service. May I help you?

早上好，送餐服务，我能为您做些什么？

2. Room Service. May I come in?

送餐服务，可以进来吗？

3. Do you have room service?

您这有送餐服务吗？

4. You can use the doorknob menu if you'd like. Please check the items you would like to have for breakfast. Mark down the time and hang it outside your door before you go to bed.

如果你愿意，你可以用门把菜单。请划下您早餐想吃的东西。记下时间，在睡觉前把它挂在门外。

5. Is there any other way to order room service?

还有其他的预定送餐方式吗？

6. You may order breakfast by the phone. The extension number for room service is 4.

你可以打电话叫早餐。客房服务的分机号是4。

7. By the way, what should I do with the plates when I finish the breakfast.

顺便问一下，当我吃完早餐后，我应该怎么处理这些盘子？

8. You may just leave them in your room or put them outside your door. We will take them away.

你可以把它们放在房间里，或者放在门外。我们会把他们带走。

9. What kind of drink would you like?

你想喝点什么？

10. And would you like croissant or toast?

你要牛角面包还是烤面包？

11. It will take about 30 minutes. Okay, Miss Wang, you have ordered a cup of Latte, toast, sunny-side up egg, sausage. Is that right?

大约需要30分钟。好的，王小姐，你点了一杯拿铁，烤面包，煎鸡蛋，香肠。对吗？

12. And you can have either sausage or bacon.

你可以吃香肠或者熏肉。

13. Please wait a moment. We will send them to your room as soon as possible.

请稍等。我们会尽快送到您的房间。

14. I've brought you your supper ordered. Where shall I put them?

我把你点的晚餐给你带来了。我把它们放在哪里？

15. Here is the green salad, one mushroom soup, one veal salmon, one sirloin steak, one ice cream and one souffle, a bottle of red wine. Here is the bill.

这是绿色沙拉、蘑菇汤、三文鱼、沙朗牛排、冰淇淋、蛋奶酥和红酒。这是账单。

M3-14 Practice

Exercises

1. Questions and Answers

(1) What is room service?

(2) What's the relationship between room service section and other departments?

(3) How to provide room service to guests?

2. Match the words or expressions in Column A with their Chinese equivalents in Column B.

A	B
(1) doorknob menu	a. 记下
(2) mark down	b. 拿铁咖啡
(3) hang	c. 羊角包
(4) English breakfast	d. 门把菜单
(5) Latte	e. 悬挂
(6) croissant	f. 蔬菜沙拉
(7) sunny-side up	g. 三文鱼

(8)green salad   h. 英式早餐
(9) mushroom soup   i. 蘑菇汤
(10) salmon   j. 单面煎的

3. Complete the following sentences with appropriate words and expression given.

selection   mark down   salmon   grilled   Room service

(1) Why don't you try the _____, madam? It's really very good.

(2) What would you prefer, _____ sausage or steak?

(3) Remember to _____the time immediately when the guest tells you when he would like his breakfast in his room.

(4) We have a good _____of drink for you to choose, orange juice, milk, tea and so on.

(5) _____ is always provide by Food and Beverage Department instead of Housekeeping Department in the hotel.

4. Read the passage and decide if the statements are true (T) or false (F).

Room service is the service of food or beverages in guests' room in hotel or order accommodation establishments, such as motels or serviced apartments. In all-suite hotels it is often referred to as "in-suite service".

In establishments of any size there is usually a specialist Room Serviced Department responsible to the Food and Beverage manager. Room Service Department must work closely with the Kitchen, Front Office and Housekeeping departments to make sure that the standard of service satisfies, or more than satisfies, guests'expectations. Hotels are often judged, as much as anything else, by the standard of the room service they provide. A five-star property will be expected to provide room service for at least 18 hours of the day, if not all hours of the day and night, and that service must at all times be friendly, quick and efficient.

Exercises:

(1) Room service is also called "in-suite service". (   )

(2) The housekeeping department is responsible for room service. (   )

(3) Room service staff must work closely with the Kitchen, Front Office and Housekeeping departments. (   )

(4) Hotels are also judged by the standard of the room service they provide. (   )

(5) Room service must at all times be friendly, quick and efficient. (   )

Challenges and Solutions

1. How would you introduce room service to your guest?
Solutions:

2. How would you introduce how to use the doorknob menu to guests?
Solutions:

3. If you were working in the room service section, when the telephone rings, what would you say?
Solutions:

4. If you sent food to guest's room, but the guest is not in the room, what will you do?
Solutions:

5. If a guest ordered some food but your hotel don't have, what will you do?

Solutions:

6. If you were a room service attendant and you brought the food to the guest's room, how would you introduce the food to guest?

Solution:

7. What qualities should a room service attendant have?

Solutions:

M3-15　Knowledge Link　　　　　M3-16　Key to Exercises

Lesson Five Maintenance Service

Objectives

➢ To help the students master useful expressions and sentences about maintenance service.

➢ To help the students familiar with the duties of maintenance service.

➢ To help the students make some dialogues about maintenance service.

Warming Up

1. Look at the following pictures and fill in the blanksaccording to the corresponding description.

Hotel Maintenance

_____is a kind of service that the hotel provides to the guest when something is broken in the room, such as the air-condition is broken, the toilet is blocked and so on.

The _____ Department is responsible for all repair and maintenance work in a hotel. The _____ should check and fix light fixtures, plugs and outlets. Also examine the bathroom for leaks or dripping and ensure that all electronic items such as air conditioners and TVs work as they should.

M3-17　Warming Up

Dialogues

Key sentences:

➢ Did you call for service? What can I do for you?

➢ Let me have a look at the toilet. Oh, it's clogged... It's all right now. You can try it.

➢ Can you describe the problem?

➢ Probably the satellite signal is not very good. It's cloudy today. Was it good yesterday?

➢ I'm very sorry, sir. Some part needs to be replaced. I will change them soon.

Pre-questions:

1. If the guest finds the air-conditioner does not work, what should he do?

2. Do you know which department is responsible for the repair and maintenance work in hotel?

3. Do you think it is necessary for hotel to provide the maintenance service? Why?

Dialogue 1

Housekeeper:	Good afternoon, Housekeeping. May I help you?
Guest:	Good afternoon. There seems to be something wrong with the toilet. It doesn't flush.
Housekeeper:	Don't worry, madam. We'll send a plumber to your room right away. Could you tell me your room number?
Guest:	Room 304.
Housekeeper:	Room 812. Please wait a moment.
	(several minutes later)
Plumber:	Plumber. May I come in?
Guest:	Yes, please.
Plumber:	Let me have a look at the toilet. Oh, it's clogged... It's all right now. You can try it.
Guest:	Oh, yes. It's working now. What efficient work! Thank you very much.
Plumber:	It's my pleasure. Wish you a pleasant stay with us!

Dialogue 2

Housekeeper:	Good afternoon, Housekeeping. How may I help you?
Guest:	Good afternoon. It's Miss Wang from 1302. I'm having a problem with the air-conditioner. It doesn't work.
Housekeeper:	Okay, Madam.Can you describe the problem?
Guest:	Well, I can't get any cool air. It so hot now.
Housekeeper:	Are you sure it's turned on?
Guest:	Okay, I'll check again...Yes, it is.
Housekeeper:	I'll inform the maintenance department at once. They'll send someone to

deal with it.

(a few minutes later)

Repairman:	Maintenance department, may I come in?
Guest:	Come in please.
Repairman:	Let me check the air-conditioner... Okay, how do you feel now?
Guest:	Oh, I can feel the cool air now. Thank you very much.
Repairman:	You are welcome. Anything else I can do for you, Madam?
Guest:	Yes, the picture on TV is not very clear. Could you help me repair it?
Repairman:	All right. Is it for every channel?
Guest:	No, just this channel.
Repairman:	Probably the satellite signal is not very good. It's cloudy today. Was it good yesterday?
Guest:	Yes, it was.
Repairman:	Then that's probably the reason.

Dialogue 3

Repairman:	Maintenance department. May I come in?
Guest:	Come in, please.
Repairman:	Did you call for service? What can I do for you?
Guest:	Oh, the water tap drips all night long. I can hardly sleep.
Repairman:	I'm very sorry, sir. Some part needs to be replaced. I will change them soon.
Guest:	Thank you.
Repairman:	It is good now. Is there anything else I can do for you?
Guest:	Yes, the light in this room is too dim. Please get me a brighter one.
Repairman:	Certainly sir. Do you mind if I move your things?
Guest:	Oh, no. Go ahead.
Repairman:	Thank you. (Later) How is the light now?
Guest:	It's much better now. Thank you.
Repairman:	You are welcome. And if you need any other things, please let us know.
Guest:	Okay, thank you.

Vocabulary

flush[flʌʃ]　*v.* 用水冲洗

plumber['plʌmə]　*n.* 水管工

clog[klɒg]　*v.* 阻塞

efficient [ɪ'fiʃ(ə)nt]　*adj.* 有效率的

air-conditioner　*n.* 空调

describe[dɪ's kraɪb]　*v.* 描述

turn on　*v.* 打开

maintenance department　*n.* 维修部

repair　*v.* 修理

channel ['tʃæn(ə)l]　*n.* 频道

satellite signal　*n.* 卫星信号

water tap　*n.* 水龙头

drip [drɪp]　*v.* 滴下

dim[dɪm]　*adj.* 暗淡的

Useful Expressions

1. Good afternoon, Housekeeping. May I help you?

下午好,客房部，有什么需要帮助的吗?

2. There seems to be something wrong with the toilet. It doesn't flush.

卫生间好像有点问题，不能冲水了。

3. Don't worry, Madam. We'll send a plumber to your room right away. Could you tell me your room number?

别担心，夫人。我们马上派一个水管工到你的房间去。你能告诉我你的房间号码吗？

4. Plumber. May I come in?

水管工，我可以进来吗？

5. Let me have a look at the toilet. Oh, it's clogged... It's all right now. You can try it.

让我看看厕所。哦，它堵住了……现在没事了。你可以试一试。

6. It's my pleasure. Wish you a pleasant stay with us!

这是我的荣幸。祝你在这里过得愉快。

7. I'm having a problem with the air-conditioner. It doesn't work.

我的空调有个问题。它不工作了。

8. Can you describe the problem?

你能描述一下问题吗？

9. Are you sure it's turned on?

你确定打开了吗？

10. I'll inform the maintenance department at once. They'll send someone to deal with it.

我马上通知维修部。他们会派人来处理的。

11. Maintenance department, may I come in?

维修部，我可以进来吗？

12. Let me check the air-conditioner... Okay, how do you feel now?

让我检查一下空调，现在您感觉怎么样？

13. You are welcome. Anything else I can do for you, Madam?

您客气了，还有什么需要我帮忙的，女士？

14. The picture on TV is not very clear. Could you help me mend it?

电视上的画面不是很清楚。你能帮我修一下吗？

15. Is it for every channel?

是这个频道吗？

M3-18　Practice

Exercises

1. Questions and Answers

(1) Is maintenance service important in hotel? Why?

(2) What are the daily jobs of the maintenance department?

(3) When the maintenance department provide service for guests, what should they pay attention to?

2. Match the words or expressions in Column A with their Chinese equivalents in Column B.

A	B
(1) flush	a. 水管工
(2) plumber	b. 用水冲洗
(3) clog	c. 描述
(4) efficient	d. 频道
(5) describe	e. 阻塞
(6) turn on	f. 有效率的
(7) maintenance department	g. 水龙头
(8) channel	h. 打开
(9) drip	i. 维修部
(10) water tap	j. 滴水

3. Complete the following sentences with appropriate words and expression given.

> check, clear, within, matter, else, understanding, inform, manager

(1) There is something wrong with the toilet. It does not _____.

(2) I'm sorry about it. I will look into the _____.

(3) The repairman will come to your room _____ ten minutes.

(4) Thank you for your cooperation and _____.

(5) I'll tell the _____ of the maintenance department.

(6) The picture of the TV in my room isn't _____.

(7) I'll _____ the maintenance department at once.

(8) I'll send a repairman to your room to _____ it at once.

4. Read the passage and decide if the statements are true (T) or false (F).

Maintenance Service is a kind of service that the hotel provides to the guest when something is broken in the room, such as the air-condition is broken, the toilet is blocked and so on.The Maintenance Department is responsible for all repair and maintenance work in a hotel. The maintenance staff should check and fix light fixtures, plugs and outlets. Also examine the bathroom for leaks or dripping and ensure that all electronic items such as air conditioners and TVs work as they should.

It is very common that the guest will be angry when something is broken in the room that she lives in. As a hotel staff, at this time, we should be patient because we have to try our best to understand our guests. As a receptionist of the Front Office, in this case, the first thing we should do is to apologize to the guest sincerely. Then, we need to ask the guest about the matter in details. Next, we must try our best to help the guest solve the problem as soon as possible. If necessary, we may make a discount for the guest so that the guest can know our sincerity. Finally, we need to apologize to the guest again and express our best wishes. As a repair man of the Maintenance Department, in this situation, first of all, we also need to apologize to the guest. Secondly, we have to ask the guest about the problem. What's more, we must try our best to repair the broken thing quickly. After repairing the thing, we need to let the guest have a check.

Exercises:

(1) When something is broken in the room, the maintenance department will help repair it. (   )

(2) The maintenance staff should often check and fix light, plugs and outlets. (   )

(3) The maintenance department has no relationship with other department. (   )

(4) When the guest complaint something is wrong, the hotel staff should be patient and helpful. (   )

(5) The maintenance staff should do the repair work quickly and efficiently. (   )

Challenges and Solutions

1. What is the daily job of the maintenance department?

Solutions:

2. If the guest complains that the light does not work, as a repairman what should you do?

Solutions:

3. If the guest complaints that the light is too dim, as a repairman what should you do?

Solutions:

4. If a guest complains that the guest next room is too noisy, what should you do?

Solutions:

5. If a guest lost his room card and ask for help from you, what should you do?

Solutions:

6. If a guest complains the bathing machine does not work, as a repairman what should you do?

Solution:

7. What qualities should a maintenance staff have?

Solutions:

M3-19   Knowledge Link

M3-20   Key to Exercises

Lesson Six   Handling Complaints

Objectives

➢ To help the students master useful expressions and sentences about complaints in housekeeping department.

➢ To help the students familiar with the common complaints in housekeeping department.

➢ To help the students analyze the reasons of complaints and handle complaints in housekeeping department.

Preamble

Friday night June 6, 2018

Dear Housekeeping Manager:

I am writing this letter to express my dissatisfaction with the service I received. I could not imagine that my staying in this hotel would be so bad.

I have been a customer of your hotel on many occasions and I have always been satisfied with the service but I had an unpleasant experience recently.

When I checked into the room, the room was very dirty and smelly. The dustbin was full of garbage. They even didn't change my bed sheets or towels. The worse part of my stay was that I had a neighbor who made noises until late-night. I complained about it to the housekeeping but they refused to improve the situation until the fourth day of my stay.

I request you to boost your housekeeping service because I don't want this experience to ruin my positive impression about your hotel. I just hope that these problems will be solved.

Sincerely yours,

(Signature) Jack

Dialogues

Key sentences:

➢ I'm so sorry. I'll ask Housekeeping come to clean it up immediately.

➢ May I change your room?

➢ We apologize for the inconvenience. I will send a maintenance worker to check it right away. For our deeply apology, we'd like to upgrade you to a suite without any costs.

➢ Thank you for bringing the matter to our attention. I'll arrange the room as soon as possible.

Pre-questions:

1. What are the common complaints in the housekeeping department of a hotel?

2. How to deal with these complaints?

3. What is the right attitude of dealing with the complaints?

Dialogue 1

Guest:	May I speak to the hotel manager please?
Manager:	Hi, this is Benny Smith, the manager of the hotel. How can I help you?
Guest:	Hi. My name is Lisa Wang. I would like to complain about the poor service of your hotel. This is my first time to stay in your hotel and it will be my last one too.

Manager:	I am sorry to hear that. Could you tell meexactly what it is all about?
Guest:	When I checked in this afternoon, I find the bed sheet is stained. And I found a room attendant was cleaning another room. I asked her to help me change the bed sheet. She said yes, but she didn't come. I called to the front desk again, but still nobody come now.
Manager:	Miss. Wang, I do apologize for what happened. I will look into it and give you a reply as soon as possible.
Guest:	Thank you for your attention in this matter.
Manager:	Gould you tell me your room number so that I can reach you later?
Guest:	1201.
Manager:	OK. Miss. Wang, thank you so much for calling. I will deal with the matter right away. Have a good day! Bye!

Dialogue 2

Receptionist:	Good morning, Miss. Is there anything I can do for you?
Guest:	What's wrong with your hotel? Do you really have Housekeeping Department?
Receptionist:	I'm so sorry. Could you tell me what's going on?
Guest:	The bathroom is a mess now. It is not cleaned after the last guest leaved.
Receptionist:	I'm so sorry. I'll ask Housekeeping come to clean it up immediately. (Several minutes later)
Room attendant:	Housekeeping. May I come in?
Guest:	Yes, please. You see you didn't clean the bathroom.
Room attendant:	I'm very sorry. I'll clean it right now.
Guest:	There is one more thing that I'm not satisfied. The weather is so hot. But the air conditioner is out of work. I can't stand it anymore.
Room attendant:	We apologize for the inconvenience. I will send amaintenance worker to check it right away. For our deeply apology, we'd like to upgrade you to a suite without any costs.
Guest:	Fine. I hope this kind of thing will not happen again.
Room attendant:	We promise.

Dialogue 3

Receptionist:	Good morning, madam. Can I help you?
Guest:	I didn't sleep a wink last night. I was botheredby mosquitoes all night.
Receptionist:	I'm terribly sorry, madam. May I have your name and room number?
Guest:	Wang Jie from room 1203. I can't stand it now.
Receptionist:	I'm sorry, Miss. Wang. I do wish you had let us know at once.
Guest:	At once? I was bothered all night by the mosquitoes. I'm considering moving to another hotel.
Receptionist:	Oh, please don't. May I change your room?
Guest:	I accept your offer if there are no mosquitoes.
Receptionist:	Of course. We will take necessary precautions. I can assure you such things won't happen again.

Guest:	All right.
Receptionist:	Thank you for bringing the matter to our attention. I'll arrange the room as soon as possible.
Guest:	Thank you.
Receptionist:	It's my pleasure. Have a good rest.

Vocabulary

exactly *adv.* 正确地	promise *v.* 允诺
stained[steɪnd] *adj.* 玷污的	wink[wɪŋk] *v.* 眨眼
apologize *v.* 道歉	bother['bɒðə] *v.* 打扰
reply [rɪ'plaɪ] *v.* 回答	mosquito [mɒ'ski:təʊ] *n.* 蚊子
mess *n.* 混乱	consider[kən'sɪdə] *v.* 考虑
clean up *v.* 清洁	precaution *n.* 预防措施
inconvenience [ɪnkən'vi:nɪəns] *n.* 不便	assure [ə'ʃʊə] *v.* 保证
upgrade[ʌp'greɪd] *v.* 使升级	arrange[ə'rendʒ] *v.* 安排

Useful Expressions

1. What seems to be the problem, sir?

有什么问题吗，先生？

2. Would you mind coming with me to my office and tell me exactly what happened there, Madam/sir?

小姐/先生，您介意跟我来一下办公室，告诉我具体发生什么事吗？

3. Excuse me, but there's a problem with the heating in my room.

对不起，我房间的暖气有点问题。

4. My wife was woken up several times by the noise the baggage elevator made.

我妻子被运送行李的电梯发出的嘈杂声弄醒了几次。

5. She said it was too much for her.

她说这对她来说太过分了。

6. The light in this room is too dim.

这个房间的灯光太暗了。

7. I've never found a room with such poor facilities.

我从来没有遇到一间设备这么差的房间。

8. I'm afraid I have to make a complaint. Some money has gone missing from my hotel room.

恐怕我得投诉。我在旅馆房间里的钱少了一些。

9. I'm afraid there's a slight problem with my room — the bed hasn't been made.

恐怕我的房间有点小问题——床还没铺好。

10. I'm terribly/awfully/extremely sorry for (my carelessness/ the inconvenience/trouble).

对于我的粗心大意/给您带来的不便/给您带来的麻烦我感到非常抱歉。

11. Please accept my sincere apology on behalf of the hotel.

请接受我代表酒店的真诚道歉。

12. I'm sorry to have caused you so much trouble.

很抱歉给你带来这么多麻烦。

13. I'm sorry to have kept you waiting.

对不起，让你久等了。

14. I'm very sorry, Madam. There must be some misunderstandings.

非常抱歉，女士。一定有误会。

15. I'll have the maintenance man come in and take a look at it.

我会让维修人员进来看看。

Exercises

1. Match each word or phrase in the column on the left with its meaning in the column on the right.

(1) reply	a. say sorry to sb.
(2) apologize	b. think about carefully.
(3) inconvenience	c. take the trouble to do something.
(4) promise	d. say sorry to somebody.
(5) wink	e. the trait of practicing caution in advance.
(6) bother	f. a difficulty that causes anxiety.
(7) consider	g. something that you say or write when you answer someone.
(8) precaution	h. look toward them and close one eye very briefly.
(9) assure	i.put into a proper or systematic order.
(10) arrange	j. make certain of.

2. Complete the following dialogue according to the Chinese in brackets and read it in roles.

RA=Receptionist   B=Guest

RA: Good evening. Housekeeping. Can I help you?

B: I just checked into the room, _____（但是我的房间还没被整理。）

RA: _____（非常抱歉，女士）We are very busy this morning. I'll send a room attendant to clean your room now. May I have your room number please?

B: Room 602. I would like to have my room made up early every day. Can you do this?

RA: Yes, madam._____（只要客人要求，我们总是早点收拾房间。）Just let us know what you need. And if we can, we'll try our best to do it.

B: All right. Thank you.

RA: It's my pleasure, _____（还有什么需要帮忙的吗？）

B: No, thank you.

3. Choose the correct attitude for dealing with guest's complaints.

a. Respond submissively.

b. Remain calm and be polite and helpful.

c. Blame another employee or department.

d. Be attentive and listen carefully.

e. Blame guests and argue back.

f. Take effective measures.

g. Take corrective and protective action.

4. Choose the best English translation for each sentence.

(1) 很抱歉给你带来这么多麻烦。（   ）

A. I'm sorry for the trouble.   B. I'm sorry to bring you the trouble.

C. I'm sorry to have caused you so much trouble.   D. I'm very sorry about so much trouble.

(2) 对不起，让你久等了。(　　)

A. I'm sorry to have kept you waiting.   B. I'm sorry to let you wait.

C. I'm sorry to wait for you.   D. I'm sorry to wait with you.

(3) 我们将立即调查此事。(　　)

A. We'll check the matter.   B. We'll attend to the matter.

C. We'll see the matter now.   D. We'll look into the matter immediately.

(4) 一切都会好的。(　　)

A. Everything is good.   B. All is ok.

C. Everything will be all right.   D. No problem.

(5) 一定有误会。(　　)

A. You are misunderstanding.   B. There must be some misunderstandings.

C. You are wrong.   D. I misunderstand you.

5. Read the passage and choose the best answers to the following questions.

How to Follow up with the customer complaints

1. Investigate the complaint. Before you find a constructive solution to your customers complain, investigate the situation further based on her description of events. Ask other employees, review correspondence or security video to help develop a complete picture of what happened; ask any employees for their perspective on what happened. They may have been directly involved or observed the event and may be able to provide additional details; read any correspondence or listen to any messages from the customer. Watch any security videos if that is necessary; forward the complaint to any superiors.

2. Formulate an acceptable solution. Once you have a more complete picture of what happened, come up with a solution to the complaint that works for everyone. Consider having alternatives in the event that a superior or the customer doesn't agree with it.

3. Contact the customer. Call or write your customer with the solution you have for her complaint. This can show that you are serious and sincere about her concerns and want to keep her as a client. Contact the customer as soon as possible, preferably within one day. Make sure to contact her on or before you said you would. Making her wait may make irritate her even more. Thank her again for reaching out. Remind your customer that your company successfully deals with many clients every year and that you enjoy a good reputation because of your dedication to customers. Enjoy some light conversation before you offer your solution. This can help diffuse the situation and calm you and your customer. You could ask her about the weather or a sporting event that happened since you last spoke.

4. Offer your solution. After breaking the ice with the customer, kindly offer the solution to her. Remember to keep your tone warm and sincere so that she knows you genuinely care about her complaint and the solution. Tell the customer that you've investigated her complaint further and are sorry that she had a bad experience. Let her know the solution that you've reached and give her a second to process it. Offer an alternative solution if she doesn't like what you've suggested. Keep your offers to two so that the solution remains acceptable to you. Listen to any other concerns she may have to make her feel valuable.

5. Thank her again. Your customer may be feeling a little embarrassed that she created a fuss. Thank her again for her concern and tell her you've available if she needs further assistance. Let your customer know how much you appreciate her and her business.

6. Learn and move on. Even though the situation may have initially been negative, you can use it as a learning experience. Take the process of addressing and following up on the complaint as a constructive way to handle future complaints.

7. Engage your customer again. After some time has passed, consider contacting your customer to make sure the resolution was satisfactory. This can show her that you value her business and allows you to address any potential problems. Call or email and say something like "I don't mean to bother you, I just want to make sure that you're satisfied with the solution we found to your complaint." Chat with your customer if everything is ok and say "We look forward to seeing you again." Address any further complaints she may have, but be aware that some people may complain on a consistent basis to get free products or services.

(1) When compliant happens, why do we need to see the security video? (　　)

A. It is more reliable than what people said.

B. It can help us develop a complete picture of what happened.

C. It is clearer.

D. Most people use it to deal with complaint.

(2) Why do we need to have alternative solutions when dealing with complaints? (　　)

A. Because the customer may not agree with one solution.

B. Because it is required by the hotel.

C. Because customer is cleverer than manager.

D. Because the government require it.

(3) Once complaint happens, when should we contact the customer? (　　)

A. When you have free time.

B. When the customer calls you again.

C. As soon as possible, preferably within one day.

D. You don't need to contact customer, just wait.

(4) Which of the following statements is TRUE according to the passage? (　　)

A. When the complaint happens, you just need to listen to the customer and don't need to do investigation.

B. After we have solved the complaint, we don't need to contact the customer.

C. Complaints is just a work and we can not get anything from it.

D. People may complain on a consistent basis to get free products or service.

Challenges and Solutions

1. If the guest complains you to your manager, what will you do?

Solutions:

2. If the guest complains that you are not professional, what will you do?

Solutions:

3. If the guest complains you and is not satisfied with your methods, what will you do?

Solutions:

4. If the guest complains that the room's light is too dim, what will you do?

Solutions:

5. If the guest complains that the water tap does not work, what will you do?

Solutions:

6. If the guest complains that he loses some money in the room, what will you do?

Solution:

7. If the guest complains that the air-conditioner does not work, what will you do?

Solutions:

M3-21　Knowledge Link

M3-22　Key to Exercises

Chapter 4

Western Food Service

Lesson One Taking Orders

Objectives

➢ To let students master useful words and expressions about taking orders.
➢ To let student familiar with the standard sequence of multicourse meal of western meal.
➢ To let student make some dialogues about taking orders service.

Warming Up

1. A multicourse meal or full-course Dinner is a meal of multiple courses, almost invariably eaten in the evening or afternoon. Most Western-world multicourse meals follow a standard sequence, influenced by traditional French haute cuisine. There are variations depending on location and custom. The following is a common sequence for a five-course meal. Look at the pictures to write down the names of meal sequence by the corresponding description.

A hors d'oeuvre (/ɔːrˈdɜːrv), _____ or _____ is a small dish served before a meal. Some hors d'oeuvres are served cold, others hot. Formerly, hors d'oeuvres were also served between courses.

The starter is followed by a clear or thick _____ course.

A _____ is the "meat course" in a meal consisting of several courses. It is most often preceded by an _____ or soup. The _____ is usually the heaviest, heartiest, and most complex or substantive dish on a menu.

Main course is often followed by a _____ selection, accompanied by an appropriate selection of wine.

_____ is a course that typically comes at the end of a meal, usually consisting of sweet food. Common desserts include cakes, cookies, fruits, pastries, ice cream, and candies.

A_____ is a dish consisting of small pieces of food mixed with a sauce. Salads can be based around a wide variety of foods including vegetables, fruits, and cooked meat, eggs, and grains.

M4-1　Warming Up

Dialogues

Key sentences:

➢ Here are your menus.

➢ I'll be back to take your order in a minute.

➢ Are you ready to order, Sir/ Madam?

➢ May I take your order, Sir/ Madam?

➢ Today's special is...

Pre-questions:

1. What do you usually do when the guest comes into the restaurant?

2. What information would you provide to the guest who comes to your restaurant first time?

3. How do you take orders?

Dialogue 1

Waiter:	May I take your order now?
David:	Have you figured out what you want, Annie?
Annie:	Yeah. I'll have the "Alice Springs Chicken".
Waiter:	And for your side dishes?
Annie:	Sauteed vegetables and a baked potato.
Waiter:	And for you sir?
David:	I want to have the sirloin steak.
Waiter:	And how would you like that cooked this evening?
David:	Make it medium rare.
Waiter:	Okay, sir. I'll put your order in right away.

Dialogue 2

Waiter:	Are you ready to order, sir?
Mr. Ryefield:	Yes, I'll have the beef stew for starters and my wife would like tomato soup.
Waiter:	One beef stew and one tomato soup. What would you like for the main course?
Mr. Ryefield:	I'll have the Cayenne Pepper Steak and my wife would like the Fried Trout with mashed potatoes.
Waiter:	I'm afraid the trout is off.
Mr. Ryefield:	Oh, dear. Err... What else do you recommend?
Waiter:	The sole is very good.
Mr. Ryefield:	OK. I'll have that. Do you have any coleslaw?
Waiter:	No, I'm sorry. We don't.
Mrs. Ryefield:	Just give me a small mixed salad then.
Mr. Ryefield:	Same for me.
Waiter:	Certainly. Would you like something to drink?
Mr. Ryefield:	Yes, please. May I see the wine list?
Waiter:	Certainly. Here you are.
Mr. Ryefield:	A bottle of Chabils'please.
Waiter:	Excellent choice!

Dialogue 3

Waiter:	Good morning, do you have a reservation madam?
Guest:	Yes, a table for two. My name is Alice Gray.
Waiter:	Would you like smoking or non-smoking?
Guest:	Non-smoking, please.
Waiter:	Fine, madam. Would you follow me please?

(*After seating the guest*)

Waiter:	Would you like to see the menu?
Guest:	Yes, I'd like to see the menu.
Waiter:	Are you ready to order?
Guest:	Yes, I'd like to appetizer a Mediterranean salad and then Duck stuffed served with orange sauce.
Waiter:	Would you like anything to drink?
Guest:	A bottle of a red wine?
Waiter:	And would you like any dessert?
Guest:	Yes, I'd like to dessert a Strawberry with whipped cream.
Waiter:	And... Would you like something else?
Guest:	Yes, a cappuccino, please.
Waiter:	Ok madam, I'll be with you in a minute.

Vocabulary

figure ['fɪɡə] out　*v.* 想出、算出、断定

sauteed [səʊ'teɪd]　*adj.* 快炒、嫩煎

baked['beɪkt]　*adj.* 烤的、烘焙的

sirloin ['sɜːlɔɪn]　*n.* 牛里脊肉

steak [steɪk]　*n.* 牛排

beef [biːf]　*n.* 牛肉

stew [stju:] *v.* 炖、焖

trout [traʊt] *n.* 鳟鱼、鲑鱼

mashed[mæʃt] *adj.* 捣碎的、捣烂的

mashed potato 土豆泥

recommend [rekə'mend] *v.* 推荐、介绍、建议

sole [səʊl] *n.* 鳎目鱼

coleslaw ['kəʊlslɔ:] *n.* 卷心菜沙拉

excellent ['eksələnt] *adj.* 卓越的、杰出的、极好的

reservation [rezə'veɪʃ(ə)n] *n.* 预订、预约

appetizer ['æpɪtaɪzə] *n.* 开胃菜、前菜

Mediterranean [ˌmɛdətə'reɪnɪən] *adj.* 地中海的 *n.* 地中海

stuff [stʌf] *v.* 填塞、填满

whipped [wɪpt] cream *n.* 生奶油

cappuccino [ˌkæpʊ'tʃi:nəʊ] *n.* 卡布奇诺咖啡、意大利泡沫咖啡

Useful Expressions

1. May I help you?
请问有什么可以帮您？

2. Can I take your coat?
我给您拿外套？

3. Have you booked a table?
请问您有预订吗？

4. How many are you?
您有几位？

5. Can I take your order, sir/ madam?
先生/女士，请问能为您点单了吗？

6. What would you like to start with?
前菜（开胃菜）您想吃点什么？

7. What would you like to drink?
您想喝点什么？

8. What would you like for dessert?
甜点您想来点什么？

9. How would you like your steak? (rare, medium, well done)
牛排您要几分熟？（一分，五分，全熟）

10. Do you want a salad with it?
您想配个沙拉吗？

11. What kind of dressing?
请问用哪种沙拉酱呢？

12. The burgers are very good.
汉堡很不错。

13. Sorry, the hamburgers are off.
抱歉，汉堡已经售罄了。

14. Is everything all right?
一切您还满意吗？

15. Did you enjoy your meal?
请问您吃的如何？

M4-2 Practice

Exercises

1. Questions and Answers

(1) What is the standard sequence of a 5-course western meal?

(2) What is dessert?

2. Match the words or expressions in Column A with their Chinese equivalents in Column B.

A	B
(1) ketchup	a. 牛肉
(2) menu	b. 盐

(3) clear soup   c. 醋

(4) pasta   d. 牛排

(5) pizza   e. 海鲜

(6) steak   f. 番茄酱

(7) beef   g. 比萨

(8) seafood   h. 清汤

(9) salt   i. 菜单

(10) vinegar   j. 意大利面

3. Choose the best English translation for each sentence.

(1) 请问您有预订吗？

A. Please pass the book to me.   B. Do you have reservation?

C. Reservation need to be maked 3 days earlier.   D. I don't have reservation.

(2) 您想喝点什么？

A. Do you like to drink a cup of tea?   B. Alcoholic drinks need to be charged.

C. What would you like to drink?   D. Which one do you prefer, orange juice or tomato juice?

(3) 我想向您推荐我们今天的特色菜。

A. I'd like to recommend our specialty for today.

B. Our specialty for today is the sweet and sour fish.

C. We don't have any specialties for today.

D. Fillet steak is our best.

(4) 请您慢慢吃。

A. Please slow down.   B. Take your time.

C. Please feel free to contact us.   D. Please enjoy your meal.

(5) 我会尽快帮您安排的。

A. I'll go there soon.   B. I'll be back as soon as possible.

C. Please wait a moment.   D. I'll arrange it for you as soon as possible.

4. Read the passage and decide if the statements are true (T) or false (F).

One of the key elements of a customer's experience in a restaurant is the level of service offered by the wait staff. If you are a server, your primary responsibility is to ensure that all your customers are happy and their needs are met. You must also have a pleasant disposition and possess the flexibility to respond to a variety of demands from your customers. However, your most important duty is to ensure that you accurately take your customer's order so he receives the dish exactly the way he wants.

Prepare your order pad. Some restaurants may have a preconfigured pad with a sequential order of seats for all the tables at your station. If not, ensure that you have your own method of order-taking, such as a clockwise system or a coding system based on the number of guests, that assures everyone receives the correct dish.

Greet the guests at the table with a smile as you make eye contact with each of them. State the specials of the day and make several recommendations. Ask if anyone has questions about an item on the menu.

Take the first order from the female guests, if applicable. If there are no women at the table, take the order based on your restaurant's sequential system or from the male guest who seems most ready to order. If your customer is trying to decide among several menu items, provide assistance by explaining how each dish is prepared.

Repeat the order back to every guest to ensure it is accurate. If someone orders a dish that can be prepared several different ways – such as a steak – ask how the guest would like the item cooked. Repeating the order also allows you to ensure that you match each guest with the proper order.

Ask the diners if they would like to add anything to the order. Thank everyone, collect the menus and state that the meal will arrive shortly.

Tip

Know your restaurant's menu well so you can make recommendations, answer meal preparation questions and advise guests about possible allergic reactions due to the presence of ingredients such as nuts, dairy or wheat.

Warning

Do not tell a guest that a meal can be prepared in a special way unless you know that the chefs or cooks can do it. Otherwise, you could create resentment in the guest and may spoil her dining experience.

Exercises:

(1) The waiter needn't to take anything to record the order. (　　)
(2) Lady first. (　　)
(3) The waiter need to explain the preparation of every dish. (　　)
(4) After taking the order, the waiter need to repeat the order back to guest. (　　)
(5) The menu is useless for the waiter to recommend dishes to guests. (　　)

Challenges and Solutions

1. How to recommend dishes to old people?
Solutions:

2. How to recommend dessert to the people who is on diet?
Solutions:

3. If a guest likes coffee, but he thinks coffee is bad for his health, what beverage can you recommend?
Solutions:

4. If a guest takes his baby and walks into your restaurant, what should you do?
Solutions:

5. When the restaurant is very busy and there is no menu, and the guests want to order, what will you do?
Solutions:

M4-3　Knowledge Link

M4-4　Key to Exercises

Lesson Two Western Breakfast Service

Objectives

➢ To help the students master useful expressions and sentences about western breakfast.
➢ To help the students familiar with all kinds of western breakfast.
➢ To help the students make some dialogues about western breakfast service.

Warming Up

1. Breakfast is the first meal of a day. Guests can choose varieties of breakfast at the hotel. Look at the pictures to write down the names of following pictures by the corresponding description.

The _____ breakfast originates in Europe, it is very light. A _____ breakfast usually consists of some sort of bread, jam, juice, coffee or tea, and some fruit.

A hotel breakfast that includes most or all of the following: two eggs (fried or poached), sliced bacon or sausages, sliced bread or toast with jam, jelly, butter, pancakes with syrup, cornflakes or other cereal, coffee, tea, orange, grapefruit juice. It's called _____ breakfast.

M4-5　Warming Up

Dialogues

Key sentences:
➢ Are you ready to order, Sir/ Madam?
➢ Would you like anything to drink?
➢ Anything else?
➢ May I get you anything else?

Pre-questions:

1. Do you have the habit of having breakfast? What do you usually have for breakfast?

2. What do you know about western breakfast?

3. How to provide the breakfast service to guests?

Dialogue 1

Waiter:	Good morning. Are you ready to order?
Bill:	Yes, thank you. I´ll have three scrambled eggs with country ham, toast and jam, please.
Waiter:	Would you like anything to drink?
Bill:	I´ll have a tomato juice and some iced tea.
Waiter:	Anything else?
Bill:	Could I have a slice of pumpkin pie?
Waiter:	Sure. Coming right up.

Dialogue 2

Waiter:	Good morning, sir. May I take your order for breakfast?
Mr. Ryan:	Yes, do you serve English style breakfast?
Waiter:	Yes, sir. We do. Which juice do you like to start with, sir, pineapple or grape fruit?
Mr. Ryan:	Pineapple, please. Fresh, of course.
Waiter:	Fresh pineapple juice, ok. How would you like your eggs, sir?
Mr. Ryan:	Scrambled.
Waiter:	Do you like porridge or cornflakes?
Mr. Ryan:	Cornflakes.
Waiter:	Do you like bread or toast?
Mr. Ryan:	Toast with honey and marmalade.
Waiter:	Do you like tea, coffee or milk?
Mr. Ryan:	None, but do you have hot chocolate?
Waiter:	Of course, we have, sir. What do you prefer Horlicks or Ovaltine?
Mr. Ryan:	Horlicks, please.
Waiter:	So, sir, your order is—fresh pineapple juice, two scrambled eggs, cornflakes, toast with honey and marmalade and Horlicks.
Mr. Ryan:	That's right. How early you can serve?
Waiter:	In 5 minutes, sir. Do you care for a local newspaper?
Mr. Ryan:	Oh, sure. Thanks.
Waiter:	You're welcome, sir.

Dialogue 3

Guest:	Is it time for breakfast?
Waiter:	Yes, we serve breakfast from 7:00 to 9:00 in the morning. What kind of breakfast do you want to have, continental or American?
Guest:	We'd like to have the continental breakfast. It'll save some time.
Waiter:	And what kind of fruit juice would you like to have? We have a variety of them, pineapple, orange, grapefruit.

Guest:	But do you serve hot coffee?
Waiter:	Certainly, what coffee do you prefer, white or black?
Guest:	A cup of white coffee and the pineapple, please.
Waiter:	And the meal?
Guest:	We'd like two egg rolls and two pieces of bread.
Waiter:	Buttered or not?
Guest:	No butter.
Waiter:	Okay. A moment, pleas.

Vocabulary

scrambled ['skræmb(ə)ld] egg　*n.* 炒鸡蛋

toast [təʊst]　*n.* 烤面包，吐

pumpkin ['pʌmpkɪn]　*n.* 南瓜

porridge ['pɒrɪdʒ]　*n.* 粥，糊，麦片粥

cornflake ['kɔ:nfleik]　*n.* 玉米片

marmalade ['mɑ:məleɪd]　*n.* 橘子酱

serve [sɜ:v]　*v.* 为……服务，供应

local ['ləʊk(ə)l]　*adj.* 当地的，地方性的

Useful Expressions

1. Excuse me, madam/sir. How many people in your party?

女士/先生，请问您几位？

2. I'll bring you the menu, sir.

我给您拿菜单，先生。

3. Would you prefer to sit inside or outside, madam/sir?

您是想坐在外面还是里面？

4. Excuse me, sir. This is our breakfast buffet.

先生，这是我们的自助早餐。

5. Is this table to your liking?

这张桌子您满意吗？（坐这里您看可以吗？）

6. Excuse me, Mr. Steven. May I please carry the plate for you?

史蒂文先生，我来帮您拿盘子。

7. Excuse me, Mr. Steven. May I please clear your plate?

史蒂文先生，盘子给您清一下吗？

8. Is the breakfast to your satisfaction?

早餐您还满意吗？

9. Hope you are enjoying our breakfast.

希望您用餐（早餐）愉快。

10. May I please offer you some more orange juice?

我给您再加点橙汁吧？

11. Would you care for some more coffee/tea?

您还来点咖啡/茶吗？

12. May I pour some coffee/ tea for you?

给您倒点咖啡/茶吗？

13. What would you like for breakfast?

早餐您想来点什么？

14. Which would you like, American breakfast or continental breakfast?

美式早餐和欧式早餐，您喜欢哪种？

15. How would you like your eggs?

您的鸡蛋怎么做？

M4-6　Practice

Exercises

1. Questions and Answers

(1) How many methods of cooking eggs?

(2) Are there any meat products in continental breakfast?

(3) What the differences between American breakfast and Continental breakfast?

2. Match the words or expressions in Column A with their Chinese equivalents in Column B.

A	B
(1) cookies	a. 火腿
(2) muffin	b. 吐司
(3) toast	c. 煎饼
(4) pancake	d. 果酱
(5) omelet	e. 蛋糕
(6) jam	f. 香肠
(7) cake	g. 松饼
(8) sausage	h. 火腿
(9) ham	i. 煎蛋卷
(10) steak	j. 牛排

3. Choose the best English translation for each sentence.

(1) 我能为您点早餐了吗？

A. May I take your order for breakfast?　　B. Do you satisfy with the breakfast?

C. Is the breakfast ready?　　D. What do you want to have?

(2) 我能为您加点果汁吗？

A. Do you want to have more water?　　B. May I offer you more juice?

C. Would you like some juice?　　D. Is the orange juice ok?

(3) 您的煎蛋要怎么做，单面煎还是双面煎？

A. How to get the eggs?

B. How many eggs would you like?

C. How would you like your eggs, fried or boiled?

D. How would you like your fried egg, sunny-side-up or over-easy?

(4) 我们有香肠和培根，您要哪种？

A. Sausages and bacon are popular in western meal.

B. Sausages or bacon, which do you want?

C. There is ham and bacon on the plate.

D. What do you have, sausage or bacon?

(5) 您吃过中式早餐吗？

A. Have you ever tasted Chinese breakfast?　　B. I'd like to try Chinese breakfast.

C. Do you have Chinese breakfast?　　　　　　D. Do you like Chinese breakfast?

4. Read the passage and decide if the statements are true (T) or false (F).

Breakfast is the first meal of a day, most often eaten in the early morning before undertaking the day's work.

As mainland China is made up of many distinct provinces each with their own unique cuisine, breakfast in China can vary significantly from province to province. In general, basic choices include sweet or salty pancakes, soup, deep fried bread sticks or doughnuts (youtiao), buns (mantou), porridge (congee), and fried or soup-based noodles. These options are often accompanied by tea or sweetened soy bean milk. However, condiments for porridge and the soup base tend to vary between provinces and regions. The types of teas that are served and spices that are used can also differ significantly between the provinces.

A typical Hong Kong style Cha chaan teng breakfast may include pan fried eggs and a bun, including a cup of milk tea. Due to its near two centuries history as a British colony and proximity to China's Canton region, both English and traditional Cantonese style breakfasts are of somewhat equal popularity in Hong Kong, as well as the hybrid form of breakfast commonly offered in Cha chaan teng. Cha Chaan Teng breakfasts often include Hong Kong-style milk tea, pan fried egg, bread, Cantonese noodles or Hong Kong style macaroni in soup. Traditional Cantonese breakfast may include dim sum, which include a variety of different ingredients and are prepared in numerous different forms from delicately wrapped baby shrimp steamed dumplings to sweet water chestnut cake. Each dish is designed to be sampled and diners can go through a large selection of dim sum quickly accompanied by a generous amount of good tea. Tieguanyin is the most common accompaniment, but other teas such as pu'er and oolong are also common. Fried and rice-based noodles and cakes are also popular. In modern times, dim sum is commonly prepared and served in Yum Cha restaurants rather than at home because of the skill and efforts involved in the preparation.

Exercises:

(1) The first meal of the day is lunch. (　　)

(2) Chinese breakfast is all the same from province to province. (　　)

(3) Youtiao is deep fried bread sticks or doughnuts. (　　)

(4) Traditional Cantonese breakfast may include dim sum. (　　)

(5) Dim sum is commonly prepared and served in Yum Cha restaurants rather than at home. (　　)

Challenges and Solutions

1. What information would you provide to the guest when you find it is the very first time to stay at your hotel?

Solutions:

2. If guests don't want to have breakfast in the restaurant, what should you do?

Solutions:

3. If the guest misses the breakfast time and he really wants to have some food to eat, what should you do?

Solutions:

4. If a guest wants to have some food that you don't have in your hotel, what will you do?

Solutions:

M4-7　Knowledge Link

M4-8　Key to Exercises

Lesson Three　Western Table Setting & Napkin Folding

Objectives

➢ To help the students master useful expressions and sentences about western table setting service.

➢ To help the students familiar with all kinds of tableware and napkin.

➢ To help the students make some dialogues about western table setting service.

Warming Up

Each restaurant has a required table setting that must be strictly followed by each server. The customers should never have to ask for china, silver, or linen. Each table should be set appropriately before the guests are seated. All glasses and silver must be spotless. The table settings must be perfectly arranged. 3 kinds of table setting will be introduced as follow.

Basic Table Setting

Setting Instruction

(1) Lay the placemat on the table.

(2) Put the dinner plate in the middle of the placemat.

(3) Lay the napkin to the left of the plate.

(4) Place the fork on the napkin.

(5) To the right of the plate, place the knife closest to the plate, blade pointing in. Place the spoon to the right of the knife. (Note: The bottoms of the utensils and the plate should all be level.)

(6) Place the water glass slightly above the plate, in between the plate and the utensils, about where 1 p.m. would be on a clock face.

Casual Table Setting

Setting Instruction

(1) Lay the placemat on the table.

(2) Put the dinner plate in the middle of the placemat.

(3) Place the salad plate on top of the dinner plate.

(4) If you're starting with a soup course, place the soup bowl on top of the salad plate.

(5) Lay a napkin to the left of the charger.

(6) To the left of the plate, place the fork on the napkin.

(7) On the right of the plate, place the knife closest to the plate and then the spoon.

(8) Directly above the knife, place the water glass.

(9) To the right and slightly above the water glass, place the wine glass or a glass for another beverage.

Formal Table Setting

Setting Instruction

(1) Lay an ironed tablecloth on the table.

(2) Set a charger at each seat.

(3) In the center of the charger, place a soup bowl.

(4) Place the bread plate to the top left of the charger (between 10 and 11 p.m. on a clock face).

(5) Lay a napkin to the left of the charger.

(6) On the left of the charger, place the salad fork on the outside, and the dinner fork on the inside. You can put the forks on the napkin, or for roomier settings, directly on the tablecloth between the napkin and the charger.

(7) On the right of the charger, place the knife closest to the charger (blade facing in towards

the charger) and then the soup spoon. Note: All vertical flatware (salad fork, dinner fork, knife, and soup spoon) should be spaced evenly, about half an inch away from each other, and the bottoms of each utensil should be aligned with the bottom of the charger.

(8) Place a butter knife horizontally, blade facing inwards on top of the bread plate with the handle pointing to the right. (Note: In all place settings the blade will face inwards towards the plate.)

(9) Directly above the charger, place a dessert spoon (a teaspoon) with the handle pointing to the right.

(10) Directly above the knife, place a water glass. To the right of the water glass and about three fourths of an inch downward, place the white wine glass. According to a 2006 issue of InStyle Home, the red wine goes to the right of—and slightly above—the white wine glass. (Note: Since people traditionally drink more water than wine during dinner, the water is closer to the diner.)

(11) If using individual salt and pepper shakers for each guest, place them above the dessert spoon. Otherwise, place them near the center of the table, or, if using a long, rectangle table, place them in the middle of each end.

(12) If using a place card, set above the dessert spoon.

M4-9   Warming Up

Dialogues

Key sentences:
➢ Would you please bring us another...?
➢ May I ...?

Pre-questions:
1. Before serving the guest, what do you need to prepare?
2. How many tableware do you know? List some of them.
3. What do you know about the western table manner?

Dialogue 1

Lily:	Excuse me, waiter, would you please bring us another place setting? A friend of mine will join us.
Waiter:	Wait a moment. Here you are.
Lily:	By the way, we would like to order some dishes for my friend.
Waiter:	Sure.

Dialogue 2

Mr. Blair:	Excuse me, waiter. I have just dropped the spoon onto the ground. Would you please bring me another one?
Waiter:	Sure. Wait for a moment. Here you are.
Mr. Blair:	Thank you. We'd like to have some dessert
Waiter:	Here is the menu.

Dialogue 3

Waiter:	How may I help you?
Guest:	Please give me a can of Coca-Cola.
Waiter:	Ok, I'll get it ready for you.

(*A few minutes later*)

Waiter:	Here you are.
Guest:	Oh, my god. This glass is so dirty.
Waiter:	I'm sorry. I'll change it for a new one.

Vocabulary

place setting   *n.* 成套餐具   drop [drɒp]   *v.* 掉下

Useful Expressions

1. Shall I change this for a smaller one?
我把这个换成小一点的碟子，好吗？

2. I'm sorry. May I have it changed into the small plate?
对不起，我把它换成小盘子好吗？

3. I'll bring you another glass right away.
我马上给您换另一个杯子。

4. OK, I'll get it for you.
好的，我去拿来。

5. Just a moment, please. I will change it right away.
请稍等，我马上为您换。

6. May I bring you a knife and a fork?
我给您拿一副刀叉好吗？

7. This glass is cracked. I'll bring you a new one.
这个杯子有裂痕，我给您换个新的。

8. I'm sorry. Can I take this plate away?
对不起，我能把这个盘子撤走吗？

M4-10   Practice

Exercises

1. Questions and Answers

(1) What utensils are required in western meal service?

(2) Do you have some ideas about Chinese table wares?

2. Match the words or expressions in Column A with their Chinese equivalents in Column B.

A	B
(1) fork	a. 沙拉叉
(2) saucer	b. 碗
(3) tea pot	c. 叉子
(4) chopsticks	d. 碟子
(5) bowl	e. 葡萄酒杯
(6) salad fork	f. 纸巾

(7) wine glass   g. 调料瓶

(8) tissue   h. 茶壶

(9) napkin   i. 筷子

(10) seasoning shaker   j. 餐巾

3. Choose the best English translation for each sentence.

(1) 我给您更换新的。

A. The new one is very expensive.   B. I'll take it for you.

C. I'll change it for a new one.   D. Here is the new one.

(2) 我能把这个盘子撤走吗？

A. Can I take the plate away?   B. Can I take the bowl away?

C. Can I take the fork away?   D. Can I take the brush away?

(3) 这个杯子有污点。

A. The glass is a little bit small.   B. The glass is stained.

C. On my point of view, this glass is very valuable.   D. This glass is so dirty.

(4) 看来您用不惯筷子。

A. It seems you are not used to chopsticks.   B. Chopsticks are not good for western people.

C. Your chopsticks are very bad.   D. Look. You are using chopsticks.

(5) 很抱歉，我马上给您换一个。

A. Sorry, the horse is on the way.

B. Sorry, I will give you another horse.

C. I'm sorry to hear that. I'll bring you another one right away.

D. Sorry, I'll buy another for you.

4. Read the passage and decide if the statements are true (T) or false(F).

As soon as the hostess picks up her napkin, pick yours up and lay it on your lap. Sometimes a roll of bread is wrapped in it, if so, take it out and put it on your side plate.

If the napkin is large, leave it folded double in your lap; if waistcoat, or rumple it in your hands. Use a corner of fingers if greasy or dirty. Never use it to wipe the silver and china.

Dinner usually begins with soup. The largest spoon at your place is the soupspoon. It will be beside your plate at the right-hand side. Do not make the mistake of using a spoon from the center of the table which may be intended for vegetable or jelly. No one should begin to eat of any course until the hostess picks up her own spoon or fork. It is usual for her to wait until everyone is served before Chinese custom. When she picks up her spoon or fork, it means the others may do so also.

If you have English and American friends, you will notice a few differences in their customs of eating. For the main course, the English keep the fork in the left hand, points downward, and bring the food to the mouth either by sticking the points into it or, in the case of soft vegetable, by placing firmly on the fork with the knife. Americans cut the meat in the same position, then lay down the knife, and take the fork in the right hand with the points turned up and push it under a smack piece of food without the help of the knife and bring it to the mouth. When the plate is empty Americans place the knife across the back-right hand edge of the plate and the fork beside it, points up. The English place the knife in the middle of the plate with its point on the plate and the fork beside it, points turned up. In no case should one rest the knife or fork with one end on the table.

It is not necessary or usual to lay down the table tools while one is speaking, as one does with chopsticks. One may carry on a talk with the fork in the hand. If the fork is laid down, the hostess may think that the guest has finished the course.

A salad is eaten with a fork only, held in the right hand with points turned up. There is usually a special fork for the salad. If the salad is served before the meat course, the fork will be on the outside of the meat fork: if after, on the inside. If a cracker or bread is served with the salad one may use a small piece in the left hand to help the fork take up the salad. If lettuce is served with the salad, one may eat it or not, as one prefers. If eaten, it should be cut only with the fork.

Bread is taken in the fingers and laid on the side plate to the edge of the large plate; it is never taken with a fork. Butter is taken from the butter dish with the butter knife and placed on the side plate. A small piece is broken from the roll or slice of bread, buttered with the knife, and eaten. The whole slice is not buttered at once. Americans usually use a butter spreader; the English often use a knife like the meat knife but smaller and placed on the outside of the dish. The butter spreader will be either on or near the side plate.

It is impolite for a guest to leave the table during a meal, or before the hostess gives the signal at the end. When the hostess says that the dinner is over, she will start to rise from her seat and all the guests should rise from theirs at the same time. It is polite for the gentlemen to men to help replace the ladies' chairs after they rise. Should it be absolutely necessary for you to leave the table during the meal, you should ask the hostess to excuse you.

Sit up straight on your chair; do not lean heavily against the back. You may lean the body the slightly forward when you eat, but never lower the head down toward the plate. Your arms should be held close to your sides, so as not to touch the person next to you, and they should not rest on the table when you are eating.

Do not put much food in your mouth at a time. Keep your lips closed while chewing. And as long as there is food in your mouth, do not try to talk. Drink only when there is no food in your mouth. It is bad manners to take a mouthful of food and then wash it down with water. Be sure your lips are not greasy when you drink from your glass. Do not make any noise when you eat. It is bad manners at a Western meal to make any noise with the mouth. If you have to cough or choke, use your napkin to cover your mouth. Do not clean your teeth at the table or anywhere in public either with your fingers or a tooth pick, not even with your tongue. If you have to get something out that is caught between your teeth, cover your mouth with your napkin while you do so: but it is better to leave it until you are alone sometimes later.

Exercises:

    (1) Napkin need to be put around your neck. (   )

    (2) Dinner usually begins with main course. (   )

    (3) Salad can be eaten with spoon. (   )

    (4) Bread can be eaten with your fingers. (   )

    (5) It's ok for the guests leave the table anytime then want. (   )

Challenges and Solutions

1. What should you do if your guest can't use fork and knife?

Solutions:

2. What kind of guests can be offered a discount from the hotel?

Solutions:

3. If your hotel doesn't have the rooms guests like, what will you do?

Solutions:

M4-11　Knowledge Link

M4-12　Key to Exercises

Lesson Four　Western Table Manner

Objectives

➢ To help the students master useful expressions and sentences about western table manner.

➢ To help the students familiar with all kinds of table manner.

➢ To help the students make some dialogues about western table manner.

Warming Up

1. Table manners are the rules used while eating, which may also include the use of utensils. Look at the pictures to write down the names of following pictures by the corresponding description.

If you are _____ to have dinner with someone, it is always a good idea to respond, even if an RSVP is not requested. This helps with planning. Don't ask if you can bring _____ if the invitation doesn't make the offer. However, if your family is invited to someone's home for dinner, it is okay to ask if your children are included. If they are, make sure your children know _____ before they go.

When you are dining at the home of a friend, it is a good idea to bring a host or hostess _____.

Some dinner parties are formal and have _____ where the host or hostess wants you to sit. If not, ask if there are seating preferences.

Wait until the host sits _____ you do. In some cultures, a blessing will be said. Even if you don't follow the beliefs of the prayer, show _____ and be silent. If the host offers a toast, lift your glass. It is not necessary to "clink" someone else's glass.

As soon as you sit down, turn to your host or hostess and take a cue for when to _____. Once the host unfolds his or her napkin, you should remove your napkin from the table or plate and place it on your_____. If you are dining out, you should place your napkin in your lap immediately.

Keep your napkin in your lap until you are finished eating. If you must get up at any time during the meal and plan to return, place the napkin on either side of your plate. After you are_____, place your napkin on the table to the left of your plate.

A typical rule of thumb is to start with the utensil that is _____ from your plate and work your way toward the center of your place setting. If you see the host or hostess doing something different, you may follow his or her lead. The important thing is to remain as inconspicuous as possible.

Never _____ when you have food in your mouth. That's just gross. Even if someone asks you a question, wait until you _____ before answering.

Don't _____ all your food before you begin eating. Cut one or two bites at a time.

If you are drinking from a _____, hold it by the stem.

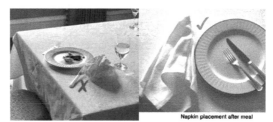

Napkin placement after meal

_____ your food before you add salt, pepper, or other _____. Doing otherwise may be insulting to the host or hostess.

After you finish eating, partially fold your napkin and place it to the _____ of your plate. Wait until the host or hostess signals that the meal is _____, you may stand.

M4-13　Warming Up

Dialogues

Key sentences:
- ➢ Are you ready to ...?
- ➢ Would you like ...?
- ➢ Anything else?
- ➢ May I get you anything else?

Pre-questions:

1. Do you know what is table manner?

2. Do you think Western table manner are different from Chinese table manners?

3. How to behave correct in western dining table?

Dialogue 1

Judy:	Hi, Betty. What's up?
Betty:	Nothing special. how about you? Are you used to the life here in the States?
Judy:	Everything has been fine for the past several months.
Betty:	Great!

Judy:	Well, I wish someone could talk to me about Western table manners.
Betty:	Sounds interesting. Where did you get the idea?
Judy:	As you know, table manners in China are quite different from those of Westerners.
Betty:	Absolutely. that's because both of us have distinctive cultural features.
Judy:	For example, in China, it's okay to talk while eating. However, you may regard it as rude.
Betty:	Yes. this must be a huge difference.
Judy:	Can you think of anything else?
Betty:	Sure. We tend to think that the slower on eats, the politer one seems.
Judy:	I didn't know that before.
Betty:	And we never sip or slurp the soup loudly. We quietly like little mouthfuls.
Judy:	I got it. I'll bear it in mind.
Betty:	Don't worry. I'm sure our etiquette will become a natural part of your behavior as time goes by.
Judy:	I hope so.

Dialogue 2

Waiter:	Welcome to Antico's . Here are your menus. Today's special is grilled salmon. I'll be back to take your order in a minute.

(*A moment later*)

Waiter:	Are you ready to order?
Mr. Ryan:	I'd like the seafood spaghetti.
Waiter:	And you?
Mrs. Ryan:	I'll have a hamburger and fries.
Waiter:	Would you like anything to drink?
Mrs. Ryan:	I'll have a coke, please.
Waiter:	And for you?
Mrs. Ryan:	Just water, please.
Waiter:	OK. So that's one seafood spaghetti, one hamburger and fries, one coke, and one water. I'll take your menus.
Waiter:	Here is your food. Enjoy your meal.

Dialogue 3

Mr. Li and his colleagues are in a restaurant with Mr. Warner, a foreign manager.

A: Mr. Li; B: Mr. Warner; C: Mr. Zhang; D: Miss Yao; H: Mr. Huang; Z: Mr. Zhao

A:	Mr. Warner, it's a pleasure to have you here.
B:	It's very kind of you to have invited me.
A:	Now, I'd like you to meet my friends. Allow me to introduce them to you. This is Mr. Zhang, the assistant manager of our company. He is in charge of the sales department. This is Mr. Zhao. He is the finance department manager and you know, this is Mr. Huang, the director of the manager office, and this is Miss Yao, the secretary of our office. They are with us this evening.
B:	Oh, how nice. I'm glad to meet you Mr. Zhang and Zhao.

C&Z:	Glad to meet you, too.
B:	It's nice to see you again, Mr. Huang and Miss Yao.
H&D:	Nice to see you again, Mr. Warner.
A:	Now, let's be seated. Have a cup of tea, please.
B:	It's good to start with a cup of Chinese tea. I like it.
A:	I'm glad to hear that. By the way, Mr. Warner, do you intend to have a long stay here?
B:	About more than one month. This is meant to be both a business and pleasure trip.
A:	That's a good idea. We hope you'll stay here for a long time.
D:	Dinner is ready. Please go to the table.
A:	This is your seat, Mr. Warner. Sit down, please.
B:	Thank you, Mr. Li. I'm really a bit nervous now. I know nothing of your table manners. It would be in bad taste for a guest to make blunders.
A:	Don't worry, Mr Warner. As for table manners, there is only one rule you must observe. That's to make yourself at home.
B:	No wonder people say the Chinese are hospitable. Now, I have seen it with my own eyes.
C:	Mr. Warner, which do you prefer, Brandy, Whiskey, Wuliangye or Wine?
B:	Brandy, Whiskey and Wuliangye are too strong for me. Just a glass of wine, please.
C:	But Shaoxing spirit doesn't go to the head. Would you like to try it?
B:	Well, I'll try a little.
D:	Would you like to use chopsticks or knife and fork, Mr. Warner?
B:	I think I'll try chopsticks and see if I can manage.
D:	Let me show you. Look, at first, place both sticks between the thumb and the forefinger, then, keep one still and move the other, so as to make them work like pincers.
B:	Let me try. Well, how is that?
D:	Fine, you are learning fast, Mr. Warner.
A:	Well, Mr. Warner, to your health and success in business. Cheers！
B:	And to yours. Cheers！
	(*Serving Dishes*)
A:	This food is Sichuan specialty. Help yourself, please.
D:	Making yourself at home and eat it while it is hot, Mr. Warner.
B：	Thank you. These dishes are all delicious, especially the chicken in chili sauce and redcooked beef.
D:	We›re glad you like it. May I help you to some more?
B:	Thank you, just a small helping.
A:	May I help you to some of the roast duck? It tastes best while it is hot.
B:	Very delicious! Tender and crisp. I've never tasted anything like that.
A:	Have some more, please.

B:	No, thank you. It's really delicious, but I must leave room for my other favorites.
A:	May I fill your glass again?
B:	Thank you, Mr. Li. What do we say in Chinese for "Bottoms up"?
A:	We say "Gan Bei". I wish to propose a toast to our friendship and cooperation. Gan Bei.
ALL:	To our friendship and cooperation. Gan Bei!

Vocabulary

manners ['mænə]   *n.* 礼貌，礼仪

distinctive [dɪ'stɪŋ(k)tɪv]   *adj.* 与众不同的，有特色的

regard [rɪ'gɑːd]   *v.* 看待，尊敬

sip [sɪp]   *v.* 小口喝，抿

slurp [slɜːp]   *v.* 出声的吃或喝

spaghetti [spə'getɪ]   *n.* 意大利式细面条

invite [ɪn'vaɪ]   *n.* 邀请

finance [faɪ'næns]   *n.* 财政，金融

secretary ['sekrətrɪ]   *n.* 秘书

blunder ['blʌndə]   *v.* 跌跌撞撞的走

observe [əb'zɜːv]   *v.* 观察

hospitable [hɒ'spɪtəb(ə)l]   *adj.* 热情好客的

pincer ['pɪnsə(r)]   *n.* 拔钉钳

tender ['tendə]   *adj.* 柔软的，嫩的

crisp [krɪsp]   *adj.* 脆的

to propose a toast   敬酒，提议干杯

Useful Expressions

1. It's a pleasure to have you here.
欢迎光临。

2. It's very kind of you to have invited me.
非常感谢你的盛情邀请。

3. I'm happy to host this dinner party in honor of our friends.
非常高兴能为朋友举办这次晚宴。

4. We are very honored to be invited to this magnificent dinner.
我们非常荣幸能被邀请参加这个盛宴。

5. Dinner is ready.
饭菜已经准备好了。

6. Please go to the table.
请入席吧。

7. I'm really a bit nervous now, for I know nothing of your table manners.
我真有点不安了，我对你们的席间礼节一点也不懂。

8. No wonder people say the Chinese are hospitable.
难怪人们都说中国人很好客。

9. I have seen it with my own eyes.
现在我算是亲眼看到了。

10. To your health and success in business.
为你的身体健康、生意兴隆干杯。

11. This food is Sichuan specialty.
这道菜是四川的特色菜。

12. Make yourself at home.
不要客气，随便吃。

13. Eat it while it is hot.
请趁热吃。

14. It's really delicious.
味道真的好极了。

15. I wish to propose a toast to our friendship and cooperation.
我提议为我们的友谊和合作干杯。

M4-14   Practice

Exercises

1. Questions and Answers

(1) Do you know of any foreign eating habits which you think are strange?

(2) Have you ever been embarrassed by someone's behavior in a restaurant?

(3) What topics should you not discuss at mealtime? Why not?

2. Match the words or expressions in Column A with their Chinese equivalents in Column B.

A	B
(1) hospitable	a. 膝盖
(2) host	b. 宗教信仰
(3) gesture	c. 用具
(4) blessing	d. 粗野的，恶劣的
(5) etiquette	e. 偏好
(6) preference	f. 礼节
(7) lap	g. 祷告
(8) religion	h. 姿态，手势
(9) utensil	i. 主人
(10) gross	j. 热情好客的

3. Choose the best English translation for each sentence.

(1) 您知道怎样正确吃面包吗？

A. Is bread good for you to eat?　　　　　B. Do you like bread?

C. Do you know how to make bread?　　　D. Do you know how to properly break bread?

(2) 奶油刀怎么用？

A. Can you tell me where is the butter knife?　B. Do you want to sharpen the butter knife?

C. How do you use the butter knife?　　　　D. How do you use the bread knife?

(3) 喝汤时不要发出声音？

A. Soup should be eaten slowly.　　　　　B. Don't slurp your soup.

C. Don't blow your soup.　　　　　　　　D. Sound is not allowed.

(4) 不要挥舞你的餐具。

A. Don't wave utensil about.　　　　　　B. Don't play your knife.

C. Don't use utensils.　　　　　　　　　D. Don't clean the knife by yourself.

(5) 我应该特别要注意些什么呢？

A. What should I get from you?　　　　　B. What should I particularly have?

C. What should I know?　　　　　　　　D. What should I pay special attention to?

4. Read the passage and decide if the statements are true(T) or false(F).

Table manners are closely associated with the characteristics of Chinese and western banquets. There are some similarities in table manners of China and the West. These rules show the consensus between Chinese and Westerners on the proper way of eating. For example, it is impolite for diners to smoke at table. Smoking is harmful to people's health and considered rude at banquet, unless permitted. It is advisable for people to sit straight up at the table to make a good impression on others. Dinners should not talk with each other when their mouth is full. It is polite.

Although there are some similarities in table manners, more obvious differences exist between Chinese and Western table manners. Chinese people pay much attention to the content and arrangement of dinner. They usually provide ten or more main courses at a formal banquet. The more pompous the dishes are prepared, the more the host's hospitality and the higher the host's status. In western countries, a banquet consists of no more than six dishes, and it is similar to common dinner. In the U.S., friends may contribute to a dinner. They take their dishes to share with each other amidst joyful exchange of ideas. What really counts is the relaxed and cheerful atmosphere at dinner. Clearly, western banquet symbolizes freedom and relaxation.

During dinner, Chinese people like to persuade others to drink and use their own chopsticks to put food in the plate or bowl of guests to show politeness and hospitality. In China, it has long been held that people should not eat alone, without considering others when many people dine together. A person should not possess one kind of dish totally and he should not jolt his hot dishes in order to make it cool quickly either, for it is not decent and polite. In the West, people do not act as enthusiastically and courteously as the Chinese when they have a banquet. Westerners pay more attention to personal independence.

Exercises:

(1) There are no similarities at all in table manners of China and the West. (   )

(2) It is impolite for diners to smoke at table. (   )

(3) In formal banquet Chinese usually provide 2 to 3 main courses. (   )

(4) In U.S, people can take their own dishes to share with others. (   )

(5) Compare with Chinese, westerners pay more attention to collectivism. (   )

Challenges and Solutions

1. When being invited to a meal, what rules should you follow?

Solutions:

2. When Inviting a client to a meal, what rules should you follow?

Solutions:

3. What do you think are some of the differences between Chinese and Western dinning etiquette?

Solutions:

4. Do you think dinning arrangement is an important part in business in the Western countries? Why or why not?

Solutions:

M4-15   Knowledge Link

M4-16   Key to Exercises

Lesson Five   Handling Complaints

Objectives

➤ To help the students master useful expressions and sentences of complaints in the western restaurant.

➤ To help the students familiar with the common complaints in the western restaurant.

➤ To help the students analyze the reasons of complaints and handle complaints in the western restaurant.

Preamble

to: email of the receiver
from: email of sender
Subject: complaint letter

Mr. Davis,

On May 4th, 2018 we organized a birthday party for my son, and all his friends were invited. I chose to arrange a party in your restaurant as I heard the food served at your place is authentic and tasty but to my surprise the food served was pathetic.

Initially, the guests were supposed to get soup and a starter, but the starter didn't come till the dinner time, and the guests were upset. After telling the waiters several times finally we got the soup and starter served to the guests, but for my shock, it was cold and tasteless. It was my sons 20th birthday, and we were in very high spirits to enjoy the day with his friends and some of my family members but because of the food everything ruined.

The dinner served was also cold, and they could not serve the dishes which we had ordered two days beforehand so that there are no confusions. But the manager seemed ignorant about the whole episode, and I felt humiliated in front of my guest. Even my son was really unhappy about the whole function. We ordered both non-vegetarian and vegetarian food, but they did not provide us with vegetarian dishes because of which some of the guests had to leave without food.

The only good thing about your restaurant was the customer service as the waiters were very patient and were listening to all our complaints. I am very disappointed with the food provided in m sons birthday and hope that in future you will maintain good standards.

Sincerely'

Rosen

Dialogues

Key sentences:

➤ Is there anything wrong with your order, sir?

➤ I'll bring you another one.

➤ I'll return your dish to the chef.

Pre-questions:

1. What are the common complaints in the western restaurant?

2. How to deal with complaints?

3. Do you think it's an important to handle complaints from the guests? Why?

Dialogue 1

Julie:	Is there a problem with your steak Andrew?
Andrew:	Yeah, there is. I ordered a rare steak because I like it when the meat is very red inside and they have brought me a well-done steak instead. I don't like it when they fry it for a long time, so it is brown on the inside and the meat doesn't have a lot of taste.
Julie:	You should ask the waiter to send it back to the kitchen, so you they can give you another steak. I'll call the waiter over.
Sally:	I have a problem with my main course as well. The roast chicken is good, but they've overcooked the carrots, so they are too soft and they don't have any taste at all. But the boiled potatoes are almost raw. They are so hard. It's like they haven't cooked the potatoes at all.
Julie:	I'll call the waiter over now. Excuse me!
Waiter:	Yes, madam. How can I help you?
Julie:	One of my friends ordered a rare steak and you've brought him a well-done steak. My other friend's carrots are overcooked and her potatoes are raw. Can you send them back to the kitchen to be replaced please?
Waiter:	I apologize for the steak. I'll replace it straight away. Both the carrots and the potatoes are supposed to be like that. I'm afraid there is nothing I can do.
Julie:	Well, in that case. I'd like to speak to the manager, please.
Waiter:	I'll go and get him for you.
Manager:	What seems to be the problem?
Julie:	The waiter is refusing to send back my friend's dish. The carrots are overcooked and the potatoes are almost raw. We're not happy with the service we have received from the waiter. He's made several mistakes with our food tonight and he's been arrogant towards us.

Manager:	Please accept my apologies. I'll send your friend's dish back to the kitchen and get it replaced. We won't charge you for the roast chicken. So, you don't have to pay for it. Also, to say sorry we'll give you a bottle of red wine on the house for all the problems you've experienced.
Julie:	A free bottle of wine! Thank you very much.

40 minutes later, after receiving the bill/check from the waiter

Julie:	The bill seems very high.
Andrew:	Let me have a look. I think they've overcharged us. They have included the roast chicken on the bill and also they are charging us for a roast duck which we didn't have or order. I'll have a word with the waiter. Excuse me!
Waiter:	Yes?
Andrew:	There seems to be a mistake with the bill. It has a roast duck on it, which we didn't have. And it has my wife's roast chicken on it which your manager said we wouldn't be charged for.
Waiter:	I'm terribly sorry. I'll bring you the correct bill now.

5 minutes later, having paid and about to leave

Andrew:	Let's leave here now we've paid the bill. It's been a disaster.
Julie:	That doesn't seem right. I think they've short changed me. The meal cost £140. I gave them £200, but I've only got £30 back in change.
Andrew:	They have short changed you. You should have got £60 back in change. You should call the waiter over again.
Julie:	I will.

Dialogue 2

Waiter:	Are you ready to order, Sir?
Guest:	I wanted to try something new today, but I don't see anything interesting on the menu.
Waiter:	What kind of food are you looking for?
Guest:	Hmm. nothing specific. I've tried all the dishes that are listed here. I was looking to explore new ones.
Waiter:	Let me to talk to the chef. I'm sure he can suggest something.
Guest:	No. That's okay. Let me just suggest that you add some more food variety to your menu. I haven't seen any changes in it, for a while now.
Waiter:	You've been one of our more regular customers. I'll definitely take your suggestion to the manager.
Guest:	That's good. For now, you can bring me the red sauce pasta and potato wedges.

Dialogue 3

Guest:	Excuse me! Are you out of vegetables today?
Waiter:	I am sorry, Sir. I don't understand...
Guest:	I ordered a Creamy Vegetable Soup and there aren't many vegetables in it. It's mainly just broth.
Waiter:	I really apologize for that. Allow me to replace it with a better one.

Guest:	No. That's alright now. I'll just fill up on the main course.
Waiter:	I assure you it won't happen again. As a token of our apologies, we won't charge you for the soup.
Guest:	That's good. I hope we won't be disappointed with the food quality.
Waiter:	You will not, Sir.

Vocabulary

taste [teɪst]　*v.* 品尝，体验

raw [rɔ:]　*adj.* 生的

refuse [rɪ'fju:z]　*v.* 拒绝

arrogant ['ærəg(ə)nt]　*adj.* 自大的，傲慢的

disaster [dɪ'zɑ:stə]　*n.* 灾难，灾祸

specific [spə'sɪfɪk]　*adj.* 特殊的，特定的

explore [ɪk'splɔ]　*v.* 探索

wedge [wedʒ]　*n.* 楔形物

broth [brɒθ]　*n.* 肉汤

Useful Expressions

1. we'll try our best to solve the problem.

我们当尽力为您解决问题！

2. I'm sure the waiter didn't mean to be rude. perhaps he didn't understand you correctly.

相信服务员并不是有意无礼，他只是可能没有听懂您的意思。

3. I'm sorry sir, there must be some misunderstanding.

很抱歉，先生（小姐）。我想这里面可能有点误会。

4. I'm afraid you have misunderstood what I said. Perhaps I can explain again.

恐怕您误会了我的意思，我能解释一下吗？

5. I'm awfully sorry for my carelessness.

对于我的粗心大意我非常抱歉。

6. Lease sir, if you calm yourself, I'll try to help you.

先生请别激动，让我来想办法。

7. What's problem, sir? Can I be of assistance?

先生，出了什么问题？我能为您做些什么？

8. This is quite unusual. I will look into the matter.

这是很少有的，我会调查此事的。

9. I will get you another one.

我再去给您重端一份上来。

10. I will have them prepare another one. Would you like some drinks while you are waiting?

我去让他们重做一份，您是不是愿意边喝饮料边等？

11. Shall I have the dish cooked again?

要不要我去把这道菜再重做一遍？

12. I will take to the chef and see what he can do.

我去和厨师长商量一下，看看他是否能给予补救。

13. I'm terribly sorry. I can give you something else if you'd like. That will be on the house, of course.

非常抱歉，如果您愿意，我可以给您上点别的菜，这当然是本店免费赠送的。

Practice

Role Play: Work in pairs or groups and create conversations according to the given situations.

Topic: This steak is raw.

You: —...

Waiter: — Is everything all right, sir?

You: —...

Waiter: — I do apologize, sir. Would you like it cooked a little more?

You: —...

Waiter: — Would you like something else while you´re waiting?

You: —...

Exercises

1. Match each word or phrase in the column on the left with its meaning in the column on the right

(1) chef   a. something that has been done in the wrong way, or an opinion or statement that is incorrect.

(2) broth   b. happening or doing something very often.

(3) rare   c. a skilled cook, especially the main cook in a hotel or restaurant.

(4) mistake   d. clearly known, seen, or stated.

(5) regular   e. to discuss or think about something carefully.

(6) definite   f. soup with meat, rice, or vegetables.

(7) explore   g. an argument or disagreement that is not very serious – often used humorously.

(8) misunderstanding   h. meat that is rare has only been cooked for a short time and is still red.

(9) disaster   i. different from what is usual or normal.

(10) unusual   j.something that is very bad or a failure, especially when this is very annoying or disappointing.

2. Complete the following dialogue according to the Chinese in brackets and read it in roles.

A=Staff   B=Guest

B: _____（这儿太吵了，能找个安静点的地方吗？）

A: Would you prefer to sit in the next-door room? It's quieter.

B: Ok.

A: _____（请稍等。）

Later

B: _____（坐那边怎么样？）They have finished their meal just now.

A: Please wait a moment. I move your meal there.

3. Choose the best English translation for each sentence.

(1)能不能换一下座位？

A. Is it possible to change tables?   B. Would you please sit here?

C. Let me change the chair for you.   D. Could you please give a chair.

(2) 对不起，我给您拿一个过来。

A. I'm sorry. I'll give you one. B. I'm sorry. I'll bring you one.

C. I'm sorry. I'll lend you one. D. I'm sorry. I'll catch you one.

(3) 抱歉，我们没有儿童椅。

A. I'm sorry. We don't have high chair. B. I'm sorry. High chair is broken.

C. I'm sorry. We just bought the high chair. D. I'm sorry. High chair is down stairs.

(4) 你的职员太慢。

A. Your staff is very slow. B. Take your time.

C. Don't be worry. D. Your waiter is on the way.

(5) 请再检查一遍好吗？

A. Would you please have a look? B. Would you please come here?

C. Would you please check it again? D. Would you mind I go first?

4. Read the passage and choose the best answers to the following questions.

A Letter of Complaints

To: manger @ tastytreat.com

Date: Monday, 7 October, 3:34 p.m.

From: raymondyuen@ canada.net

Subject: Complaint

Dear Mr. Price,

I have eaten in your restaurant many times and have always been happy with the food and service. This makes what happened last Saturday even more disappointing.

It was my son's birthday so we booked a non-smoking table at your restaurant for 7:30 p.m. We arrived on time but were told that our table was not yet ready. At 8:00 p.m., we were given a table in the smoking section. I asked to move but I was told that there were no other tables. A lot of people were smoking so it was uncomfortable and unhealthy.

Our first waitress, Janet, was very polite and helpful. She gave us free drinks for waiting so long. Our food also came quickly and looked fresh and tasty. When my wife had eaten most of her meal, she found a dead cockroach (蟑螂) in her vegetables. She was shocked and wanted to leave. At first, the waitress told us it was a piece of garlic. When we told her that garlic does not have legs, she apologized and took the food away.

We asked for the bill, expecting not to pay for my wife's meal. Nobody came. After 15 minutes, I asked to see the manager. The head waiter told us that you were on holiday I complained again about the horrible cockroach. He told me Janet had finished work. He didn't believe my story and gave me a bill for three meals. I argued with him but was forced to pay.

The waitress, Janet, was always friendly, but I would like an apology from your impolite head waiter and a full repayment for our meal. It cost $68. Until then, I will not be eating at your restaurant or recommending it to anyone.

You can contact me at 742-3254 or through e-mail if you want more information.

Thank you for your attention.

Yours Sincerely,

Raymond Yuen

1.We learn from the text that, before Saturday, Mr. Yuen .

A. was satisfied with the restaurant   B. was disappointed with the restaurant

C. had to wait for his table   D. rarely ate at the restaurant

2. The head waiter didn't believe Mr. Yuen because _____.

A. the waitress stopped working and hadn't told him about it

B. he believed that the cockroach was garlic

C. he didn't want to pay Mr. Yuen back

D. the manager was on holiday

3. Mr. Yuen demanded that Mr. Price_____ .

A. say sorry to his family   B. let the head waiter stop working in the restaurant

C. get the head waiter to say sorry   D. get the head waiter and Janet to say sorry

4. What does Mr. Yuen want to pay for now?

A. Two meals.   B. Their meals.   C. Nothing.   D. Only the drinks.

Challenges and Solutions

1. If the guest is not satisfied with the taste of dish, what will you do?

Solutions:

2. What will you do if you spilt the drinks on the guest?

Solutions:

3. If the guest complains that the facilities are not complete, what will you do?

Solutions:

4. If the guest change seat because of the poor enviornmet, what will you do?

Solutions:

M4-17   Knowledge Link

M4-18   Key to Exercises

Chapter 5

Chinese Food Service

Lesson One   Chinese Cuisine

Objectives

➤ To help the students master useful expressions and sentences about Chinese cuisine service.

➤ To help the students familiar with all kinds of Chinese cuisine.

➤ To help the students make some dialogues about Chinese cuisine service.

Warming Up

1. There are many kinds of Chinese cuisine. Look at the following pictures and write down the correct names of the Chinese cuisine by the corresponding description.

_____ is a well-known dish in Beijing. It was a famous dish on Chinese imperial court menus.

_____ is a common Sichuan cuisine. It is a tradional dish with fish flavour.

_____ is a Hangzhou dish which is made by pan-frying and red cooking pork belly. The pork consist of fat and lean meat.

_____ is a classical Chinese made from a piece of dough wrapped around a filling.

_____ is a Chinese cooking method, prepared with a simmering pot of soup stock at the dining table, containing a variety of East Asian foodstuffs and ingredients.

_____ is a popular Chinese dish from Sichuan province. It consists of tofu set in a spicy sauce.

Dialogues

Key sentences:

➢ How many people are there in your party?

➢ Have you got a table for two?

➢ Would you like the table near the corner?

➢ May I have your order?

➢ What do you recommend?

Pre-questions:

1. Do you know about Chinese cuisine?

2. Do you know how to serve guests in the restaurant?

3. Do you know how to recommend dishes to guests?

Dialogue 1

Waiter:	Can I take your order now?
Guest:	What's today's special?
Waiter:	Here is the menu of our specials, madam.
Guest:	Thank you. Let me have a look. I like West Lake Fish in Sweet Sour Sauce and Mapo Tofu.
Waiter:	Anything else?
Guest:	Beggar's Chicken and two bottles of beer please. Thank you.

Dialogue 2

Waiter:	Would you like to order now?
Guest:	Yes, please.
Waiter:	Which flavor would you prefer, sweet or spicy?
Guest:	We are not used to spicy food, so please don't put any chili in the meal.

Dialogue 3

Waiter:	Hello, Madam. May I help you?
Guest:	Yes. I'd like something typically Chinese.
Waiter:	Fine. We serve a wide range of typical Chinese food. Here is the menu.
Guest:	Oh, I Know Beijing Roast Duck is popular in China. I'd like to try it.
Waiter:	OK, I'll bring your order right now.

Vocabulary

roast [rəʊst]　*v.* 烤制

cuisine [kwɪˈziːn]　*n.* 菜肴；烹饪

duck [dʌk]　*n.* 鸭子

sauce [sɔːs]　*n.* 酱汁

chili [ˈtʃɪli]　*n.* 辣椒

garlic [ˈɡɑːlɪk]　*n.* 大蒜

tofu ['təʊfu:] *n.* 豆腐	spicy ['spaɪsi] *adj.* 辛辣的
noodle ['nu:dl] *n.* 面条	salt[sɔ:lt] *n.* 盐
rice [raɪs] *n.* 大米；米饭	order ['ɔ:də(r)] *v.* 订购；*n.* 订单
dumpling ['dʌmplɪŋ] *n.* 饺子	recommend[ˌrekə'mend] *v.* 推荐
bun [bʌn] *n.* 馒头	menu['menju:] *n.* 菜单
hotpot ['hɒtpɒt] *n.* 火锅	beverage['bevərɪdʒ] *n.* 饮料
soup [su:p] *n.* 汤	typical['tɪpɪkl] *adj.* 典型的
sweet [swi:t] *adj.* 甜的	

Useful Expressions

1. Is there anything I can do for you?
有什么我可以帮助您的吗？

2.How many people are there in your party?
你们一共有多少人？

3.Have you got a table for two?
你有两人桌吗？

4.Would you like the table near the corner?
您想要靠近角落的桌子吗？

5.May I have your order?
您可以点菜了吗？

6. What do you recommend?
您有什么可以推荐的？

7. Can I take your order now?
您可以点菜了吗？

8. What's today's special?
今天的特色是什么？

9. You like Chinese food or Western food?
您喜欢中餐还是西餐？

10. Which flavor would you prefer, sweet or spicy?
您喜欢什么口味的？甜的还是辣的？

M5-2 Practice

Exercises

1. Questions and Answers

(1) Chinese and Western food, which one do you prefer?

(2) Could you list five famous Chinese cuisine?

(3) What's the famous local snacks in your home town?

2. Match the words or expressions in Column A with their Chinese equivalents in Column B.

A	B
(1) Guangdong cuisine	a. 饺子
(2) Fish-Flavored Shredded Pork	b. 包子
(3) Shandong cuisine	c. 馒头
(4) Chinese cuisine	d. 汤
(5) Dumplings	e. 面条
(6) Steamed stuffed bun	f. 火锅
(7) Soup	g. 中国菜

(8) Noodles   h. 鲁菜

(9) Bun   i. 粤菜

(10) Hot pot   j. 鱼香肉丝

3. Choose the best English translation for each sentence.

(1) 您准备好点菜了吗？

A. What food do you like more?   B. May I have your order?

C. Do you like Chinese food?   D. Are you ready?

(2) 您喜欢中餐还是西餐？

A. Do you like Chinese food?   B. You like Chinese food or Western food?

C. Do you like China?   D. What kind of food do you like best?

(3) 今天的特色菜是什么？

A. Is it special?   B. What's today's special?

C. Do you like it?   D. What's the color of it?

(4) 您推荐什么？

A. What's that?   B. I'm so sorry to be waiting.

C. Can you help me?   D. What do you recommend?

(5) 你们一共多少人？

A. How many people in your party?   B. How many people in your family?

C. Who are you?   D. How many books do you have?

4. Read the passage and decide if the statements are true (T) or false (F).

China's long history, vast territory and rich culture have given birth to the distinctive Chinese culinary art. With several thousand years of creative and accumulative efforts, Chinese cuisine has become increasingly popular among more and more overseas gourmets.

As the top three cuisines in the world (the other two are French cuisine and Turkish cuisine), Chinese cuisine has a deep influence to East Asia. Originated from different regions and ethnic groups of China, Chinese cuisine can be divided into many categories, like the Eight Famous Cuisines, local snacks, ethnic foods and so on. Rooted in the traditional Chinese philosophy, Chinese food represents the harmony and balance of nature, not only satisfy a gourmet appetite, but also preserve people's health.

Exercises:

(1) The history of Chinese food is short. (   )

(2) Chinese is popular worldwide. (   )

(3) Chinese cuisine is not one of the top three cuisines in the world.(   )

(4) Chinese cuisine can be classified into different styles by region. (   )

(5) Chinese food is not good for our health. (   )

Challenges and Solutions

1. Do you like Chinese food?

Solutions:

2. Which Chinese food do you like best?

Solutions:

3. Can you cook?

Solutions:

4. What is dumpling?

Solutions:

5. What is hotpot?

Solutions:

6. If the guest don't know which one to choose, can you recommend?

Solution:

7. If the guest wants to eat seafood, what will you recommend?

Solutions:

8. If the guest eat Chinese food for the first time, what should you do?

Solutions:

M5-3　Knowledge Link

M5-4　Key to Exercises

Lesson Two　Chinese Breakfast Service

Objectives

➢ To help the students master useful expressions and sentences about Chinese breakfast service.

➢ To help the students familiar with all kinds of Chinese breakfast.

➢ To help the students make some dialogues about Chinese breakfast service.

Warming Up

1. There are many kinds of breakfast in China. Look at the following pictures and write down the correct names of Chinese breakfast by the corresponding description.

_____ is a type of filled bun. There are many versions in filling, such as meat and vegetables.

_____, often referred to as Chinese steamed bun, is a type of cloud-like steamed bread or bun popular in Northern China. The name mantou is said to have originated from a tale about Zhuge Liang.

_____ , also called fried breadstick, is a long golden-brown deep-fried strip of dough eaten in China.

_____ is a Chinese snack made with very soft tofu. It is also referred to as tofu pudding and soybean pudding.

_____ is a type of dumpling-like Chinse breakfast. It is commonly boiled and served with soup.

_____ is a type of baked and layered food in Northern Chinese cuisine. It can be made with or without stuffing and sesame.

_____ is a coffee drink made with espresso and steamed milk.

_____ is a typical Chinese savory food commonly sold as a snack, in which a boiled egg is cracked slightly and then boiled again in tea, sauce and/or spices.

M5-5　Warming Up

Dialogues

Key sentences:

➢ What are the specials for today?

➢ What kind of food do you prefer?

➢ Do you like Chinese food?

➢ How would you like the egg?

➢ What sauce do you like?

Pre-questions:

1. Do you know about Chinese breakfast?

2. Do you know how to provide room service to the guests?

3. Do you know how to recommend breakfast to guests?

Dialogue 1

Clerk:	Room service. Can I help you?
Mr. Steven:	Yes. Would you please bring me some breakfast?
Clerk:	Sure. When would you like it, sir?
Mr. Steven:	Now, please.
Clerk:	What's your room number, sir?
Mr. Steven:	My room number is 1212.
Clerk:	For how many people, sir?
Mr. Steven:	One.
Clerk:	Porridge and steamed stuffed bun?
Mr. Steven:	Yes. And bring me a cup of coffee and some fruit.
Clerk:	We will bring it up now.
Mr. Steven:	Thank you.

Dialogue 2

Guest:	Hi, waiter, I want to order some food.
Waiter:	What would you like?
Guest:	Kung Pow chick, Yuxiang shredded pork and tomatoes fried with egg.
Waiter:	Something to drink?
Guest:	Yes, two bottles of Tsingtao beer, no MSG and only a little spicy, please.
Waiter:	No problem, sir.

Dialogue 3

Waitress:	Good evening. Welcome to our restaurant.
Guest A:	Good evening. Do you have a table for two.
Waitress:	Yes. This way, please. Here is the menu.
Guest A:	Thank you. Let me see what you have.
Waitress:	Excuese me, sir. May I take your order now?
Guest B:	What are the specials for today?
Waitress:	Beggar's Chicken is today's special.
Guest B:	That's good. I'll try it.

Guest A:	I'd like to try barbecued pork, seaweed soup.
Waitress:	Would you like some vegetables?
Guest A:	Yes, bring us some cabbages and potatoes.
Waitress:	OK. Would you like something to drink?
Guest A:	Tea, please.
Waitress:	What else?
Guest A:	No, thanks.
Waitress:	So Beggar's Chicken, barbecued pork, seaweed soup, cabbages and potatoes.
Guest A:	That's right.
Waitress:	Thank you, sir. Your dishes will take about 10 minutes to prepare. Please wait a moment.
Guest A:	OK.

Vocabulary

stir-fry ['stɜ:fraɪ] *v.* 炒

culinary ['kʌlɪnəri] *adj.* 厨房的；烹饪的

pan-fry [pæn frai] *v.* (用平底锅)油煎

deep-fry ['di:p'fraɪ] vt. 油炸

aroma [ə'rəʊmə] *n.* 芳香；香味

ingredient [ɪn'gri:diənt] *n.* 原料

fragrant ['freɪgrənt] *adj.* 芳香的

appetite ['æpɪtaɪt] *n.* 胃口；欲望

odor [əʊdə] *n.* 气味

soy [sɔɪ] *n.* 大豆

seasoning ['si:zənɪŋ] *n.* 调味品

shred [ʃred] *v.* 切丝

crisp [krɪsp] *adj.* 脆的

simmer ['sɪmə(r)] *v.* 炖

greasy ['gri:si] *adj.* 油腻的

stew [stju:] *v.* 炖

syrup ['sɪrəp] *n.* 糖浆

Useful Expressions

1. Can I help you?
有什么需要帮助的？

2. Would you please bring me some breakfast?
可以给我带点早餐吗？

3. What are the specials for today?
今天特色菜是什么？

4. What kind of food do you prefer?
你更喜欢什么食物？

5. Do you like Chinese food?
你喜欢中餐吗？

6. How would you like the egg?
鸡蛋打算怎么做？

7. What sauce do you like?
您想要什么调料？

8. What would you like to drink?

您喝点什么？

9.Would you please bring me some breakfast?
可以给我来份早餐吗？

10. When would you like your breakfast?
您想什么时候吃早餐？

11. What is your room number?
您的房间号是多少？

12. For how many people?
一共多少人？

13. Do you have a table for two?
你有两人桌吗？

14. Would you like some vegetable?
想要点蔬菜吗？

15. Something to drink?
想要点喝的吗？

M5-6 Practice

Exercises

1. Questions and Answers

(1) What's breakfast?

(2) Could you list fivefamous Chinese food of breakfast?

(3) What's bun?

2. Match the words or expressions in Column A with their Chinese equivalents in Column B.

A	B
(1) Noodles	a. 鸡蛋
(2) Deep fried dough stick	b. 炸糕
(3) porridge	c. 油条
(4) Egg	d. 包子
(5) Steamed stuffed bun	e. 馒头
(6) Bun	f. 豆腐脑
(7) fried cake	g. 馄饨
(8) Tofu jelly	h. 粥
(9) Bean soup	i. 豆浆
(10) Wonton	j. 面条

3. Choose the best English translation for each sentence.

(1) 您想要点蔬菜吗？

A. Do you like vegetables?　　　　B. Vegetable or meat?

C. Would you like some vegetables?　　D. Do you have dumplings?

(2) 你们有两人桌吗？

A. Do you have a table for two?　　B. Can I book a table?

C. what is on the table?　　　　D. can I use this table?

(3) 您的房间号是多少？

A. Who is in the room?　　　　B. Do you need room service?

C. Where can you find it?　　　　D. What's your room number?

(4) 您想喝点什么？

A. I want to drink some water.　　B. Do you want to try this?

C. Would you like something to drink?　　D. Do you like drinking milk?

(5) 有什么可以帮助你的？

A. Can you show me the way?　　B. Can you tell me where is it?

C. What can I do for you?　　　　D. Can you help him?

4. Read the passage and decide if the statements are true (T) or false (F).

This breakfast set usually appears together. The two components are the most common breakfast combination. Some locals also like to have deep-fried dough sticks with rice congee.

Soybean milk is made with a blender. You can find freshly blended or boiled soy milk in disposable cups at most breakfast stalls. It's very convenient for a take-out.

Deep-fried dough sticks are long, brown, deep-fried sticks of dough. You can eat one as it is or dip it in some soybean milk, which has a better taste.

Exercises:

(1) The breakfast set usually appears individually. (　　)

(2) People usually eat deep-fried dough sticks with bun. (　　)

(3) Soybean milk is not a kind of milk. (　　)

(4) Soybean milk is not convenient to take out.(　　)

(5) Deep-fried dough sticks is a kind of deepfried food. (　　)

Challenges and Solutions

1. What kind of Chinese break do you know?

Solutions:

2. Do you Chinese breakfast is good for health?

Solutions:

3. What is soybean milk?

Solutions:

4. What is steamed stuffed bun?

Solutions:

5. Do you eat breakfast everyday?

Solutions:

6. If the guest wants to have some Chinese breakfast, what will you recommend?

Solution:

7. If you go to Beijing, what breakfast will you try?

Solutions:

8. What Chinese breakfast do you like best?

Solutions:

M5-7　Knowledge Link

M5-8　Key to Exercises

Lesson Three   Chinese Table Setting

Objectives

➤ To help the students master useful expressions and sentences about table setting.
➤ To help the students familiar with different kinds of table setting.
➤ To help the students make some dialogues about table service in restaurants.

Warming Up

1. There are many kinds of Chinese tableware. Look at the following pictures and write down the correct names of tableware by the corresponding description.

_____ are shaped pairs of equal-length sticks that have been used as kitchen and eating utensils in virtually all of East Asia for over 2000 years.

_____ is a round open-top container used to serve food. It can also be used to drink water.

_____ is a tableware used for setting a table, serving food and dining.

_____ is used for eating liquid or semi-liquid foods. It can also be used in food preparation to measure, mix, stir ingredients.

_____ is a small stick of wood or other substance used to remove detritus from the teeth.

_____ is a rectangle of cloth used at the table for wiping the mouth and fingers while eating. It is usually small and folded, sometimes in intricate designs and shapes.

Dialogues

Key sentences:

➢ Would you like a table in the main restaurant or in a private room, sir?

➢ What time would you like your table?

➢ What is it going to be, Chinese food or Western food?

➢ Do you have a children's menu?

➢ May I have your name and telephone number?

Pre-questions:

1. Do you know how to greet and seat guest?

2. Do you know how to take orders?

3. Do you know how to recommend food to guests?

Dialogue 1

Waiter:	Good evening, sir. Can I help you?
Guest:	I think I have a reservation for 6 people. My name is James Lee.
Waiter:	Yes, Mr. Lee. We have a very nice table reserved for you. This way, please.
Guest:	Oh, I'm sorry. I want a private room for 8 people.
Waiter:	All right. Then downstairs, please.
Guest:	Thank you.
Waiter:	You are welcome. Do you like this room?
Guest:	It's a nice and cozy room. Yes, that will do.
Waiter:	Be seated, please. Have a cup of tea please.

Dialogue 2

Waiter:	Good evening, Sir. Here is the menu.
Guest:	Thanks.
Waiter:	What would you like?
Guest:	I'm really confused with all the Chinese food here. Do you have any suggestions?
Waiter:	It's my pleasure. How about Beijing Roasr Duck?
Guest:	Roast Duck?
Waiter:	It is the speciality of this restaurant, and many foreign guests like it.
Guest:	That sounds good. I'll take one.
Waiter:	Anything else to go with the duck?
Guest:	Some vegetables would be OK.

Dialogue 3

Guest:	I will take beef steak and Beijing Roast Duck as the main course.

Waiter:	OK.
Guest:	And some vegetables.
Waiter:	The Roast Duck will be ready in twenty minutes. Would you like something to drink while waiting?
Guest:	Sure.
Waiter:	House wine or anything special?
Guest:	Do you have Maotai?
Waiter:	Yes, it's one of the most popular drinks in China.
Guest:	Then Maotai for the gentlemen, champagne for the ladies and soda for children.
Waiter:	Maotai, champagne and soda. A moment, please.

Vocabulary

spoon [spu:n] *n.* 勺子

chopsticks ['tʃɒpstɪks] *n.* 筷子

toothpick ['tu:θpɪk] *n.* 牙签

bowl [bəʊl] *n.* 碗

plate [pleɪt] *n.* 碟子

cutlery ['kʌtləri] *n.* 刀叉；餐具

napkin ['næpkɪn] *n.* 餐巾

tissue ['tɪʃu:] *n.* 纸巾；餐巾纸

thermos ['θɜ:məs] *n.* 保温杯

ashtray ['æʃtreɪ] *n.* 烟灰缸

vase [vɑ:z] *n.* 花瓶

tea[ti:] *n.* 茶

teapot ['ti:pɒt] *n.* 茶壶

lighter ['laɪtə(r)] *n.* 打火机

suggestion[sə'dʒestʃən] *n.* 建议

Useful Expressions

1. Would you like a table in the main restaurant or in a private room, sir?
您想要在主餐厅吃还是在雅间吃？

2. I'd like to book a table for two this evening.
我想订今晚的两人桌。

3. What time would you like your table?
您几点需要桌子？

4. What is it going to be, Chinese food or Western food?
您想要什么风格的？中餐还是西餐？

5. How many people in your party?
您一共多少人？

6. How many people do you want a table for?
定一个几人桌？

7. Do you have a children's menu?
您有儿童菜单吗？

8. May I have your name and telephone number?
我可以要您的名字和电话吗？

9. How about Beijing Roast Duck?
北京烤鸭如何？

10. Anything else to go with the duck?

想要点什么和烤鸭搭配的吗？

11. Would you like something to drink while waiting?

等待期间您想要喝点什么吗？

12. Anything special?

想来点特别的吗？

M5-10　Practice

Exercises

1. Questions and Answers

(1) Why do we need to set the table?

(2) What Chinese tablewares do you know?

(3) Can you fold napkin flowers?

2. Match the words or expressions in Column A with their Chinese equivalents in Column B.

A	B
(1) Teapot	a. 筷子
(2) chopsticks	b. 茶杯
(3) Spoon	c. 茶壶
(4) Dish	d. 牙签
(5) Bowl	e. 桌子
(6) Cup	f. 碗
(7) Table	g. 碟子
(8) Ashtray	h. 汤匙
(9) Towel	i. 手巾
(10) Toothpick	j. 烟灰缸

3. Choose the best English translation for each sentence.

(1) 想来点特别的吗？

A. Is it special?　　　　　　　　　　B. Anything special?

C. What's special?　　　　　　　　　D. Where is it?

(2) 来点炸鸡怎么样？

A. Do you want smoked chicken?　　　B. How about curry chicken?

C. Do you like roast duck?　　　　　D. How about some friend chicken?

(3) 我可以问一下你的电话和房间号吗？

A. May I ask your name?　　　　　　　　　　　　B. May I help you?

C. May I have your phone number and room number?　D. Can you show me the way?

(4) 有儿童菜单吗？

A. Do you have a children menu?　　　B. Do you have a baby?

C. Where is the menu?　　　　　　　D. Is it children's day?

(5) 您喜欢中餐还是西餐？

A. You like Chinese food or Western food?　　B. Do you like Chinese?

C. Are you a westerner?　　　　　　　　　　D. Are you in China?

4. Read the passage and decide if the statements are true (T) or false (F).

Chopsticks are two long, thin, usually tapered, pieces of wood. Bamboo has been the most popular material of chopsticks because it is inexpensive, readily available, easy to split, resistant to heat, and has no perceptible odor or taste.

Chopsticks are called "Kuaizi" in Chinese which resembles the pronunciation of other two words, soon and son. Therefore, it is a tradition in some areas to give chopsticks as a gift to newly-married couples, wishing them to have a baby soon.

Chinese food seems to taste better eaten with chopsticks which are the special utensil Chinese use to dine. It will be an awkward experience for foreigners to use chopsticks to have a meal. Fortunately, learning to eat with chopsticks is not difficult.

Exercises:

(1) Chopsticks are commonly made of wood.(　　)

(2) Bamboo is very precious. (　　)

(3) Bamboo is hard to split.(　　)

(4) In China, people usually give chopsticks to newly married people. (　　)

(5) For foreigners, using chopsticks is difficult. (　　)

Challenges and Solutions

1. What are chopsticks?

Solutions:

2. What is a bowl?

Solutions:

3. What is a plate?

Solutions:

4. What is the difference between Chinese and Western tableware?

Solutions:

5. Do you know how to use chopsticks?

Solutions:

6. Do you know how to set the table?

Solution:

7. If foreign guest don't know how to use chopsticks, what will you do?

Solutions:

8. If the chopsticks fall on the floor, what will you do?

Solutions:

M5-11　Knowledge Link

M5-12　Key to Exercises

Lesson Four　Taking the Bill Service

Objectives

➢ To help the students master useful expressions and sentences about taking the bil service.
➢ To help the students familiar with the working procedure of taking the bill.
➢ To help the students make some dialogues about taking the bill service.

Warming Up

1. There are many kinds of facilities in the restaurants. Look at the following pictures and write down the correct names of facilities by the corresponding description.

_____ is a kind of food cart. It is typically used by restaurants to deliver or display food.

_____ is made for the carrying of items. It can be used in the restaurants to carry dishes.

_____ is a list of prepared foods in restaurants.

_____ is a commercial paper issued by a seller to buyers. Payment terms are usually stated on the invoice.

M5-13　Warming Up

Dialogues

Key sentences:

➤ Could I have a receipt?

➤ Do you charge for drinks?

➤ Could we have separate check?

➤ It is my treat.

➤ What's this for?

Pre-questions:

1. Do you know about payment and checking out??

2. Do you know how to serve guests in the restaurant when they need to check out?

3. Do you know how to help guests to check out?

Dialogue 1

A:	Waiter,would you bring me the check, please?
B:	Would you like to pay by cash or by credit card?
A:	Cash.
B:	One second, please. That will be 130 Yuan.
A:	This is the money.
B:	Thank you.

Dialogue 2

A:	Can I have my bill?
B:	Certainly, sir.
A:	I'm afraid there has been a mistake.
B:	I'm sorry sir. What seems to be the trouble?
A:	I believe you have charged me twice for the same thing. Look, the figure of 6.5 dollar appears here, then again here.
B:	I just go and check it for you, sir.

Dialogue 3

A:	Are you all through, madam?
B:	Yes, everything is very good. Can I have my bill, please?
A:	Yes, one moment, please. Here you are.
B:	Thanks for your nice service. Here is 70 dollars. Keep the change, please.
A:	Thank you, madam.
B:	By the way, I think I need a food bag.
A:	OK, no problem.

Vocabulary

bill [bɪl]　*n.* 账单；清单

credit card ['kredɪt kɑːd]　*n.* 信用卡

debit card ['debɪt kɑːd]　*n.* 借记卡

dollar ['dɒlə(r)]　*n.* 美元

euro ['juərəʊ]　*n.* 欧元

pound [paʊnd]　*n.* 磅；英镑

visa ['viːzə]　*n.* 签证；维萨信用卡

mastercard ['mɑːstə(r)kɑː]　*n.* 万事达卡

check [tʃek]   *n.* 支票
POS machine   *n.* POS机
wechat [witʃæt]   *n.* 微信
alipay [alipeɪ]   *n.* 支付宝
cash [kæʃ]   *n.* 现金

currency['kʌrənsi]   *n.* 货币
exchange rate [iks'tʃeindʒ reit]   *n.* 汇率
tip[tɪp]   *n.* 小费
interest ['ɪntrəst]   *n.* 利率

Useful Expressions

1. Could I have the bill?
我可以结账吗？
2. Could I have a receipt?
我可以要个收据吗？
3. Do you charge for drinks?
饮料收费吗？
4. Could we have separate check?
可以分别结账吗？
5. Let's go Dutch.
让我们AA吧。
6. It is my treat.
算我请客。
7. What's this for?

这一项是什么？
8. Can I have a doggy bag?
我可以要个打包袋吗？
9. Would you bring me the check?
可以帮我结账吗？
10. Would you like to pay by cash or by credit card?
您是付现金还是信用卡支付？
11. Can I have my bill?
我可以结账吗？
12. Can I have a food bag?
我可以打包吗？

M5-14   Practice

Exercises

1. Questions and Answers

(1) What kind of payment method do you use often?

(2) Could you list five payment method you know?

(3) What's bill?

2. Match the words or expressions in Column A with their Chinese equivalents in Column B.

A	B
(1) Air conditioner	a. 托盘
(2) Tray	b. 空调
(3) Trolly	c. 美国运通卡
(4) Menu	d. 吉士美卡
(5) Bill	e. 万事达卡
(6) Visa	f. 银联卡
(7) American Express	g. 维萨卡
(8) JCB	h. 手推车

(9) Master Card   i. 账单

(10) Unionpay   j. 菜单

3. Choose the best English translation for each sentence.

(1) 我可以结账吗？

A. Can I take your order now?   B. Could I have the bill?

C. Can I use it?   D. Where is the menu?

(2) 我们可以分别结账吗？

A. Can I check in?   B. Can I check out?

C. Can I have the bill?   D. Could we have separate check?

(3) 这次我请客。

A. Invite the guests this time, please.   B. It's my treat.

C. Here is the menu.   D. Let's go Dutch.

(4) 我可以要一个打包袋吗？

A. Can I have a doggy bag?   B. Do you need steamed stuffed bun?

C. Where is your bag?   D. May I ask?

(5) 饮料收费吗？

A. Do you need some drinks?   B. Do you want some beer?

C. Do you charge for drinks?   D. Do you want to try it?

4. Read the passage and decide if the statements are true (T) or false (F).

When you apply for a credit card, you apply to borrow money from the card issuer, usually a bank or building society. The issuer then looks at your credit history to consider your application – and if you have a low credit score you could be refused credit, or perhaps given a less attractive deal on interest rate.

If you have a good credit rating, then you will be accepted and the bank will set a credit limit, which is the maximum amount you can spend on the card. The card company will send you a statement every month, detailing any transactions on your card, plus the amount owing. It also provides details on the minimum payment you need to make (this depends on how much you have your balance) and the payment due date.

Exercises:

(1) When we apply for credit card to save money to the card issuer. (   )

(2) The credit card issuer is usually a bank or building society. (   )

(3) The card issuer will not look at the applier's credit history. (   )

(4) If you have good credit rating, you can easily get a credit card. (   )

(5) The card company will send a statement twice a month. (   )

Challenges and Solutions

1. Do you have a credit card?

Solutions:

2. How to apply for a credit card?

Solutions:

3. What credit card company do you know?

Solutions:

4. Do you have a wechat account?

Solutions:

5. Wechat and Alipay, which one do you use more often?

Solutions:

6. If a guest wants use credit card but there is POS machine, what shall you do?

Solution:

7. If guest wants to take the bill, what will you do?

Solutions:

8. Whan there is something wrong with the bill, what will you do?

Solutions:

M5-15　Knowledge Link

M5-16　Key to Exercises

Lesson Five　Chinese Table Manner

Objectives

➤ To help the students master useful expressions and sentences about table manners of Chinese food.

➤ To help the students familiar with table manners of Chinese food.

➤ To help the students make some dialogues about table manners of Chinese food.

Warming Up

1. There are many kinds of Chinese tableware. Look at the following pictures and write down the correct names of tableware by the corresponding description.

_____ is used for collecting ash from cigarettes and cigars.

_____ is tableware, similar to a knife rest or a spoon rest, used to keep chopstick tips off the table and to prevent used chopsticks from contaminating or rolling off tables.

_____ is a small wet piece of paper or cloth that often comes folded and individually wrapped for convenience. Wet wipes are used for cleaning purposes like personal hygiene and household cleaning.

_____ is a tableware used to carry cooked fish.

M5-17　Warming Up

Dialogues

Key sentences:

➢ Please help yourself to anything you like.

➢ Do you have a dress code?

➢ Don't talk with your mouthful.

➢ Children should above all learn table manners.

➢ Every culture has its own rules of table etiquette.

Pre-questions:

1. Do you know about Chinese table manners?

2. Do you know how to use different tablewares?

3. What's the difference between Chinese and Western table manners?

Dialogue 1

A:　　　　　　I read an article about Chinese table manners.

B:　　　　　　What does it say?

A:　　　　　　When you have your meals, you should try your best to make less sound and action.

B:　　　　　　Anything else?

A:　　　　　　And even in restaurants it requires people stop smoking.

B:　　　　　　 I've heard it before.

A:　　　　　　Yes, it's very exquisite in China.

B:　　　　　　So it is. We have a lot to learn.

Dialogue 2

A:　　　　　　As you know, table manners in China are quite different from those of Westerners.

B: Absolutely. That's because both of us have distinctive cultural features.

A: For example, in China, it's OK to talk while eating. However, you may regard it as rude.

B: Yes. Also, we tend to think that the slower one eats, the more polite one seems.

A: I've never heard that before.

B: Yes, and we never sip or slurp the soup loadly. We quietly like little mouthfuls.

Dialogue 3

A: Now that you have been to our Guangzhou Fair, Mr. King, what's your impression?

B: Well, there is really a wide range of goods on display and the prices are reasonable.

A: Quite true. I hope your business does well, and I look forward to working with you in the future.

B: Well, here is a toast to your health and success in business.

A: And to yours. Time flies. You are leaving tomorrow. We hope you will come again soon.

B: Thank you for a wonderful evening and thank you for all your help during my stay here.

Vocabulary

chopstick ['tʃɒpstɪk]   *n.* 筷子

ashtray ['æʃtreɪ]   *n.* 咖啡；咖啡豆；咖啡色

hopstick rest   筷架

towel ['taʊəl]   *n.* 毛巾

spoon [spu:n]   *n.* 汤匙

bottle opener   *n.* 起子；开瓶器

saucer ['sɔ:sə(r)]   *n.* 茶碟；茶托

deep-fried dough stick   *n.* 油条；果子

steamed stuffed bun   *n.* 包子

spring roll   *n.* 春卷

pancake [ə,mɛrɪ'kɑno]   *n.* 煎饼

fried twist [,mækɪ'ɑ:təʊ]   *n.* 麻花

moon cake ['mokə]   *n.* 月饼

glue pudding   *n.* 元宵；汤圆

Useful Expressions

1. To our health.

为我们健康干杯！

2. Cheers!

干杯！

3. Please help yourself to anything you like.

请随意吃。

4. Do you have a dress code?

对着装有要求吗？

5. Don't talk with your monthful.

不能一边嚼饭一边说话。

6. Children should above all learn table manners.

孩子们应该学习餐桌礼仪。

7. Every culture has its own rules of table etiquette.

每个文化都有自己的餐桌礼仪。

8. How to put and use the napkin?

餐巾纸怎么放？怎么用？

9. Table manners in China are quite different from those of Westerners.

中国的餐桌礼仪和西方的很不一样。

10. I hope your business does well.

祝您生意兴隆！

11. I look forward to working with you in the future.

期待将来和您一起工作。

12. Here is a toast to your health and success in business.

为您的身体健康和工作顺利而干杯！

M5-18　Practice

Exercises

1. Questions and Answers

(1) What good table manners do you know?

(2) What bad table manners do you know?

(3) What's the difference betwwen Chinese and Western table manners?

2. Match the words or expressions in Column A with their Chinese equivalents in Column B.

A	B
(1) Saucer	a. 筷架
(2) Moon cake	b. 茶杯托
(3) Bottle Opener	c. 毛巾
(4) Glass	d. 纸巾
(5) Spring roll	e. 玻璃杯
(6) Chopstick rest	f. 起子
(7) Tissue	g. 麻花
(8) Donkey burger	h. 春卷
(9) Towel	i. 驴肉火烧
(10) Fried twist	j. 月饼

3. Choose the best English translation for each sentence.

(1) 对着装有要求吗？

A. Do I have to wear formal dress?　　　B. Do I have to wear suit?

C. Do you have a dress code?　　　D. Can I wear jeans?

(2) 嘴里有饭时不要说话。

A. Don't eat junk food.　　　B. Don't eat on the bed.

C. Don't talk with your mouthful.　　　D. You can call room service.

(3) 餐巾怎么放？怎么用？

A. Where is the napkin?　　　B. Can I use your towel?

C. How to put and use the napkin?　　　D. Where is the restaurant?

(4) 孩子们都应该学习餐桌礼仪。

A. She is setting at the table.　　　B. The waiter is cleaning the table.

C. Table manner is important.　　　D. Children should all learn table manner.

(5) 为我们的健康干杯！

A. To our health!　　　B. You should drink more.

C. I want a cup of wine.　　　D. This is red wine.

4. Read the passage and decide if the statements are true (T) or false (F).

When eating a meal in China, people are expected to behave in a civilized manner (according to Chinese customs), pay attention to table manners and practice good dining habits. In order to avoid offense diners should pay attention to the following points:

Let older people eat first, or if you hear an elder say "let's eat", you can start to eat. You should not steal a march on the elders.

You should pick up your bowl with your thumb on the mouth of the bowl, first finger, middle finger the third finger supporting the bottom of the bowl and palm empty. If you don't pick up your bowl, bend over the table, and eat facing your bowl, it will be regarded as bad table manners. Moreover, it will have the consequence of compressing the stomach and restricting digestion.

Exercises:

(1) Table manner is not impirtant in China. (　　)

(2) When you eat, you should pay attention to others. (　　)

(3) The youngers should eat first. (　　)

(4) You are not allowed to pick up the bowl when you eat. (　　)

(5) Bowl is a kind of tableware. (　　)

Challenges and Solutions

1. Do you thing table manner is important in China?

Solutions:

2. What good table manners do you know?

Solutions:

3. What kind of behaviors can be considered as a bad table manner?

Solutions:

4. What's the difference between Chinese and Western table manner?

Solutions:

5. If you have dinner with old man, who will eat at fitst?

Solutions:

6. What table manners of other countries do you know?

Solution:

7. Why do you think we should follow table manners?

Solutions:

Lesson Six　Handling Complaints

Objectives

➢ To help the students master useful expressions and sentences about complaints in the Chinese restaurants.

➢ To help the students familiar with the common complaints in the Chinese restaurants.

➢ To help the students analyze the reasons of complaints and handle complaints in the Chinese restaurants.

Preamble

Monday October 13, 2018

Dear Sir,

I visited your restaurant on 10 September 2016 for dinner with my family. We ordered Chinese food and requested the waiter for spring roll first.

The starter came in after a long wait and turned out to be stale. Despite reporting the same to your supervisor, he denied our claim and was rude when he asked us to look for another restaurant instead.

The children started complaining of discomfort and we rushed them to a hospital wherein doctors declared food poisoning. We could avert-serious damages due to timely medical attention.

I request you to kindly investigate and take action against the staff on duty for their negligence and rude behavior. I am sending a copy of hospital bills for reimbursement failing which I will take up the case to the Customer Forum for stringent action against your restaurant.Sincerely yours,

Thanking you.

James King

Dialogues

Key sentences:

➢ What's wrong with your food sir?

➢ Do you wish to try some other dishes?

➢ What happened, sir?

➢ Could you tell me exactly what it is all about?

➢ Would you please wait for a minute? I'll go to have a check for you right now.

Pre-questions:

1. What are the common complaints in the Chinese restaurant?

2. How to deal with complaints?

3. What's the procedure of handling complaints?

Dialogue 1

A:	Excuse me, but this is not what I ordered.
B:	What did you order?
A:	Bacon and eggs.
B:	I'll get you the right order. Sorry about the mix up.
A:	No big deal.

Dialogue 2

Waiter:	Do you enjoy your meal?
Guest:	No, the steak is under-cooked.
Waiter:	I'm sorry about that.
Guest:	You know I want my steak well done.
Waiter:	I'm sorry, madam. I'll take it away and bring you another steak.
Guest:	OK
(After the meal)	
Waiter:	Madam, I am sure everything will be good next time. Please give us another chance.
Guest:	All right. I'll come again.
Waiter:	Thank you very much, madam.

Dialogue 3

A:	Hi, Waiter. Can I come over here?
B:	Of course, what is the matter, sir?
A:	Can you make out what this it?
B:	Oh my god. I think that's hair.
A:	So there is nothing wrong with my my eyes.
B:	I'm terribly sorry. We will replace the dish and refund your money.
A:	Good. That will help me calm down a little.

Vocabulary

complaint [kəmˈpleɪnt]　*n.* 投诉

steak [steɪk]　*n.* 牛排

bacon [ˈbeɪkən]　*n.* 培根

undercooked [ˈʌndəkʊkt]　*adj.* 没熟的

Useful Expressions

1. What's wrong with your food, sir?
先生，您的食物有什么问题？

2. Do you want to try some other dishes?
您想尝一尝其他的菜吗？

3. I am sorry that you didn't enjoy it.
很抱歉，您不喜欢它。

4. What happened sir?
先生，发生了什么？

5. Could you tell me exactly what it is all about?
您可以详细告诉我发生了什么吗？

6. Would you please wait for a minute? I'll go to have a check for you right now.
请稍微等我一下，我马上为您查一下。

7. The beer is flat.
这啤酒没气了。

8. I didn't enjoy it at all.
我觉得味道一点也不好。

9. The meat is too tough.
肉太老了。

10. The fish is not fresh.
鱼不新鲜了。

Exercises

1. Match each word or phrase in the column on the left with its meaning in the column on the right.

(1) complaint

(2) disappointed

(3) situation

(4) survey

(5) sympathy

(6) perspective

(7) regretful

(8) pale

(9) superior

(10) upset

a. being not happy with the result.

b. sharing the feeling of others.

c. supervisor.

d. a reason for not being satisfied.

e. white.

f. a detailed inspection.

g. a way of regarding situations.

h. a condition that you are facing.

i. a sense of loss over something done.

j. being unhappy.

2. Complete the following dialogue according to the Chinese in brackets and read it in roles.

Mr. Green: I want to complain about the terrible service in this hotel.

Manager: _____（对于您的不满意我很难过。）What has happened? _____

Mr. Green: This morning I wanted a wake-up call at 7 a.m., but I didn't get one so I was late for my meeting.

Manager: _____（很抱歉先生。）

Mr. Green: Also, your staff are very slow. I waited an hour for service in your restaurant and when the waiter came he was very rude and he upset my wife.

Manager: I am so sorry.

Mr. Green: I would like to know what you are going to do about this awful service.

Manager: _____ (我会和我的员工们说，让这种事情不再发生)

Mr. Green: Good. If the service doesn't get better I will never stay here again.

Manager: It will get better. I promise.

3. Choose the correct steps for settling guest's complaints in the Chinese restaurant.

A. Make an apology to the guest.

B. Inquire the problem.

C. When the problem is settled, report it guests and record the handling process.

D. Promise to solve the problem.

E. Ask someone who is in charge of this issue to solve the problem.

F. Say sorry again.

G. If the problem is not handled and you are going to get off duty, hand it over to the next duty.

H.If the problem can not be solve, as supervisor for help.

4. Choose the best English translation for each sentence.

(1)您的牛排怎么了，先生？（   ）

A. What's wrong with you, sir?   B. What's wrong with your streak, sir?

C. What is the problem, madam?   D. what is your name, sir?

(2)我可以跟经理谈一谈吗？（   ）

A. Can I speak with the manager?   B. Can I talk with you?

C. Can I use your phone?   D. can I use the internet?

(3)服务生，可以过来一下吗？（   ）

A. Wait me a moment.   B. Waiter, can you do me a favour?

C. Come in please.   D. Waiter, could you come here for a while?

(4)我马上给您换。（   ）

A. I'm terrible sorry, we'll give you another glass of sherry.

B. I'm terrible sorry, we'll give you another glass of sherry for free.

C. I want to change

D. I will change for you immediately.

(5)请慢用。（   ）

A. Please do it slowly.   B. Please do it alone.

C. Please help me.   D. Enjoy your meal.

5. Read the passage and choose the best answers to the following questions.

How to Handle Customer Complaints Quickly

Customer service is the interaction a person experiences when conducting business with a company or an individual. The experience can be positive or negative. Successful businesses train their staff on how to handle customer complaints quickly.

1. Understanding the Problem

Listen to the customer concerns. Generally, concerns over an issue can be handled without it becoming a complaint. The manner in which the concern is handled will determine the intensity of the problem. Get the customer's name, address, phone number, and any other applicable information like an account number or username. The important part here is to respond quickly and professionally. Give the customer a chance to air their grievances as soon as possible. Be proactive in looking for a resolution to the issue.

Give the customer an opportunity to explain the problem without interruptions. Constantly interrupting the customer will only add fuel to the problem and may end in a shouting match. It also simply make the customer think that you don't genuinely care about the issue. When they're done, repeat their major points of concern back to them to let them know that you've understood.

Don't challenge their complaint. Even if what the customer is saying has no basis in reality and you immediately want to completely reject everything they've said, don't tell them they are wrong. This won't help you resolve the problem. Instead, let them know that you understand their complaint without agreeing with them.

Ask questions to clarify the problems and the causes. Next, you'll have to identify exactly where the customer ran into an issue. Many times, customers will assess the entire customer service experience negatively, even if they only had a problem with one part of it. Ask them more questions to determine exactly where something went wrong. Many times the problem may not be with the price, merchandise, or service, but with an employee's negative attitude while dealing with the customer.

Transfer the customer to someone else if necessary. In some cases, you may be unable to handle the customer's complaints directly. If this is the case, immediately transfer them to someone who can, like a manager or customer service specialist. This should be done as soon as you determine the need to transfer, not after you've already asked the customer a ton of questions. If language is a problem, find someone that speaks the customer's language for clear communication to expedite matters.

2. Resolving the Issue

Apologize sincerely. Extend your regrets that the service or product did not meet the customer's expectations. Make your apology as sincere as possible. If there business is directly at fault, be the first to acknowledge this. However, if the customer is at fault, allow them to realize this on their own and then gracefully move past it.While it may be tempting, don't automatically take an employee's side against the customer or vice versa. You'll have to investigate the problem further to determine who is at fault.

Empathize with their problem. Put yourself in the customer's place. Everyone has experienced bad service at some point. Saying that you understand and feel for the customer's problem will help diffuse a situation. Doing so lets the customer know that you're with them and will work with them to solve the problem at hand.

Find out how the customer wants the issue resolved. Simply ask the customer what they want, even if you are unsure if you can provide it. The resolution could be in the form of a replacement, refund, exchange, store credit or discount on price.

Reassure them that the problem will be taken care of. Explain to the customer that all feedback by a customer is valued by the company. The customer will be unsure whether or not you will actually solve their problem, so be clear that you intend you reach a mutually beneficial solution.

Do your best to remedy the complaint. If possible, go through with what the customer has asked for. If this is not possible, you should offer them other sufficient solutions that may remedy the issue. Focus on what you can offer them instead of on what you can't. Decide on a solution and execute that solution as quickly as possible.

Thank the customer. Express your genuine appreciation to the customer for sharing their complaint. Explain that customer complaints serve as constructive criticism and can allow the company to better serve other customers. Be sure that you include that you hope to serve them again soon.

Follow up with them. Call or email the customer to make sure that they felt as though their issue was completely resolved. Give them a contact number to call if they feel as though their problem was not resolved.You can also follow up with a customer service survey that you can use to assess your business's ability to resolve customer complaints. This should be done 24 to 48 hours after the complaint was resolved.

Record the customer interaction. Write down information regarding the interaction with the customer and how the situation was handled, if applicable. You should also note whether or not the interaction resulted in a resolution of the complaint and what that resolution entailed. Then, compile similar complaints by grouping them under similar categories based on cause or the product/service complained about.

3. Following General Guidelines

Know what not to say to the customer. Some phrases will just anger customers more and are not particularly useful in resolving complaints. Here are some examples: According to our policy...; Let me transfer you to the manager.

Don't take it personally. It may be tempting to take all customer complaints personally. If you're a small business owner they will get to you and make you question many aspects of your operation. However, you have to know that customer complaints are a simple truth of business and that they occur regularly even for the most well-run and successful businesses. Keep in mind that every complaint can be an opportunity for improvement.

(1) Why is it necessary to listen to the customers? (   )

A. So the customer can have a chance to air their grievance.

B. Because the customers are very angry.

C. It is an requirement of supervisor.

D. Because the problem is very serious.

(2) If the customer's saying has no reality basis, what shall we do? (   )

A. We should reject everything they say.

B. We should tell them that they are wrong.

C. Let them know that we understand their complaint.

D. We should agree with them.

(3) Why should we ask customers more questions? (   )

A. Because they are wrong.   B. So we can determine the problam.

C. Because they have a negative attitude.   D. Because the problem is with the price.

(4) How to put yourself in the customer's place? (   )

A. We should ignore their problem.   B. We work with them to solve the problem at hand.

C. We should say nothing.   D. We should empathize their problems..

Challenges and Solutions

1. If the guest is not satisfied with the taste of dumplings, what will you do?

Solutions:

2. What will you do if your customers complain about your being late for presenting food?

Solutions:

3. If the guest complains that the beer is stale, what will you do?

Solutions:

4. If the guest complains that the waiter is rude, what will you do?

Solutions:

5. If the customer found a fly in the food, what will you do?

Solutions:

6. If the guest complains that the tea is not hot enough, what will you do?

Solution:

7. If the guest complains that there is a hair in the dish, what will you do?

Solutions:

8. If the guest complains that the food is not delicious, what will you do?

Solutions:

M5-21　Knowledge Link

M5-22　Key to Exercises

Chapter 6

Bar Service

Lesson One   Wine Service

Objectives

➢ To help the students master useful expressions and sentences about wine service.

➢ To help the students familiar with all kinds of wine.

➢ To help the students make some dialogues about wine service.

Warming Up

1. There are many kinds of wine. Look at the following pictures and write down the correct names of wine by the corresponding description.

_____ is a red wine grape variety of the species Vitis vinifera. It is derived from the French words for pine and black, and it's also a primary variety used in sparkling wine production in Champagne and other wine regions.

_____ is a green-skinned grape variety used to make white wine. It originated in the Burgundy wine region of eastern France but is now grown wherever wine is produced, from England to New Zealand.

_____ is one of the world's most widely recognized red wine grape varieties. It is grown in nearly every major wine producing country among a diverse spectrum of climates from Canada's Okanagan Valley to Lebanon's Beqaa Valley.

_____ is a dark blue-colored wine grape variety, that is used as both a blending grape and for varietal wines. It is thought to be a diminutive of merle, the French name for the blackbird, probably a reference to the color of the grape.

_____ is a white grape variety which originated in the Rhine region of Germany. It is an aromatic grape variety displaying flowery, almost perfumed, aromas as well as high acidity. It is used to make dry, semi-sweet, sweet and sparkling white wines.

_____ is one of France's main wine producing areas. It is well known for both its red and white wines, mostly made from Pinot noir and Chardonnay grapes.

_____ is a port city in southwest France, also a major center of the wine trade. its name form the famous wine that has been produced in the region since the 8th century.

_____ is a variety of black-skinned wine grape. a Californian wine grape originally transplanted from Europe and producing a quick-maturing fruity red wine.

M6-1　Warming Up

Dialogues

Key sentences:
➢ Would you like to have some drink?
➢ Where would you like to sit?
➢ What can I get you to drink?
➢ How would you describe what you do?
➢ Does it go with red wine, white wine?

Pre-questions:

1. Do you know about wine?
2. Do you know how to offer wine service for guests at the bar?
3. Do you know how to recommend wine?

Dialogue 1

Barman:	Would you like to have some drink, sir?
Guest:	Yes, please.
Barman:	Here is our wine list.
Guest:	Gamay, please.
Barman:	With ice or not, sir?
Guest:	Ice, please.
Barman:	So, a Gamay with ice.
Guest:	Yes, please.
Barman:	I'll be right back.

Dialogue 2

Guest:	This is a great bar.
Barman:	Welcome, this is a great idea to come here. Where would you like to sit?
Guest:	By the window.
Barman:	How are you today?
Guest:	Pretty good.
Barman:	What can I get you to drink?
Guest:	Please give me a cup of Merlot.
Barman:	Certainly, I'll be right back to take your order.

Dialogue 3

Guest:	Hello! How are you now?
Barman:	I'm fine, thanks.
Guest:	Now, you are a wine connoisseur. Or wine teacher?
Barman:	A wine connoisseur. No, that's sort of a snobby.
Guest:	Oh, ok. So, how would you describe what you do?
Barman:	A wine professional.
Guest:	A wine professional. OK, so what does a wine professional do?
Barman:	Try to make money from wine.
Guest:	So, I'm a wine writer, a wine columnist. I teach wine.
Barman:	OK, so let's say if I'm going to have friends over, and I'm making let's say steak. I'm having a grilling steak. Can I serve wine with steak?
Guest:	Yes. Steak goes with almost any red wine.
Barman:	Oh, really. So, red. How about if I want to mix wines. Does it go with red wine, white wine?
Guest:	You always start out with white wines going towards red wines.
Barman:	OK, always go white wine first, then the red wine. And how about for dessert. Is there a special dessert wine?
Guest:	There are many great dessert wines, so it depends on what you like, how

Barman:	OK, so how about I'm making Terimisu.
Guest:	Terimisu, then I would probably have a tawny port, either from Portugal or from Australia, which makes great ports, or you might even go for a fruity and oaky Zinfandel, which is dry wine from California.
Barman:	How much will that cost me?
Guest:	Depends on how much you want to spend. For a port, a tawny port, anywhere in between RMB 3,500 to 10,000. And for a California Zinfandel, a good one probably about RMB 3,000.
Barman:	Wow, it's a pleasant conversation. Have a nice day.
Guest:	Have a nice day.

Vocabulary

Gamay [gæ'me]　*n.* 加美葡萄酒（产于法国南勃艮第）

Merlot ['mɜ:lɒt]　*n.* 梅乐，梅鹿汁（红葡萄酒名）

connoisseur [ˌkɒnə'sɜ:]　*n.* 鉴赏家；内行

snobby ['snɒbi]　*n.* 虚荣；势力

professional [prə'feʃ(ə)n(ə)l]　*n.* 专业人员；职业运动员　*adj.* 专业的；职业的；职业性的

columnist ['kɒləm(n)ɪst]　*n.* 专栏作家

Terimisu　*n.* 提拉米苏（一种带咖啡酒味儿的意大利甜点）

oaky ['əʊkɪ]　*adj.* 橡木味的；橡木桶味的

Zinfandel ['zinfəndel]　*n.* 仙粉黛(一种葡萄酒名称)

Pinot Noir　*n.* 黑皮诺／黑比诺（一种葡萄酒名称或葡萄品种之一）

Chardonnay [ˌʃɑ:dən'ei]　*n.* 霞多丽（一种类似夏布利酒的无甜味白葡萄酒）

Cabernet Sauvignon　*n.* 卡百内红葡萄酒；卡百内红葡萄；赤霞珠

Riesling ['raɪslɪŋ; 'raɪz-]　*n.* 雷司令（一种干白葡萄酒的商标名称）

Bourgogne[bur'gɔ:nj]　*n.*（法）勃艮地；勃艮第产区的红葡萄酒（等于Burgundy）

Bordeaux[bɔ:'dəu]　*n.* 波尔多葡萄酒；波尔多（法国西南部港市）

wine list　　酒单

red wine　　红葡萄酒

white wine　　白葡萄酒

tawny port　　黄褐色波尔图葡萄酒；波特酒

wine connoisseur　　葡萄酒鉴赏家

wine columnist　　葡萄酒专栏作家

Useful Expressions

1. Would you like to have some drink, sir?
先生，您想喝点什么？

2. Where would you like to sit?
您想坐在哪里？

3. Would you like to have another bottle?
您想再要一瓶吗？

4. What can I get you to drink?
您想喝点什么酒？

5. I'll be right back to take your order.
我马上回来下单。

6. Would you taste it, sir/madam?
先生/女士，您愿意品尝一下这个酒吗？

7. How would you describe what you do?

你如何形容你做的工作？

8. Steak goes with almost any red wine.

牛排几乎和任何红葡萄酒都可以搭配食用。

9. Would you like wine with your meal?

你想要点葡萄酒配餐吗？

10. It's a pleasant conversation. Have a nice day.

这是一次愉快的对话，祝你过得愉快！

M6-2　Practice

Exercises

1. Questions and Answers

(1) What's wine?

(2) What's the red wine, white wine and rose wine?

(3) Could you list some famous brands of wine in China?

2. Match the words or expressions in Column A with their Chinese equivalents in Column B.

A	B
(1) crisp	a. 鲜香
(2) earthy	b. 花香
(3) easy	c. 水果味
(4) flowery	d. 橡木味
(5) fresh	e. 蜜糖味
(6) fruity	f. 易入口
(7) honey	g. 土香
(8) oaky	h. 酸爽
(9) Well-balanced	i. 优雅
(10) elegant	j. 平衡

3. Choose the best English translation for each sentence.

(1) 这酒尝起来很易入口，是非常好的一款葡萄酒。(　　)

A. It tastes very good, it is a very good wine.　B. It tastes very good, it is a pretty good wine.

C. It tastes elegant, it is a very good wine.　D. It tastes easy, it is a very good wine.

(2) 这酒尝起来很糟，有股霉塞味。(　　)

A. It tastes good, it is corky.　B. It tastes bad, it is corky.

C. It doesn't taste right, it is oaky.　D. It does taste right, it is oaky.

(3) 我再给您拿一瓶。(　　)

A. I'll take you one bottle.　B. I'll take you more bottle.

C. I'll bring you another bottle.　D. I'll bring another bottle.

(4) 您想要点葡萄酒配餐吗？(　　)

A. Would you like wine with your meal?　B. Would you like wine with your order?

C. Would you like to order wine and food?　D. Would you like to order wine and meal?

(5) 这是我们的酒单。(   )

A. There is our wine list.

B. Here is list.

C. Here you are list.

D. Here is our wine list.

4. Read the passage and decide if the statements are true (T) or false (F).

Serving wines by glass

The wine may be opened at the bar previously.

It is not customary to have guest taste the wine; this should be done by observation (aroma/bouquet, colour and date opened) at the bar.

If you are suggesting wines for guests you may wish to give sample taste to involve them in the decision, and therefore their enjoyment of the dining experience.

Announce the wine to the guest and hold the bottle so they can read the label when pouring, pour to the right of the guest, "twist and lift".

You may need to carry several bottles to the table when guests are drinking wine by glass; it is OK to place them neatly on the table if you are having difficulty balancing them.

Remember guests drink at different rates, so keep an active eye on the table when they are drinking by the glass.

All wines by the glass should be dated and pumped at the end of every service, a wine stored correctly can hold for 2-3 days.

Exercises:

(1) The guest can open the wine previously at the bar.(   )

(2) It is customary to have guest taste the wine. (   )

(3) The waiter should show the label to the guest before pouring the wine.(   )

(4) Pouring to the left of the guest. (   )

(5) All wines by the glass should be dated and pumped at the end of every service. (   )

Challenges and Solutions

1. Do you know what are wines classified by color?

Solutions:

2. Do you know what are wines classified by sugar? (Dry)

Solutions:

3. Do you know what are wines classified by food? (Aperitif)

Solutions:

4. If the guest wants to have a cup of wine at the bar, how to recommend the wine?

Solutions:

5. If the guest has drunk at the bar, what should you do?

Solutions:

6. If the guest comes to your bar for the first time, what should you do?

Solution:

7. If the guest takes his baby come to your bar, what will you do?

Solutions:

8. If the guest wants to chat without ordering wine at the bar, what will you do?

Solutions:

Lesson Two　Champagne Service

Objectives

➤ To help the students master useful expressions and sentences about champagne service.
➤ To help the students familiar with all kinds of champagne.
➤ To help the students make some dialogues about champagne service.

Warming Up

1. There are many kinds of champagne . Look at the following pictures and write down the correct names of champagne by the corresponding description.

_____ is a Champagne house located in Reims, founded in 1760 by a magistrate François Delamotte.

_____ is situated in Reims in northern France. It is one of the largest Champagne producers.

_____ is a notable producer of champagne. The brand is still owned and run by the descendants of Pol Roger.

_____ was founded in 1668 by the French monk Dom Pierre Perignon.

_____ is one of the world's largest champagne producers and a prominent champagne house. It was established in 1743 by Claude Moët.

_____ is a Champagne house founded in 1812 and is the main company of the Laurent-Perrier Group.

_____ is a producer of champagne based in Reims, France.Founded in 1776, it was inherited and renamed by Louis Roederer in 1833.

_____ is a French champagne house based in Reims, specializing in premium products. Founded in 1772 by Philippe Clicquot-Muiron.

M6-5　Warming Up

Dialogues

Key sentences:
➢ Where would you like to sit?
➢ What do you want?
➢ Is the extra dry/ dry/ medium dry?
➢ Can I see the drink list?
➢ What kinds of Champagne do you have?

Pre-questions:
1. Do you know about Champagne?
2. Do you know how to offer Champagne service for guests at the bar?
3. Do you know how to recommend Champagne to guests?

Dialogue 1

Guest:	This is a great bar. It's really hopping.
Barman:	Yes, it's a great idea to come here. I'm glad to see you.
Guest:	I'm glad to see you again.
Barman:	Where would you like to sit?
Guest:	By the window.
Barman:	what do you want?
Guest:	I'd like to order a bottle of Champagne.
Barman:	Is the extra dry/ dry/ medium dry?
Guest:	Yes, it is.
Barman:	Certainly, I'll be right back to take your order.

Dialogue 2

Barman:	May I help you?
Guest:	Can I see the drink list?
Barman:	Certainly, here it is. Have you decided?
Guest:	I think so. Do these come by the glass?
Barman:	Yes, except for the Champagne.
Guest:	What kinds of Champagne do you have?
Barman:	We have Lanson, Pol Roger, Louis Roederer and Veuve Clicquot.
Guest:	I'll take a bottle of Pol Roger, and make it a cold one.
Barman:	Perfect. I'll bring them right to you.

Dialogue 3

Barman:	Hello, this is your Champagne, sir. Enjoy, please.
Guest:	Oh. No, this is not the Champagne I ordered. What I want is Moet et Chandon, not Mumm.
Barman:	I'm sorry. Terribly sorry. I'll change it for you immediately. Sir, here you are. I hope I'm right this time.
Guest:	Let me have a look. That's right. You know, both of them are Champagne but their taste is different. By the way, are there other Champagne?
Barman:	Yes, I think there is Dom Perignon.
Guest:	It must be as good as Moet et Chandon. Give me another one.
Barman:	Ok, please. There are some dessert, and they are free please enjoy.

Vocabulary

Lanson   *n.* 岚颂香槟；兰颂香槟

champagne [ʃæm'peɪn]   *n.* 香槟酒；香槟酒色

Pol Roger   *n.* 宝禄爵香槟；保罗杰香槟

Louis Roederer   *n.* 路易王妃

Veuve Clicquot   *n.* 凯歌香槟

Moet et Chandon   *n.* 酩悦香槟

Mumm   *n.* 玛姆香槟

Dom Perignon   *n.* 唐培里侬香槟

Brut [bryt]　　*adj.* 极干的（尤指香槟酒）；粗糙的

Sec [bryt]　　*adj.* 干的

Demi-[d(ə)mi]　　*adj.* 表示"半"；"不完全"的意思

Doux[du，dus]　　*adj.* 甜的；甜味的

extra dry　特干的

dry　干的

medium dry　半干的；半甜的

label ['leɪb(ə)l]　　*n.* 标签；商标；签条　*vt.* 标注；贴标签

unlock [ʌn'lɒk]　　*vt.* 开启；开……的锁　*vi.* 解开；解除锁定

Useful Expressions

1. Can I see the drink list?

我可以看一下酒单吗？

2. Have you decided?

您决定了吗？

3. Do these come by the glass?

这些酒都是按杯售的吗？

4. What kinds of Champagne do you have?

您想要哪种香槟？

5. I'll take a bottle of Pol Roger, and make it a cold one.

我想点一瓶宝禄爵香槟，要冰的。

6. This is not the Champagne I ordered.

这不是我点的香槟。

7. I'll change it for you immediately.

我马上给您换。

8. It must be as good as Moet et Chandon.

它一定和酩悦香槟一样好。

9. Give me another one.

再给我来一杯。

10. There are some dessert, and they are free please enjoy.

这里有一些甜点，它们是免费的，请享用。

11. Let me pour this for you。

我给您倒酒。

12. You're drunk。

您喝醉了。

13. This is a great bar. It's really hopping.

这是一个很不错的酒吧。他们可真忙。

14. Where would you like to sit?

您想坐在哪里？

15. Is the extra dry/ dry/ medium dry?

是特干的、干的，还是半干的？

M6-6　Practice

Exercises

1. Questions and Answers

(1) What's champagne?

(2) Could you list five famous brands of champagne?

(3) What's the extra dry/dry/medium dry?

2. Match the words or expressions in Column A with their Chinese equivalents in Column B.

A	B
(1) Taittinger	a. 凯歌
(2) Piper Heidsieck	b. 泰亭哲
(3) Louis Roederer	c. 白雪
(4) Krug	d. 唐培里侬
(5) Perrier Jouet	e. 酩悦
(6) Veuve Clicquot	f. 路易王妃
(7) Dom Pérignon	g. 库克
(8) Moet et Chandon	h. 巴黎之花
(9) Mumm	i. 罗兰百悦
(10) Laurent Perrier	j. 玛姆

3. Choose the best English translation for each sentence.

(1) 我们美餐了一顿，还喝了一瓶香槟。(   )

A. We had a meal with a bottle of champagne.

B. We had a nice meal with drinking a bottle of champagne.

C. We had a nice meal with a bottle of champagne.

D. We had a meal with drinking a bottle of champagne.

(2) 史蒂夫打开几瓶香槟酒庆功。(   )

A. Steve uncorked a bottle of champagne to toast the achievement.

B. Steve uncorked bottles of champagne to toast the achievement.

C. Steve breaked bottles of champagne to toast the achievement.

D. Steve breakeda bottle of champagne to toast the achievement.

(3) 香槟是英国在新年前夜的传统酒类。(   )

A. Champagne is the traditional drink for New Year's Eve in Britain.

B. Champagne is the old drink for New Year's Eve in Britain.

C. Champagne is the traditional drink for New Yearin Britain.

D. Champagne is the old drink for New Year in Britain.

(4) 我想点一瓶特干的香槟酒。(   )

A. I'd like to order the dry champagne.

B. I'd like to order the extra dry champagne.

C. I'd like to order the medium dry champagne.

D. I'd like to order champagne.

(5) 可别告诉我没有香槟！(   )

A. Don't told me there's no champagne!   B. Don't tell me there's no champagnes!

C. Don't told me there's champagne!   D. Don't tell me there's no champagne!

4. Read the passage and decide if the statements are true (T) or false (F).

Champagne is a sparking wine. It is produced within the Champagne region of France, from which it takes its name. Most countries limit the use of the term to only those wines that come from the Champagne appellation. In Europe, this principle is enshrined in the European Union by Protected Designation of Origin (PDO) status. As a general rule, grapes used must be the white Chardonnay, or the dark-skinned "red wine grapes", Pinot Noir of Pinot Meunier.

The taste of champagne is described by Sweetness:

The amount of sugar added will dictate the sweetness level of the Champagne.

Brut (less than 15 grams of sugar per liter)

Sec (17 to 35 grams of sugar per liter)

Demi-Sec (33 to 50 grams of sugar per liter)

Doux (more than 50 grams of sugar per liter)

Take a look at the label on the champagne bottle. If it says Brut the champagne is EXTRA DRY. The French word DRY is Sec. Demi-sec means MEDIUM DRY which Doux means SWEET. The dry champagne has the highest quality and more expensive, the sweet one is lower in quality and less expensive.

Exercises:

(1) Champagne is a spirit wine. (   )

(2) In Europe, this principle is enshrined in the United States by Protected Designation of Origin (PDO) status. (   )

(3) As a general rule, grapes used must be the white Chardonnay, or the dark-skinned "red wine gra pes", Pinot Noir of Pinot Meunier. (   )

(4) Brut the champagne isDRY. (   )

(5) The dry champagne has the highest quality and more expensive, the sweet one is lower in quality and less expensive. (   )

Challenges and Solutions

1. Do you know about champagne?
Solutions:

2. Do you know what kinds of grapes is used to make champagne?
Solutions:

3. Do you like drinking champagne, why?
Solutions:

4. Do you know how to recommend champagne for the guest?
Solutions:

5. Do you know how to describe the taste of champagne?
Solutions:

6. Do you know which country is Lanson made from?
Solution:

7. If you are waiter at the bar, how to serve champagne for the guest?
Solutions:

8. If you spill the champagne on the guest's clothes, what will you do?
Solutions:

M6-7　Knowledge Link

M6-8　Key to Exercises

Lesson Three   Whiskey Service

Objectives

➤ To help the students master useful expressions and sentences about whisky service.
➤ To help the students familiar with all kinds of whisky.
➤ To help the students make some dialogues about whisky service.

Warming Up

1. There are many kinds of whisky. Look at the following pictures and write down the correct names of whisky by the corresponding description.

_____ is Scotch Whisky, it is the most widely distributed blended Scotch Whisky in the world.

_____ is a brand of blended Scotch whisky originally produced by Arthur Bell & Sons Ltd and now owned by Diageo.

_____ is made at The Old Bushmills Distillery in Bushmills, County Antrim, Northern Ireland.

_____ is a blended Irish whiskey produced by the Irish Distillers subsidiary of Pernod Ricard.

_____ is a brand of whisky from Canada. Popularly known as C.C., Canadian Club began production in 1858.

_____ was born in 1866 in linchburg, Tennessee. It is the first registered distillery in the United States.

_____ is a Kentucky Straight Bourbon Whiskey brand owned by the Kirin Brewery Company of Japan.

_____ is made by a member of the Kentucky bourbon hall of fame.

M6-9   Warming Up

Dialogues

Key sentences:

➤ How would you like your Bourbon, straight or on the rock?

➤ How much do I owe you?

➤ Which brand do you like best?

➤ Can you give me some suggestions?

➤ What would you prefer?

Pre-questions:

1. Do you know about whisky?

2. Do you know what kinds of whisky?

3. Do you know how to recommend whiskey to guests?

Dialogue 1

Barman:	Good evening, sir. What can I do for you?
Guest:	Bourbon, please.
Barman:	How would you like your Bourbon, straight or on the rock?
Guest:	With iced water, please.
Barman:	Here you are, sir. Bourbon with iced water.
Guest:	Thank you. Now how much do I owe you?
Barman:	The Bourbon is i5 dollars plus 10% service charge. So the total is 16.5 dollars.
Guest:	That is OK. Here is 20 dollars and you can keep the change.
Barman:	Thanks a lot.

Dialogue 2

Guest:	Hello! Boy, come here!
Barman:	Yes, sir! What can I do for you?
Guest:	Give me Scotch, please.

Barman:	Which brand do you like best?
Guest:	I've no idea. Can you give me some suggestions?
Barman:	It's my pleasure. Actually, it's really hard to say as individual tastes are different. We have many brands, such as Jonny Walker, Ballantine's, Chivas Regal, Bell's, J&B and White Horse. How do you like Bell's?
Guest:	Ok, I'll take Bell's.
Barman:	Soda or water?
Guest:	Just plain water with plenty of ice rock.
Barman:	Alright. Please wait for a minute.

Dialogue 3

Barman:	What would you prefer, sir?
Guest:	Whisky, please.
Barman:	Here is our drink list. We've got Scotch whisky, Irish whisky, Canadian whisky, Bourbon whisky. Which one would you prefer?
Guest:	I prefer this one. Old Bushmills.
Barman:	Would you like it with or without ice?
Guest:	On the rocks, please.
Barman:	Yes. One Old Bushmills on the rocks.
Guest:	Right.
Barman:	Please, enjoy it!If you need any helps, you can call me any time.
Guest:	Ok, thank you.

Vocabulary

whiskey ['wɪskɪ]　*n.* 威士忌酒　*adj.* 威士忌酒的

whisky ['wɪskɪ]　*n.* 威士忌酒　*adj.* 威士忌酒的

change [tʃeɪn(d)ʒ]　*n.* 变化；找回的零钱　*vt.* 改变；交换　*vi.* 改变；兑换

straight [streɪt]　*adj.* 直的；连续的；笔直的；正直的；直接饮用的

Jonny Walker　*n.* 尊尼获加（一种威士忌）

Ballantine's　*n.* 百龄坛（一种威士忌）

Chivas Regal　*n.* 芝华士（一种威士忌）

Bell's　*n.* 金玲（一种威士忌）

J&B　*n.* 珍宝（一种威士忌）

White Horse　*n.* 白马（一种威士忌）

Scotch whisky　苏格兰威士忌

Irish whisky　爱尔兰威士忌

Canadian whisky　加拿大威士忌

Bourbon whisky　波旁威士忌

on the rock　加冰

malt [mɔːlt; mɒlt]　*n.* 麦芽；麦芽酒

wheat [wiːt]　*n.* 小麦

rye [raɪ]　*n.* 黑麦

malted rye　黑麦芽

Useful Expressions

1. How would you like your Bourbon, straight or on the rock?

您要的波旁威士忌，直接饮用还是要加冰块？

2. Bourbon with iced water.

加冰水的波旁威士忌。

3. How much do I owe you?

我该付您多少钱？

4. The bourbon is i5 dollars plus 10% service charge. So the total is 16.5 dollars.

威士忌是15美元，加10%的服务费，一共是16.5美元。

5. Here is 20 dollars and you can keep the change.

这是20美元，多余的是你的小费。

6. Which brand do you like best?

你最喜欢哪个品牌？

7. Can you give me some suggestions?

您能给我一些建议吗？

8. It's my pleasure. Actually, it's really hard to say as individual tastes are different.

这是我的荣幸。事实上，很难说因为每个人的品位是不同的。

9. We have many brands, such as Jonny Walker, Ballantine's, Chivas Regal, Bell's, J&B and White Horse.

我们有许多品牌，例如：尊尼获加、百龄坛、芝华士、金玲威、珍宝以及白马威士忌品牌。

10. How do you like Bell's?

你觉得金玲威士忌如何？

11. Soda or water?

加苏打水还是水？

12. Just plain water with plenty of ice rock.

加水和多一点冰块。

13. What would you prefer, sir?

先生，您想要什么？

14. Here is our drink list. We've got Scotch whisky, Irish whisky, Canadian whisky, Bourbon whisky and American whisky.

这是我们的酒单。我们有苏格兰威士忌、爱尔兰威士忌、加拿大威士忌、波旁威士忌和美国威士忌。

15. If you need any helps, you can call me any time.

如果您需要任何帮助，您可以随时叫我。

M6-10　Practice

Exercises

1. Questions and Answers

(1) What's whisky?

(2) Could you list five famous brands of whiskey?

(3) What's single malt whisky?

2. Match the words or expressions in Column A with their Chinese equivalents in Column B.

A	B
(1) malting	a. 混合
(2) mashing	b. 木桶
(3) fermenting	c. 发芽
(4) distilling	d. 搅碎
(5) maturing	e. 粮食
(6) blending	f. 单一麦芽
(7) cask	g. 大麦
(8) single malt	h. 蒸馏
(9) barley	i. 成年
(10) grain	j. 发酵

3. Choose the best English translation for each sentence.

(1) 一杯威士忌酒立刻就使她醉了。（   ）

A. A glass of whisky soon drink him.　　B. A bottle of whisky soon drink her.

C. A glass of whisky soon muddled her.　　D. A bottle of whisky soon muddled her.

(2) 他喜欢喝了威士忌酒以后紧接着又喝啤酒。（   ）

A. He likes to drink whiskywith beer.　　B. He likes to drink whisky chased down with beer.

C. He likes to drink whisky near by the beer.　　D. He likes to drink whisky after beer.

(3) 喝了一小杯威士忌酒之后，他忘记了所有的事情。（   ）

A. After drinking a cup of whisky,he remember everything..

B. After drinking a small cup of whisky,he remember everything.

C. After drinking a small cup of whisky,he forgot nothing.

D. After drinking a small cup of whisky,he forgot everything.

(4) 我又喝了一杯威士忌酒之后，就觉得头晕目眩。（   ）

A. After another glass of whisky I begin to feel dizzy.

B. After one glass of whisky I begin to feel dizzy.

C. After another glass of whisky I begin to feel sick.

D. After one glass of whisky I begin to feel sick.

(5) 酒保，再来一杯威士忌加苏打。（   ）

A. Waiter, one more whisky and soda, please.　　B. Waiter, more whisky and soda, please.

C. Bartender, one more whisky and soda, please.　　D. Bartender, more whisky and soda, please.

4. Read the passage and decide if the statements are true (T) or false (F).

Whisky refers to a broad range of alcoholic beverages that are distilled from fermented grain mash and aged in oak casks. Different grains are used for different varieties, including barley, malted barley, rye, malted rye, wheat, and corn.

Whisky is produced in most grain-growing areas. Malted barley is an ingredient of some whiskies.

Malt is whisky mad entirely form malted barley.

Grain is made from malted and unmalted barley along with other grains.

Single malt whisky is malt whisky from a single distillery.

Blended whiskies are made from a mixture of malt and grain whiskies. A blend is usually from many distilleries.

The name "whisky" itself is a translation of the Latin phrase aquavitae, meaning "Water of Life". Today, the spelling whisky is generally used for whiskies distilled in Scotland, Canada, and Japan, while whisky is used for the spirits distilled in Ireland and America.

Exercises:

(1) Whisky is a kind of non-alcoholic beverage. (   )

(2) Whisky is made by wheat and corn. (   )

(3) Malt is whisky mad entirely form malted barley. (   )

(4) Single malt whisky is malt whisky from a single distillery.(   )

(5) The name "whisky" itself is a translation of the Latin phrase aquavitae, meaning "Water of Love". (   )

Challenges and Solutions

1. Do you know about the whisky?

Solutions:

2. Do you know how to make whisky?

Solutions:

3. Do you know what's the classification of whisky?

Solutions:

4. Would you like to introduce some famous whisky?

Solutions:

5. If the guest has ordered whiskey with ice, but here's not ice, what should you do?

Solutions:

6. If the guest wants to have a glass of Canadian whisky, can you give some suggestions?

Solution:

7. If the guest has a bad mood, but he wants to have a whiskey. What will you do?

Solutions:

8. If the guest is very angry with noisy sound at the bar, what will you do??

Solutions:

M6-11   Knowledge Link

M6-12   Key to Exercises

Lesson Four   Brandy Service

Objectives

➤ To help the students master useful expressions and sentences about brandy service.
➤ To help the students familiar with all kinds of brandy.
➤ To help the students make some dialogues about brandy service.

Warming Up

1. There are many kinds of brandy. Look at the following pictures and write down the correct names of brandy by the corresponding description.

_____ is a famous brand in the cognac industry. It has a brewing history of more than 170 years and ranks among the largest distilleries in Europe.

_____ is one of the world's leading cognac wineries, founded by Richard Hennessy in 1765.

_____ is a favorite of many cognac lovers, its Chinese name comes from the name of its founder who became a licensee of the French court at the beginning of the 19th century.

_____ is the oldest and most famous cognac in the world. It started the great cognac family in the martell district.

_____ has been brewed since 1724 and its French name comes from the name of its founder, Remy Martin.

_____ was found by Louis ROYER, it has been managed by four generations of families. The company was later acquired by Japan's Suntory group in 1989.

_____ is a family enterprise with a history of more than 150 years, and it is also one of the few cognac brands managed by the family.

_____ was founded by Baron Jean Baptiste Otard, a British exiler.

M6-13　Warming Up

Dialogues

Key sentences:

➢ Can I get you something to drink?

➢ Do you have any drink special?

➢ Do you want a double?

➢ What's the differences between XO and VSOP?

➢ What's your favorite brandy?

Pre-questions:

1. Do you know about brandy?

2. Do you know how to offer brandy service for guests at the bar?

3. Do you know how to recommend brandy to guests?

Dialogue 1

Barman:	Can I get you something to drink?
Guest:	What kinds of Cognac do you suggest?
Barman:	We have Bisquit, Hennessy, Courvoisier, Martell and Remy Martin. Which one do you like?
Guest:	Hennessy XO, how much is it?
Barman:	1199 yuan for a 350ml bottle of Hennessy XO.
Guest:	Do you have any drink special?
Barman:	Sorry, we haven't.
Guest:	That's ok. Please give me a glass of Hennessy XO firstly.
Barman:	Yes. I'll be back soon.

Dialogue 2

Barman:	What about you, sir? Something different?
Guest:	Courvoisier XO.

Barman:	Yes. One Courvoisier XO. On the rock?
Guest:	Yes, please.
Barman:	Ok, do you want a double?
Guest:	No, thanks.

Dialogue 3

Barman:	What would you like to drink, sir?
Guest:	Brandy. I always have it.
Barman:	XO or VSOP? Here is the list.
Guest:	What's the differences between XO and VSOP?
Barman:	They are grades of Cognac. XO is Extra Old, where the youngest brand is stored at least six, average upwards of 20 years. While VSOP is Very Superior Old Pale, where the youngest brandy is stored at least four years in cask, but the average wood age is much older.
Guest:	Ok. Thank you for your patient explanation. Are they the same price?
Barman:	No, it's different. XO is higher price than VSOP, have you any idea?
Guest:	Yes, I will try VSOP.
Barman:	What's your favorite brandy?
Guest:	My favorite is Remy Martin VSOP.
Barman:	Yes, one Remy Martin VSOP.
Guest:	That's right. Ice please.
Barman:	Ok. Please enjoy it!

Vocabulary

Cognac ['kɒnjæk]   *n.* 法国白兰地；（法国 Cognac 地区产的）干邑白兰地酒

brandy ['brændɪ]   *n.* 白兰地酒

Bisquit   *n.* 百事吉（一种白兰地）

Hennessy   *n.* 轩尼诗（一种白兰地）

Courvoisier   *n.* 拿破仑（一种白兰地）

Martell   *n.* 马爹利（一种白兰地）

Remy Martin   *n.* 人头马（一种白兰地）

VS=Very Special   贮藏年代在 2 年以上

VO=Very Old   贮藏年代在 5 年左右

VSO=Very Superior Old   贮藏年代在 10 年以上

VOP=Very Old Pale   贮藏年代在 10 年以上

VSOP=Very Special Old Pale   贮藏年代在 20 年以上

XO=Extra Old   贮藏年代在 50 年以上

X=Extra   贮藏年代在 70 年以上

Useful Expressions

1. Can I get you something to drink?
您想喝点什么？

2. What kinds of Cognac do you suggest?
您推荐哪款干邑白兰地？

3. Do you have any drink special?
你们有什么特价酒饮吗？

4. What about you, sir? Something different?
先生，你要什么？

5. One Courvoisier XO. On the rock?
一瓶拿破仑，加冰吗？

6. Do you want a double?
好的，酒要加倍吗？

7. What would you like to drink, sir?
你想喝点儿什么？

8. Brandy. I always have it.
白兰地，我不喝别的。

9. XO or VSOP? Here is the list.
你要优质陈酿白兰地还是要优质白兰地？这是酒单。

10. They are grades of Cognac.
它们是干邑白兰地的等级。

11. Thank you for your patient explanation.
感谢您耐心的讲解。

12. Are they the same price?
它们的价格一样吗？

13. Have you any idea?
您想好了吗？

14. What's your favorite brandy?
您最喜欢哪种白兰地？

15. Please, enjoy it!
请慢用！

M6-14　Practice

Exercises

1. Questions and Answers

(1) What's brandy?

(2) Could you list five famous brands of brandy?

(3) What's Cognac?

2. Match the words or expressions in Column A with their Chinese equivalents in Column B.

A	B
(1) P.Pale	a. 优越的；柔顺的
(2) S.Superior	b. 好的、精美的
(3) V.Very	c. 浅色、清澈的、指米加焦糖色
(4) X.Extra	d. 干邑
(5) F.Fine	e. 老陈
(6) C.Cognac	f. 非常
(7) E.Especial	g. 格外的，特高档的
(8) O.Old	h. 特别的
(9) Vintage	i. 品牌
(10) Brand	j. 年份

3. Choose the best English translation for each sentence.

(1) 白兰地酒是用葡萄酿的。（　　　）

A. Brandy makes from grapes.　　　　　B. Brandy is made from grapes.

C. Brandy makes from grape.　　　　　D. Brandy is made from grape.

(2) 我给他喝了些白兰地以减轻疼痛。（　　）

A. I gave him some brandy to have no the pain.　　B. I gave him some brandy to relieve the pains.

C. I gave him some brandy to have the pain.　　D. I gave him some brandy to relieve the pain.

(3) 干邑白兰地也用于浸泡食材，给砂锅炖菜提味。（　　）

A. Cognac is made from macerate and flavour ingredients and casseroles.

B. Cognac is made by macerate and flavour ingredients and casseroles.

C. Cognac is also used to macerate and flavour ingredients and casseroles.

D. Cognac used to macerate and flavour ingredients and casseroles.

(4) 所有的雪利酒都是在葡萄酒中加入白兰地勾兑成的。（　　）

A. All sherry is made from wine fortified with Cognac.

B. All sherry is made from wine fortified with brandy.

C. All sherry is made from wine distilled with Cognac.

D. All sherry is made from wine distilled with brandy.

(5) 葡萄酒不同的是，白兰地只能在木制容器而非玻璃容器里酿。（　　）

A. Unlike wine, brandy matures only in wood, not glass.

B. Unlike wine, brandy matures only in glass, not wood.

C. like wine, brandy matures only in wood, not glass.

D. like wine, brandy matures only in glass, not wood.

4. Read the passage and decide if the statements are true (T) or false (F).

Cognac is the most famous variety of brandy, produced in the wine-growing region surrounding the town of Cognac in France, from which it takes its name. Cognac is one of the three officially demarcated brandy regions in Europe; the others are the French town of Armagnac and the Spanish town of Jerez.

According to French Law, in order to have the name, Cognac must meet rigid legal requirements, ensuring that the 300-year old production process remains unchanged.It must be made from at least 90% Ugni Blanc, Folle Blanche, or Colombard grapes.

It must be distilled twice in copper pot stills and aged at least two years in French oak barrels.

The region authorized to produce Cognac is divided up into six zones, they are a Grande Champagne, Petite Champagne, Borderies, Fins Bois, Bon Bois and finally Bois Ordinaire.

Exercises:

(1) Brandy is the most famous variety of Cognac. (　　)

(2) Cognac is produced in the wine-growing region surrounding the town of Cognac in France. (　　)

(3) Cognac must meet rigid legal requirements, ensuring that the 300-year old production process remains changed.(　　)

(4) It must be made from at least 90% Ugni Blanc, Pinot Noir, or Colombard grapes. (　　)

(5) The region authorized to produce Cognac is divided up into six zones. (　　)

Challenges and Solutions

1. Do you know about brandy?

Solutions:

2. Do you know what's the differences between brandy and Cognac?

Solutions:

3. Do you know how to make brandy?

Solutions:

4. Do you know what's the grades of Cognac?

Solutions:

5. If the guest has drunk, but he wants to have more brandy, what should you do?

Solutions:

6. If the guest has no enough money, but he has finished brandy, what should you do?

Solution:

7. If you have XO and VSOP, which one do you recommend? Why?

Solutions:

8. If the guest has ordered Remy Martin, but you gave wrong brandy, what should you do?

Solutions:

M6-15   Knowledge Link   M6-16   Key to Exercises

Lesson Five   Cocktail Service

Objectives

➢ To help the students master useful expressions and sentences about cocktail service.
➢ To help the students familiar with all kinds of cocktail.
➢ To help the students make some dialogues about cocktail service.

Warming Up

1. There are many kinds of cocktail. Look at the following pictures and write down the correct names of cocktail by the corresponding description.

_____ is mixed by vodka, tomato juice, lemon juice, black pepper, salt, worcestershire and tabasco sauce.

_____ is mixed by light rum, bule curacao, pineapple juice, cream of coconut and ice.

_____ is mixed by light rum, coca cola and lime juice.

_____ is mixed by Irish whisky, hot coffee, fresh cream and brown sugar.

_____ is mixed by bourbon (or rye whisky), sweet vermouth and bitters.

_____ is mixed by tequila, orange curacao or cointreau and juice of half lime.

_____ is mixed by gin, cherry brandy, lemon juice, sugar, soda water and sweet cherry.

_____ is mixed by tequila, orange juice and grenadine syrup.

M6-17　Warming Up

Dialogues

Key sentences:

➢ How about one of our non-alcoholic fruit cocktails?

➢ I wonder if you could recommend some Chinese cocktails?

➢ Can we have the beverage list first?

➢ Do you have any preference, alcoholic, non-alcoholic, or soft drinks?

➢ Do you want some snacks with the drinks?

Pre-questions:

1. Do you know about cocktail?

2. Do you know how to how to offer cocktail service for guests at the bar?

3. Do you know how to recommend cocktail to guests?

Dialogue 1

Guest:	My doctor told me to stop drinking.
Barman:	How about one of our non-alcoholic fruit cocktails? A Pussy Foot or Shirley Temple?
Guest:	What's the different between Pussy Foot and Shirley Temple?
Barman:	Pussy Foot is mixed by grenadine, pineapple juice, orange juice and grapefruit juice. While Shirley Temple is mixed by ginger ale and grenadine.
Guest:	Ok. Pussy Foot sounds very nice. I will take Pussy Foot.
Barman:	That's good idea.

Dialogue 2

Barman:	Good evening, welcome to our bar. What can I do for you?
Guest:	Well, I wonder if you could recommend some Chinese cocktails?
Barman:	Well, we have the Shanghai cocktail. This is a new cocktail especially created for our bar. It's based on our famous Chinese spirit.
Guest:	It sounds interesting. What's in it?
Barman:	It consists of Maotai, mineral water, ice and lemon.
Guest:	How do you make it?
Barman:	Oh, it's easy to make. Put some Maotai into the glass, and then add some mineral water. Stir well and then add ice and a piece of lemon. That's the Shanghai cocktail.
Guest:	Very nice. Let's have three glasses to try please.
Barman:	Yes, please.

Dialogue 3

Barman:	What can I get for you?
Guest:	Can we have the beverage list first?
Barman:	Sure. There you go. Take your time.
Guest:	Thank you. We'd like to have something sweet to drink. Could you please recommend something?
Barman:	Do you have any preference, alcoholic, non-alcoholic, or soft drinks?
Guest:	We'd prefer cocktails. Do you have anything with a fruity flavor, not too sharp?
Barman:	Yes. How about a Blue Hawaii? Most ladies like its fruity taste and beautiful color.
Guest:	Well...a Blue Hawaii for my friend. I'd like a Bloody Mary.
Barman:	All right. Do you want some snacks with the drinks?
Guest:	Then, how about some popcorn and peanuts? Please also bring some ice. Thanks.
Barman:	Ok. Your drinks and snacks will be ready in a moment.

Vocabulary

non-alcoholic   *adj.* 不含酒精的

alcoholic [ælkə'hɒlɪk]   *adj.* 酒精的，含酒精的

cocktail ['kɒkteɪl]   *n.* 鸡尾酒；开胃食品

grenadine['grenədi:n]   *n.* 石榴汁糖浆；石榴汁红   *adj.* 石榴汁红的

Maotai   *n.* 茅台镇；茅台酒；五粮液

stir [stɜ:]   *n.* 搅拌；轰动   *vt.* 搅拌；激起；惹起

fruity ['fru:tɪ]   *adj.* 圆润的；有果味的；果实状的

flavor ['fleɪvə]   *n.* 情味，风味；香料；滋味

snack [snæk]   *n.* 小吃，快餐；一份，部分

popcorn ['pɒpkɔ:n]   *n.* 爆米花，爆玉米花

Pussy Foot   波斯猫脚鸡尾酒

Shirley Temple   雪莉鸡尾酒

pineapple juice   菠萝汁

orange juice   橙汁

grapefruit juice.   葡萄汁

ginger ale   姜味较淡的姜汁汽水；姜汁无酒精饮料

mineral water   矿泉水

Blue Hawaii   蓝色夏威夷（一种鸡尾酒名称）

Bloody Mary   血腥玛丽（一种鸡尾酒名称）

Useful Expressions

1. My doctor told me to stop drinking.

我的医生告诉我要戒酒。

2. How about one of our non-alcoholic fruit cocktails?

我们这里不含酒精的水果鸡尾酒怎么样？

3. Pussy Foot is mixed by grenadine, pineapple juice, orange juice and grapefruit juice.

猫爪鸡尾酒是由石榴汁、菠萝汁、橙汁、西柚汁调制而成。

4. Shirley Temple is mixed by ginger ale and grenadine.

秀兰邓波鸡尾酒是由姜汁和石榴汁调制而成。

5. Welcome to our bar.

欢迎光临我们的酒吧。

6. I wonder if you could recommend some Chinese cocktails?

我想知道您是否可以推荐一些中国鸡尾酒？

7. It sounds interesting. What's in it?

听起来非常有趣，里面有什么？

8. Let's have three glasses to try please.

请给我们三杯尝尝。

9. What can I get for you?

有什么可以为您效劳？

10. Can we have the beverage list first?

我们可以先看酒单吗？

11. We'd like to have something sweet to drink. Could you please recommend something?

我们想喝点甜的，能不能请您推荐一下？

12. Do you have any preference, alcoholic, non-alcoholic, or soft drinks?

你有什么喜好，酒精、不含酒精还是软饮料？

13. Do you have anything with a fruity flavor, not too sharp?

你们有水果口味，不太辣的鸡尾酒吗？

14. Do you want some snacks with the drinks?

您要点些零食配酒吗？

15. Your drinks and snacks will be ready in a moment.

您点的饮料和零食马上来。

M6-18　Practice

Exercises

1. Questions and Answers

(1) What's cocktail?

(2) Could you list five famous brands of cocktail?

(3) What's base liquor?

2. Match the words or expressions in Column A with their Chinese equivalents in Column B.

A	B
(1) gin	a. 朗姆酒
(2) rum	b. 餐前开胃酒
(3) vodka	c. 杜松子酒
(4) tequila	d. 龙舌兰酒
(5) digestif	e. 伏特加酒
(6) aperitif	f. 餐后甜酒
(7) spirit	g. 烈酒
(8) short drink	h. 调酒
(9) long drink	i. 长饮
(10) mix	j. 短饮

3. Choose the best English translation for each sentence.

(1) 这是一种不含酒精的鸡尾酒，它不会上头。(　　)

A. It is a kind of alcoholic cocktail, and it never goes to the head.

B. It is a kind of non-alcoholic cocktail, and it never goes to the head.

C. It is a kind of alcoholic cocktail, and it goes to the head.

D. It is a kind of non-alcoholic cocktail, and it goes to the head.

(2) 这是酒单，先生，您要喝点什么？（　　）

A. Here is the menu list, Sir. What would you like to have?

B. Here is the menu list, Sir. What would you like to drink?

C. Here is the drink list, Sir. What would you like to have?

D. Here is the drink list, Sir. What would you like?

(3) 有人邀请我去鸡尾酒会。（　　）

A. I will go to a cocktail party.　　　　B. I will take part in a cocktail party.

C. I am inviting to a cocktail party.　　D. I am invited to a cocktail party.

(4) 我们有爱尔兰咖啡、蓝色夏威夷、龙舌兰日出等鸡尾酒。（　　）

A. We have Irish Coffee, Blue Hawaii, Tequila and other cocktails.

B. We have Irish Coffee, Blue Hawaii, Tequila Sunrise and other cocktails.

C. We have Irish Coffee, Blue Diablo, Tequila Sunrise and other cocktails.

D. We have Irish Coffee, Blue Diablo, Tequila and other cocktails.

(5) 我们想喝点甜的，能不能请你推荐一下？（　　）

A. We'd like to have something sweet to drink. Could you please recommend something?

B. We'd like to have something sweet. Could you please recommend something?

C. We'd like to have something sweet. Please recommend something?

D. We'd like to have something sweet to drink. Please recommend something?

4. Read the passage and decide if the statements are true (T) or false (F).

The American cocktail dress could be anything from a "little black dress" to a floral-printed dress or a plain, short evening gown, as long as it was worn with accessories. These might be earrings, pearl necklaces, bracelets, or brooches (stylish in the 1950s). However, it was most common to wear costume jewelry. Although they were inexpensive, wearing large amounts was seen as daring and luxurious, especially when wearing a modest dress. In addition, the jewelry would be worn along with hats: velvet, lace, or horsehair; little turbans or close-fitting caps of brocade, taffeta, or satin. Gloves needed to be fashionably up-to-date and could be any length, material, or color. Shoes were usually high heels, but evening satin sandals were also common and could be dyed to match the color of the dress.

Exercises:

(1) Every one has a cocktail dress in American. （　　）

(2) The American cocktail dress is only a "little black dress". （　　）

(3) It was worn with accessories. （　　）

(4) It was most common to wear costume jewelry. （　　）

(5) Shoes weren't usually high heels. （　　）

Challenges and Solutions

1. Do you know the differences between long drink and short drink?

Solutions:

2. Do you know what's the main essential spirits of cocktail?

Solutions:

3. Would you like to introduce some famous cocktail?

Solutions:

4. Do you know how to mix cocktail? Can you give some examples?

Solutions:

5. Do you know how to make Gin & Tonic?

Solutions:

1. If the guest likes to have non-alcoholic cocktail, what kinds of cocktail can you recommend?

Solutions:

2. If the guest likes to have alcoholic cocktail, what kinds of cocktail can you recommend?

Solution:

3. If the guest wants to quit drinking, what will you do?

Solution:

M6-19　Knowledge Link   M6-20　Key to Exercises

Lesson Six   Coffee Service

Objectives

➢ To help the students master useful expressions and sentences about coffee service.

➢ To help the students familiar with all kinds of coffee.

➢ To help the students make some dialogues about coffee service.

Warming Up

1. There are many kinds of coffee. Look at the following pictures and write down the correct names of coffee by the corresponding description.

_____ is coffee brewed by expressing or forcing out a small amount of nearly boiling water under pressure through finely ground coffee beans.

_____ is based on espresso and hot milk, but with added chocolate, typically in the form of sweet cocoa powder, although many varieties use chocolate syrup.

_____ is an Italian coffee drink that is traditionally prepared with double espresso, and steamed milk foam.

_____ is an espresso coffee drink with a small amount of milk, usually foamed.

_____ is also called soluble coffee, coffee crystals, and coffee powder, is a beverage derived from brewed coffee beans that enables people to quickly prepare hot coffee by adding hot water to powder or crystals and stirring.

_____ is also called brewed coffee that is made by pouring hot water onto ground coffee beans, then allowing to brew in a filter.

_____ is a coffee drink made with espresso and steamed milk.

_____ is cold coffee with ice.

M6-21　Warming Up

Dialogues

Key sentences:
- ➢ What can I do for you?
- ➢ What have you got?

> Would you like some coffee?/Do you want some coffee?

> Would you like another cup of coffee?

> What kind of coffee would you like?

> Do you want whole bean or ground?

> Would you like a refill?

> Do you have a vacant seat?

Pre-questions:

1. Do you know about coffee?

2. Do you know how to how to offer service for guests in the coffee shop?

3. Do you know how to recommend coffee to guests?

Dialogue 1

Cafe Attendant:	Good morning, sir. What can I get you?
Guest:	I'd like a coffee please.
Cafe Attendant:	Certainly sir, what kind of coffee would you like?
Guest:	What have you got?
Cafe Attendant:	Well we have Espresso, Cappuccino, Latte,Americano or Irish coffee.
Guest:	What a choice! I think I'll have a cappuccino please.
Cafe Attendant:	Here you are. You'll find the sugar just over there.

Dialogue 2

Cafe Attendant:	Would you like a refill?
Guest:	Yes, please.
Cafe Attendant:	All right. Do you want some chocolate or cinnamon powder in your coffee?
Guest:	No, thanks. Black is fine. By the way, do you sell coffee beans? I'd like to have half-pound of Espresso roast.
Cafe Attendant:	Sorry, we are out of Espresso roast. Would you like Italian roast instead?
Guest:	Sure. I'll go for Italian roast. A quarter pound, please.
Cafe Attendant:	Ok. Do you want whole bean or ground?
Guest:	Umm...Whole beans. I also want some filters, please.
Cafe Attendant:	All right. I'll bring them when you finish your coffee.

Dialogue 3

Cafe Attendant:	Good afternoon, madam. What can I do for you?
Guest:	Good afternoon. Do you have a vacant seat?
Cafe Attendant:	Yes, this way, please. Is this table all right?
Guest:	Good. Thank you.
Cafe Attendant:	Would you like some coffee?
Guest:	Yes, please.
Cafe Attendant:	sorry to have kept you waiting, madam. Please enjoy it.
Guest:	It is good taste.
Cafe Attendant:	Would you like another cup of coffee?
Guest:	Yes, one more cup of coffee, please. If I have finished. Where can I pay for my meal?
Cafe Attendant:	Please pay the cashier.

Guest: Ok, thank you. Good bye.
Cafe Attendant: It's my pleasure. Come again, madam.
Guest: Thanks. I will.

Vocabulary

coffee ['kɔfi]   *n.* 咖啡；咖啡豆；咖啡色

caffeine ['kæfin]   *n.* [有化][药] 咖啡因；茶精（兴奋剂）

decaffeinated [ˌdiˈkæfinetid]   *adj.* 脱去咖啡因的

brew [bru:]   *vt.* 酿造；酝酿   *vi.* 酿酒；被冲泡

filter ['fltə]   *vi.* 滤过；渗入；慢慢传开   *n.* 过滤器

cream [krim]   *n.* 奶油，乳脂；精华；面霜；乳酪

roast [rəust]   *vt.* 烤，焙；烘，烘烤；*vi.* 烤；烘；*n.* 烤肉；烘烤

Espresso [eˈspresəu]   *n.*（用汽加压煮出的）意式浓咖啡

Latte ['lɑ:teɪ]   *n.* 拿铁咖啡

Cappuccino [ˌkæpəˈtʃi:nəu]   *n.* 卡布奇诺咖啡

Americano [əˌmerɪˈkɑno]   *n.* 美式咖啡

Macchiato [ˌmækɪˈɑ:təu]   *n.* 玛奇朵咖啡（意式浓缩咖啡加少量泡沫牛奶而成的咖啡）

Mocha['mɒkə]   *n.* 摩卡咖啡

chocolatey ['tʃɒklɪti,'tʃɒklət̬i]   巧克力味

bland [blænd]   *adj.* 清淡的

caramelly   焦糖味

drip [drɪp]   *v.* 冲泡

steamed milk   奶泡

foamed milk   奶沫

coffee bean   咖啡豆

freshly ground coffee   现磨咖啡

Useful Expressions

1. Good morning/afternoon/evening. Welcome to coffee shop, may I help you?

您好，欢迎来到咖啡厅，请问有什么可以帮您吗？

2. Any more request?

还有什么要求吗？

3. May I repeat your order now?

我可以重复一下您的点单吗？

4. Can I take this away?

我可以帮您把这个收走吗

5. Excuse me, sir. Would you like one more coffee.

打扰一下，先生。要不要再来点咖啡呢？

6. May I settle your bill now?

请问现在可以为您结账吗？

7. I am very sorry to have kept you waiting, sir.

很抱歉，先生，让您久等了。

8. Would you prefer tea or coffee.

请问喜欢咖啡还是茶？

9. What kind of coffee would you like to have?

您想要哪种咖啡？

10. The coffee is free for you.

这咖啡是为您免费提供的。

11. Sir, take/ have a seat, please.

先生，请坐。

12. Thank you for you coming. Hope to see you next time.

谢谢请慢走，欢迎下次光临。

13. Would you like to pay together or separately?

您是要一起结账还是要分开结账？

14. You may pay in cash/credit card/cheque/charge.

您可以用现金、信用卡、支票或记账。

15. How does coffee taste?

咖啡的味道如何？

M6-22　Practice

Exercises

1. Questions and Answers

(1) What's coffee?

(2) Could you list five famous brands of coffee?

(3) What's Espresso?

2. Match the words or expressions in Column A with their Chinese equivalents in Column B.

A	B
(1) Latte	a. 摩卡咖啡
(2) Mocha	b. 白咖啡
(3) Americano	c. 卡布奇诺咖啡
(4) Cappuccino	d. 美式咖啡
(5) Flat White	e. 浓缩（意式）咖啡
(6) Black Coffee	f. 拿铁咖啡
(7) Con Panna	g. 维也纳咖啡
(8) Macchiato	h. 黑咖啡；不加牛奶的咖啡
(9) Viennese	i. 焦糖玛奇朵咖啡
(10) Espresso	j. 康宝莱

3. Choose the best English translation for each sentence.

(1) 您想要喝咖啡吗？ (　　)

A. Would you like some coffee?　　B. Could you have some coffee?

C. Would you have a coffee?　　D. Do you have some coffee?

(2) 你们有什么咖啡？ (　　)

A. Do you have anything else?　　B. Do you have coffee?

C. What have you got?　　D. What coffee do you know?

(3) 我们有意式浓缩咖啡、卡布奇诺、拿铁咖啡。(　　)

A. We have Latte, Espresso and Americano.　　B. We have Espresso, Cappuccino and Latte.

C. We have Cappuccino, Latte and Mocha.　　D. We have Espresso, Latte and Viennese.

(4) 抱歉，让您久等了。(　　)

A. Sorry to have kept you waiting.　　B. I'm so sorry to be waiting.

C. Sorry to make you waiting.　　D. I'm sorry to waiting for you.

(5) 您要在咖啡里加黄糖还是加奶？（　　）

A. Do you want sugar or milk in your coffee?

B. Do you like brown sugar or milk?

C. Do you want some brown sugar or milk in your coffee?

D. Do you choose some brown sugar or milk in your coffee?

4. Read the passage and decide if the statements are true (T) or false (F).

Coffee has become the most popular drink in America. Today American people drink more coffee than people in any other countries.People drink coffee at breakfast, at lunch, at dinner and between meals. They drink hot coffee or coffee with ice in it. They drink it at work and at home.

People around the world drink coffee. Some people like coffee that is black（纯）and strong （浓），but other people like coffee with cream or sugar, or both cream and sugar in it. In all the ways it is served, coffee has become an international drink.

Exercises:

(1) The most popular drink in the United States is milk. (　　)

(2) People drink coffee at any time. (　　)

(3) In this passage there are three different kinds of coffee. (　　)

(4)"Coffee has become an international drink. " means "People all over the world drink coffee nearly." (　　)

(5) Coffee isn't a kind of food, but a kind of drink. (　　)

Challenges and Solutions

1. Do you know the differences between Espresso and Latte?

Solutions:

2. Do you know what's Irish coffee?

Solutions:

3. Do you know what's the taste of Mocha?

Solutions:

4. If the guest likes coffee, but he thinks coffee is bad for his health, what will you do?

Solutions:

5. If the guest has finished his coffee, what should you do?

Solutions:

6. Do you know how to make coffee?

Solution:

7. If you are cafe attendant, how to clean the table?

Solutions:

8. If the guest drinks coffee for the first time, what will you do?

Solutions:

M6-23　Knowledge Link

M6-24　Key to Exercises

Lesson Seven   Beer Service

Objectives

➢ To help the students master useful expressions and sentences about beer service.
➢ To help the students familiar with all kinds of beer.
➢ To help the students make some dialogues about beer service.

Warming Up

1. There are many kinds of beer. Look at the following pictures and write down the correct names of beer by the corresponding description.

_____ is the world's best selling German beer, sold in nearly 90 countries.

_____ is a pale lager beer with 5% alcohol by volume produced by the Dutch brewing company Heineken International.

_____ is a cold filtered light beer. It is one of American beers.

_____ is one of the most successful beer brands worldwide. It is brewed in almost 60 countries and is available in over 120.

_____ is a beer sold by Pabst Brewing Company, originally established in Milwaukee, Wisconsin in 1844 but now based in Los Angeles.

_____ was Australia's first taste of true refreshment.

_____ is one of Japanese beers.

_____ is China's most famous beer. The German style Chinese lager, with great flavors, a smooth taste and always recommended when eating Asian food.

M6-25　Warming Up

Dialogues

Key sentences:

➢ Would you like local beer or imported?

➢ What local beer is available?

➢ What else would you like?

➢ Would you care for something to drink?

➢ Would you like some beer?

➢ What should you recommend?

Pre-questions:

1. Do you know about beer?

2. Do you know what's the famous brand of beer in China?

3. Do you know how to recommend beer to guests?

Dialogue 1

Barman:	How are you, Mr.Davis?
Guest:	Very well, thanks.
Barman:	Some wine, please?
Guest:	I'll have a change today I'd like to try your beer.
Barman:	That's good. Would you like local beer or imported?
Guest:	What local beer is available?
Barman:	We've got Beijing beer and Tsingtao beer and both of them taste good. Maybe Tsingtao beer is a little bit more popular than Beijing beer.
Guest:	Then, what is your suggest?
Barman:	My idea? You are in Beijing now, and why not consider Beijing beer first?
Guest:	Good idea. Beijing beer, please.
Barman:	Ok. What else would you like?

Guest:	Nothing at the moment.
Barman:	One Beijing beer.
Guest:	Right.
Barman:	I'll be back soon.

Dialogue 2

Barman:	Would you care for something to drink?
Guest:	Yes, I'd like beer.
Barman:	Would you care for local or imported beer?
Guest:	Imported beer, please.
Barman:	We have Heineken and Carlsberg.
Guest:	I will take Heineken.
Barman:	Ok, here is your beer. Please enjoy it.
Guest:	Thank you!

Dialogue 3

Barman:	Good evening! Would you like some beer? There are many kinds of beer.
Guest:	Yes, what should you recommend?
Barman:	Budweiser.
Guest:	Are there any differences between the Budweiser and Beck's?
Barman:	Budweiser is made from American, while Beck's is made from Germany.
Guest:	Which is the best taste?
Barman:	Budweiser is made by rice, malted barley and hops. it tastes easy. It ranks the first among the world's ten beers top.
Guest:	It sounds great! I will order Budweiser.
Barman:	Well, how many do you want?
Guest:	Two bottles of Budweiser, please.
Barman:	Ok, please wait for a moment.
Guest:	Thank you.

Vocabulary

beer [bɪə]　*n.* 啤酒　*vi.* 喝啤酒

change [tʃeɪn(d)ʒ]　*n.* 变化；找回的零钱　*vt.* 改变；交换　*vi.* 改变；兑换

available [ə'veɪləbəl]　*adj.* 可获得的；可购得的；可找到的；有空的

Tsingtao['tʃɪŋ'tau]　*n.* 青岛（Tsingtao beer 青岛啤酒）

Heineken　*n.* 喜力啤酒

Carlsberg ['ka:sbə:g]　*n.* 嘉士伯啤酒公司；嘉士伯啤酒

Budweiser　*n.* 百威啤酒

Beck's　*n.* 贝克斯啤酒

malted ['mɔ:ltid]　*n.*（美）麦芽酒　*v.* 作成麦芽

barley ['ba:lɪ]　*n.* 大麦

hops　*n.* 啤酒花

local beer　本地啤酒；当地啤酒

imported beer　进口啤酒

pale beer　淡色啤酒

brown stout　黑啤

canned beer　听装啤酒

green beer　新啤酒

malt liquor　麦芽酒；啤酒

Useful Expressions

1. I'll have a change today I'd like to try your beer.

今天我想换换口味，我想尝尝你们的啤酒。

2. Would you like local beer or imported?

您想要当地的啤酒还是进口的啤酒？

3. What local beer is available?

当地的啤酒有哪些？

4. what is your suggest?

您的建议是什么？

5. You are in Beijing now, and why not consider Beijing beer first?

您现在在北京，为什么不先考虑北京啤酒呢？

6. What else would you like?

您还想要什么吗？

7. Would you care for something to drink?

您想喝点什么吗？

8. Would you like some beer?

您想喝点啤酒吗？

9. Are there any differences between the Budweiser and Beck's?

百威啤酒和贝克斯啤酒有什么不同吗？

10. Budweiser is made by rice, malted barley and hops.

百威啤酒是由大米、麦芽和啤酒花制作而成。

11. It tastes easy.

味道很好。

12. It ranks the first among the world's ten beers top.

它在世界十大啤酒排行榜中名列第一。

13. How many do you want?

你想要多少？

14. Two bottles of Budweiser, please.

请来两瓶百威。

15. What brand of beer would you like?

您要想什么牌子的啤酒？

M6-26　Practice

Exercises

1. Questions and Answers

(1) What's beer?

(2) Could you list five famous beer in the world?

(3) What's hops?

2. Match the words or expressions in Column A with their Chinese equivalents in Column B.

A	B
(1) beer tin	a. 瓶装啤酒
(2) black beer	b. 听装啤酒
(3) bottled beer	c. 黑啤酒
(4) light beer	d. 矿泉水；苏打水；姜汁啤酒
(5) minerals	e. 淡啤酒，低酒度啤酒
(6) draft beer	f. 烈性啤酒
(7) ale	g. 生啤酒
(8) barley broth	h. 黄啤（酒）；强麦酒
(9) lager	i. 啤酒酵母
(10) yeast	j. 陈贮啤酒

3. Choose the best English translation for each sentence.

(1) 先生，你要哪一种杯子乘啤酒，净饮杯还是扎啤杯？（　　）

A. Would you like that in a glass or a mug, sir?

B. Would you like a straight or a mug, sir?

C. Would you like that in a straight or a jug, sir?

D. Would you like a straight or a jug, sir?

(2) 你想要什么牌子的啤酒，青岛，还是健力士？（　　）

A. Which one do you like best, Tsingtao or Guinness?

B. What brand of beer would you like, Tsingtao or Guinness?

C. Which one do you like best, Tsingtao or Carlsberg?

D. What brand of beer would you like, Tsingtao or Carlsberg?

（3）我想要一瓶当地啤酒。（　　）

A. I care for a bottle of imported beer.　　B. I want for a bottle of imported beer.

C. I want a bottle of local beer.　　D. I care for a bottle of local beer.

（4）请来两瓶啤酒。（　　）

A. Please give me two beers.　　B. Please give me two bottles beer.

C. Two beers, please.　　D. Two bottles beer, please.

（5）我的酒量小。（　　）

A. I get drunk easily.　　B. I am drinking easily.

C. I get drink quickly.　　D. I am drinking quickly.

4. Read the passage and decide if the statements are true (T) or false (F).

Production and consumption of beer in China has occurred for around nine thousand years, with recent archaeological findings showing that Chinese villagers were brewing beer-type alcoholic drinks as far back as 7000 BC on small and individual scales. Made with rice, honey, and grape and hawthorn fruits, this early beer seems to have been produced similarly to that of ancient Egypt and Mesopotamia.Ancient Chinese beer was important in ancestral worship, funeral and other rituals of Xia, Shang and Zhou dynasties, and the beer was called as Lao Li (醪醴 in oracle bone script). However, after the Han Dynasty, Chinese beer faded from prominence in favor of huangjiu, which remained the case for the next two millennia. Modern beer brewing was not introduced into China until the end of 19th century, when Russians established a brewery in Harbin, with another three following (also in Harbin),set up by Germans, Czechoslovaks and Russians respectively. Japanese also established in 1934 in Mukden Manchurian Beer, which later became Shenyang Snow Beer and the origin of Snow Beer when it was absorbed in 1994 by China Resources Enterprises.

Exercises:

(1) Beer is produced before nine thous and years in China. (　　)

(2) Beer is made with rice, honey and grape in modern society. (　　)

(3) Ancient Chinese beer was important in ancestral worship. (　　)

(4) Modern beer brewing was introduced into China until the end of 19th century. (　　)

(5) Japanese also established in 1994 in Mukden Manchurian Beer. (　　)

Challenges and Solutions

1. Do you know what's the basic ingredients of beer?

Solutions:

2. Do you know how to make beer?

Solutions:

3. Do you know about the beer festival?

Solutions:

4. How to celebrate the beer festival in your country?

Solutions:

5. Do you like drinking beer, why?

Solutions:

6. Do you know where does Carlsberg come from?

Solution:

7. If the guest has ordered Tsingtao beer, but it is sold out, what should you do?

Solutions:

8. If your parents like to drink beer, do you agree? Why?

Solutions:

M6-27　Knowledge Link

M6-28　Key to Exercises

Lesson Eight   Tea Service

Objectives

➤ To help the students master useful expressions and sentences about tea service.
➤ To help the students familiar with all kinds of tea.
➤ To help the students make some dialogues about tea service.

Warming Up

1. There are many kinds of tea. Look at the following pictures and write down the correct names of tea by the corresponding description.

_____ is one of famous green tea in China. It is produced in hangzhou, zhejiang province.

_____ is one of famous green tea in China. It is produced in suzhou dongting mountain biluofeng.

_____ is one of famous green tea in China. It is produced in lushan, jiangxi province.

_____ is one of famous qingcha tea in China. It is produced in anxi, fujian province.

_____ is one of famous yellow tea in China. It is produced in yueyang, hunan province.

_____ is one of special green tea in China. It is produced in liuan, anhui province.

_____ is one of famous green tea in China. It is produced in xinyang, henan province.

_____ is one of famous green tea in China. It is produced in huangshan, anhui province.

_____ is one of famous oolong tea in China. It is produced in wuyishan, wujian province.

_____ is one of famous black tea in China. It is produced in qimen, anhui province.

M6-29   Warming Up

Dialogues

Key sentences:

➢ Which do you prefer, please?

➢ Shall I make the tea for you?

➢ What is it called?

➢ It is said that different tea has different benefits to human body, isn't it?

➢ What is special about it?

Pre-questions:

1. Do you know about tea?

2. Do you know how to help the guest order tea?

3. Do you know how to recommend the tea to guests?

Dialogue 1

Waiter:	Excuse me. Would you like some tea,madam? I have some quality China tea including green tea, jasmine tea and black tea. Which do you prefer, please?
Guest:	That sounds nice. What kind of tea would you recommend it to me?
Waiter:	I think you'd like to try the green tea, it is good health for people in summer.

Guest:	Ok, How much is it?
Waiter:	It is 45 Yuan for one pot.
Guest:	Ok, please give me a pot of green tea.
Waiter:	I'll fetch you a teacup in a moment.(Back with the teacups on a tray.)Here's a teacup for you. Shall I make the tea for you, madam?
Guest:	Yes, please. It's very thoughtful of you.
Waiter:	(Offering the tea.)Enjoy your tea, madam.
Guest:	Thank you.

Dialogue 2

Guest:	Thank you. The tea smells good. What is it called?
Waiter:	It is called "Tie Guanyin", belonging to Oolong tea.
Guest:	I heard of this name before. I could never understand the classification of tea.
Waiter:	There are many different kinds of tea. Generally, there are four kinds of tea according to processing methods. They are green tea, black tea,Oolong tea, and scented tea.
Guest:	It is said that different tea has different benefits to human body, isn't it?
Waiter:	Yes, it is. But there are time and personal health condition to be considered. For example, green tea is good in summer. It seems to dispel the heat and bring on a feeling of relaxation. However, it is not proper for pregnant woman.
Guest:	There seems to be a lot of knowledge about tea.
Waiter:	Of course. That's why we have "tea culture".
Guest:	You must tell me more about tea culture in the future.
Waiter:	No problem.

Dialogue 3

Guest:	So, I heard that Iran is very famous for it's coffee?
Waiter:	Well, not coffee actually, the tea.
Guest:	The tea? What is special about it?
Waiter:	Well, we love tea. We have to drink tea. Some of the people, if they don't drink two or three glasses of tea, cups of tea, they have headaches.
Guest:	Headaches.
Waiter:	Yeah, yeah, yeah. And they are very much picky about the color of the tea. Everybody orders differently. Some people say pour very colored strong tea. Some people say, "No,I don't want it that strong." The medium. Everybody has their own taste.
Guest:	So, I guess you got a lot of tea shops.
Waiter:	Yeah, yeah, we have traditional one, which is very interesting for the tourists I believe, where you go in and you sit down, no chairs there, and it's actually cushions just behind you, so you can lie on this cushions and you know, kind of like lying position. You can straighten your legs and the servant will bring you tea. Actually, the drinking tea in Iran is a little different from other countries.
Guest:	Different? How?

Waiter: Well, we have a glass or a cup of tea, and beneath that we have something called saucer, which you put the glass or cup on that, and, well, the way you drink it is that you have to pick up the cubic sugar. It is a cubic. It's not like other powder of sugar. You pick it up and then you tip it inside the tea a little bit. When it gets the most, you put it inside your mouth, and you drink tea when the cubic sugar is in your mouth.

Guest: It takes time.

Waiter: That's the way you drink it. You will get used to it. Just try once. It's actually good.

Guest: Do you go there often?

Waiter: Once a year. Yeah.

Guest: Once a year! Okay. It's interesting. I will try.

Vocabulary

fetch [fetʃ]　*n.* 取得；诡计　*vt.* 取来；接来　*vi.* 拿；取物

classification [ˌklæsɪfɪ'keɪʃ(ə)n]　*n.* 分类；类别，等级

dispel[dɪ'spel]　*vt.* 驱散，驱逐；消除（烦恼等）

heat [hiːt]　*n.* 高温；压力；热度；热烈　*vt.* 使激动；把……加热

relaxation [riːlæk'seɪʃ(ə)n]　*n.* 放松；缓和；消遣

pregnant ['pregnənt]　*adj.* 怀孕的；富有意义的

tourists ['tʊərɪsts]　*n.* 旅游者（tourist 的复数）　*v.* 旅游；观光

cushion ['kʊʃən]　*n.* 垫子　*vt.* 给……安上垫子；把……安置在垫子上

straighten ['streɪt(ə)n]　*vt.* 整顿；使……改正；使……挺直　*vi.* 变直；好转

Iran 英 [iˈrɑːn; iˈræn]　*n.* 伊朗（亚洲国家）

beneath [bɪˈniːθ]　*prep.* 在……之下　*adv.* 在下方

saucer ['sɔːsə]　*n.* 茶托，浅碟；浅碟形物

green tea　绿茶

jasmine tea　茉莉花茶

black tea　红茶

scented tea　花果茶

Tie Guanyin　铁观音

Oolong tea　乌龙茶

cubic sugar　方糖

Useful Expressions

1. Which do youprefer, please?
请问，您更喜欢哪一种？

2. How much is it?
多少钱？

3. Here's a teacup for you. Shall I make the tea for you, madam?
这是您的茶杯。夫人，我给您沏茶好吗？

4. It's very thoughtful of you.

你真是太周到了。

5. The tea smells good. What is it called?

这茶闻起来很香。这叫什么茶?

6. I heard of this name before.

我以前听说过这个名字。

7. It is said that different tea has different benefits to human body, isn't it?

据说不同的茶对于人体有不同的益处,不是吗?

8. It seems to dispel the heat and bring on a feeling of relaxation.

它似乎能够驱散炎热并带来放松的感觉。

9. I heard that Iran is very famous for it's coffee?

我听说伊朗的咖啡很有名?

10. What is special about it?

它有什么特别之处?

11. They are very much picky about the color of the tea.

他们对茶的颜色很挑剔。

12. You can straighten your legs and the servant will bring you tea.

你可以伸直你的腿,服务员会给你上茶。

13. The way you drink it is that you have to pick up the cubic sugar.

你喝茶时,一定要配方糖。

14. You pick it up and then you tip it inside the tea a little bit.

喝茶时,拿起一块方糖,放到茶水里稍微一沾。

15. That's the way you drink it. You will get used to it.

这就是伊朗人喝茶的方法。你会习惯的。

M6-30　Practice

Exercises

1. Questions and Answers

(1) What's tea?

(2) Could you list some famous brands of tea in china?

(3) What's the green tea/ black tea?

2. Match the words or expressions in Column A with their Chinese equivalents in Column B.

A	B
(1) tea pad	a. 壶垫
(2) tea plate	b. 茶盅
(3) tea pitcher	c. 杯托
(4) tea towel	d. 茶匙

(5) tea pot   e. 茶船

(6) cup saucer   f. 茶桌

(7) tea spoon   g. 茶壶

(8) tea table   h. 茶巾

(9) seat cushion   i. 茶碗

(10) tea bowl   j. 坐垫

3. Choose the best English translation for each sentence.

(1) 人们常常会把"茶点"和"下午茶"搞混，其实茶点通常相当于晚餐。（ ）

A. Tea is same with afternoon tea, usually takes the place of supper.

B. Tea is same with afternoon tea, usually takes the place of supper.

C. Tea, a term often confused with afternoon tea, usually takes the place of supper.

D. Tea is confused with afternoon tea. It usually takes the place of supper.

(2) 在中国，饮茶的历史可以追溯到公元前3000年。（ ）

A. The custom of tea dates is the third millennium BC in China.

B. The custom of tea dates back to the third millennium AD in China.

C. The custom of tea dates back to the third millennium BC in China.

D. The custom of drinking tea dates back to the third millennium BC in China.

(3) 下午茶是由第七任贝德福公爵夫人安娜在1840年创造出来的。（ ）

A. Afternoon tea was prod in England by Anna，the seventh Duchess of Bedford，in the year 1840.

B. Afternoon tea was introduced in England by Anna，the seventh Duchess of Bedford，in the year 1840.

C. Afternoon tea was introduced in England by Anna，in the year 1840.

D. Afternoon tea was introduced in England by Anna，in the year 1840.

(4) 通常，下午茶会安排在起居室，时间大约是在下午四点到五点。（ ）

A. Afternoon tea which must be served in the drawing room between four and five o'clock.

B. Afternoon tea which must be served in the dining room between four and five o'clock.

C. Afternoon tea which was usually served in the drawing room between four and five o'clock.

D. Afternoon tea which was usually served in the dining room between four and five o'clock.

(5) 传统的下午茶包括精选的三明治，英式奶油松饼，还有蛋糕和其他甜点。（ ）

A. Traditional afternoon tea consists of asandwiches, cream,cakes and pastries.

B. Old afternoon tea includes a sandwiches, cream,cakes.

C. Old afternoon tea consists of a selection of dainty sandwiches,scones served with clotted cream,cakes and pastries are also served.

D. Traditional afternoon tea consists of a selection of dainty sandwiches,scones served with clotted cream,cakes and pastries are also served.

4. Read the passage and decide if the statements are true (T) or false (F).

Different Types of Tea

Green tea is also called unfermented tea. It is made with the new shoots of appropriate tea trees as raw materials, by applying the typical techniques of inactivation, rolling and drying. According to the drying and inactivation techniques, it is sub-divided into stir-fried green tea, roasted green tea, sun-dried green tea and steamed green tea. Green tea has the characteristics of "green leaves in a clear soup with a strong astringent taste". It is the tea category with the longest history (more than 3,000 years) and also the one has the largest output in China. Famous green teas include West Lake Dragon Well Tea, Xinyang Maojian Tea and Biluochun Tea.

Red Tea is also called fermented tea. Only the new shoots of tea leaves are suitable for use as the raw material for making this tea. It is exquisitely made through the typical technical processes of wilting, rolling, fermentation and drying. Its infusion is mainly red in tone. Hence what is known as black tea elsewhere is known as red tea in China.. Famous red teas include 武夷山正山小种，福安功夫 black tea, 滇虹 black Tea, Yixing 宜兴 black Tea, and Qimen 祁门 black Tea. Wulong (Oolong) Tea is also called blue tea, and is an unfermented tea. It is a tea category with some unique and distinctive characteristics. Wulong tea, as a blend of green tea and red tea, has qualities of both green tea and red tea. It not only has the thick and fresh flavor of red tea, but also has the pleasant fragrance of green tea.

White tea is uncured, unfermented, fast-dried green tea. It is a specialty of Fujian province. It got its name from the recourse of poor Chinese of offering boiled water to guests if they didn't have any tea, which they called "white tea" (the word for white can mean plain in Chinese). Thus they would save face and come across as routinely hospitable. As might be imagined white tea is lighter in color and flavor than other teas. Famous white teas include 白毫银针 Baihao Yinzhen and 白牡丹 Bai Mudan (White Peony).

Yellow Tea is produced by letting damp tea leaves naturally turn yellow. It has an original smell, which could be mistaken for red tea if it is cured with herbs, but its taste is most similar to green and white teas. Yellow Tea is also a term used to describe the top-quality tea served to the emperor, because the imperial color has traditionally been yellow. Famous yellow teas include 君山银针 Junshan Yinzhen, 蒙顶黄芽 Mengding Huangya, and Dayeqing.

Tea products which are made by taking teas from the categories above as materials and reprocessing them, is called reprocessed tea. The product range includes scented tea 花茶, pressed tea 紧压茶, instant tea 速溶茶, extracted tea 提取的茶, fruit tea 水果茶, medicinal tea 药用茶 and health tea 保健茶, which have a variety of flavors and effects.

Exercises:

(1) Tea is divided into green tea and red tea. (　　)

(2) Red Tea is also called unfermented tea. (　　)

(3) White tea is cured, fermented, fast-dried green tea. (　　)

(4) Yellow Tea is produced by letting damp tea leaves naturally turn yellow. (　　)

(5) Reprocessed tea which are made by taking teas from different teas as materials and reprocessing them. (　　)

Challenges and Solutions

1. Do you know the differences between red tea and black tea?

Solutions:

2. Do you know what's the tea ceremony?

Solutions:

3. Do you know what is the etiquette of tea in China?

Solutions:

4. If the guest comes to China for the first time, but he wants to have a cup of tea, how to recommend the tea to the guest?

Solutions:

5. If the guest thinks drinking tea is bad for his health, what should you do?

Solutions:

6. Do you know about the health benefits of drinking tea?

Solution:

7. If you are waiter at tea cafe, how to serve the guest?

Solutions:

8. Do you know how to maketea?

Solutions:

M6-31　Knowledge Link　　　　　M6-32　Key to Exercises

Lesson Nine　　Handling Complaints

Objectives

➤ To help the students master useful expressions and sentences about complaints at the bar.

➤ To help the students familiar with the common complaints at the bar.

➤ To help the students analyze the reasons of complaints and handle complaints at the bar.

Preamble

Friday night November 3, 2018

Dear Manager,

I would like to inform you of unpleasant experiences during my recent stay at your hotel. I wanted to have a drink in your hotel, it was a challenge to start with. The bartender had great difficulties in both understanding me and expressing himself in English. I believe either he is given more training in language or he should be transferred to a position less demanding on English skills. I wanted to be alone and quiet for a while after working all day. But the bartender always recommended beverages to me, obviously in an effort to get tipped. I don't mind his help and tip him if I am in real need. But a greedy boy irritates many customers like me. I hope some effort is made by your hotel to improve the service quality and standard, if you want your customers to come back to your hotel again. Last but not the least, I give you my cell phone number in case you would like to hear from me for suggestions. Cell phone: 1234567890.

Sincerely yours,
(Signature) Bob Smith

Dialogues

Key sentences:

➢ Is everything to your satisfaction?

➢ Is there anything unsatisfying?

➢ Could you tell me exactly what it is all about?

➢ Do you have any criticism on our service?

Pre-questions:

1. What are the common complaints at the bar of a hotel?

2. How to deal with complaints at the bar?

3. Do you think it's an important to handle complaints from the guests at the bar? Why?

Dialogue 1

Supervisor:	Is everything to your satisfaction?
Guest:	No, I ordered a orange juice, but it is wrong that the staff give me lemon juice. And it is not fresh orange.
Supervisor:	Oh, I'm terribly sorry to hear that! I'll go and get your orange juice right away. This is quite unusual as we have fresh fruit from the market every day! I'll look into the matter.
Guest:	So what? It is wrong drink and not fresh that I'm not happy about it.
Supervisor:	I'm sorry, sir. Do you wish to try something else? How about a delicious dessert then, with our compliments?
Guest:	No, I don't want to try something else, and find it's not fresh again! This is very annoying.
Supervisor:	I see, sir. Just give. Another chance, I'm sure everything will be all right next time you come.
Guest:	All right. May be I'll come again.
Supervisor:	Thank you very much, sir.

Dialogue 2

Guest:	May I speak to the hotel manager please?
Hotel manager:	Hi, this is Ben Smith, the manager of Holiday inn. How can I help you?
Guest:	Hi, my name is Lisa Wang. I would like to find a complaint of the poor service of your hotel. This is my first time to stay in your hotel and it will

be my last one too.

Hotel manager:	I am sorry to hear that. Could you tell me exactly what it is all about?
Guest:	When I had a drink in the bar of your hotel, the staffs at the bar desk were quite rude. I wanted to ask some information of the beverages, but they were chatting and laughing with each other. They just threw a pamphlet at the desk and went on their chatting. That is very unprofessional.
Hotel manager:	Mrs.Wang, I apologize for what had happened. I will look into it and give you a reply as soon as possible.
Guest:	Thank you for your attention in this matter. I really appreciate that.
Hotel manager:	Could you give me a number that I can reach you?
Guest:	124-456-789
Hotel manager:	OK, Mrs.Wang , thank you so much for calling. I sincerely ask you to come back to our hotel again and I promise you that what had happened to you yesterday will not repeat. Have a good day! Bye.
Guest:	Bye.

Dialogue 3

Guest:	Hey, bartender, come here.
Staff:	What is the matter, sir?
Guest:	I have a complaint. Please ask your manager here.
Staff:	Sir, Do you have any criticism on our service?
Guest:	Look at the drink, there is a fly floating over it.
Staff:	That is impossible, I have checked it carefully.
Guest:	Anyway, I want to see your manager.
Staff:	OK, I go to find our manager.
Guest:	I need you give me a reasonable explanation.
Staff:	We will, please wait a moment.

Vocabulary

satisfaction [sætɪsˈfækʃ(ə)n]　*n.* 满意，满足；赔偿；乐事；赎罪

supervisor [ˈsuːpəvaɪzə]　*n.* 监督人；指导人；主管人

unsatisfy [ʌnˈsætisfai]　*vt.* 不满意；不安心；不履行

fresh [freʃ]　*adj.* 新鲜的；清新的；淡水的；无经验的

unusual [ʌnˈjuːʒl]　*adj.* 不寻常的；与众不同的；不平常的

compliment[ˈkɒmplɪm(ə)nt]　*n.* 恭维；称赞；问候；致意；道贺　*vt.* 恭维；称赞

annoying[əˈnɔɪɪŋ]　*adj.* 讨厌的；恼人的

pamphlet [ˈpæmflɪt]　*n.* 小册子

rude[ruːd]　*adj.* 粗鲁的；无礼的；狂暴的；未开化的

chat [tʃæt]　*vi.* 聊天；闲谈　*vt.* 与……搭讪；与……攀谈　*n.* 聊天；闲谈

unprofessional[ʌnprəˈfeʃ(ə)n(ə)l]　*adj.* 非职业性的，非专业的；外行的

reply [rɪˈplaɪ]　*vi.* 回答；[法] 答辩；回击　*vt.* 回答；答复　*n.* 回答

attention [əˈtenʃ(ə)n]　*n.* 注意力；关心；立正！（口令）

appreciate [əˈpriːʃɪeɪt; -sɪ-]　*vt.* 欣赏；感激；领会；鉴别　*vi.* 增值；涨价

sincerely [sɪn'sɪəlɪ]　*adv.* 真诚地；由衷地，诚恳地

repeat [rɪ'pi:t]　*vt.* 重复；复制；背诵　*vi.* 重做；重复发生　*n.* 重复；副本

staff [stɑːf]　*n.* 职员；参谋；棒；支撑

bartender ['bɑːtendə]　*n.* 酒保，酒吧间销售酒精饮料的人；酒吧侍者

criticism ['krɪtɪsɪz(ə)m]　*n.* 批评；考证；苛求

float [fləʊt]　*vt.* 使漂浮；实行　*vi.* 浮动；飘动；*n.* 漂流物

reasonable ['riːz(ə)nəb(ə)l]　*adj.* 合理的，公道的；通情达理的

promise ['prɒmɪs]　*n.* 许诺，允诺；希望　*vt.* 允诺，许诺；*vi.* 许诺；有指望，有前途

orange juice　奶泡

lemon juice　奶沫

hotel manager　酒店经理

Useful Expressions

1. Is everything to your satisfaction?

一切还合您的意吗？

2. I'm terribly sorry to hear that!

听到这样的事情，我真的非常遗憾！

3. How about a delicious dessert then, with our compliments?

来一份甜点怎么样，以表示我们的歉意。

4. Do you wish to try something else?

您是否想吃点别的什么？

5. I'm sure everything will be all right next time you come.

我保证下次来的时候一切都会很好的。

6. May I speak to the hotel manager please?

我可以和你们酒店经理讲话吗？

7. Could you tell me exactly what it is all about?

您能告诉我这到底是怎么回事吗？

8. I apologize for what had happened.

我为所发生的事情道歉。

9. I will look into it and give you a reply as soon as possible.

我将调查此事，并尽快给您答复。

10. Thank you for your attention in this matter. I really appreciate that.

谢谢您关注此事。我真的很感激。

11. I promise you that what had happened to you yesterday will not repeat.

我向您保证，昨天发生在您身上的事情不会再发生了。

12. What is the matter, sir?

怎么了，先生？

13. Do you have any criticism on our service?

您对我们的服务有什么批评意见？

14. I need you give me a reasonable explanation.

我需要你给我一个合理的解释。

Exercises

1. Match each word or phrase in the column on the left with its meaning in the column on the right.

(1) bartender   a. recognize with gratitude; be grateful for.

(2) compliment   b. a remark that shows you admire someone or something.

(3) appreciate   c. one who supervises or has charge and direction.

(4) criticism   d. speaking or behaving in a way that is not polite.

(5) pamphlet   e. to tell someone that you are sorry that you have done something .

(6) rude   f. showing reason or sound judgment.

(7) supervisor   g. someone who makes, pours, and serves drinks in a bar.

(8) reasonable   h. remarks that say what you think is bad about someone.

(9) satisfy   i. a book with paper covers, that gives information about something.

(10) apologize   j. to make someone feel pleased by doing what they want.

2. Complete the following dialogue according to the Chinese in brackets and read it in roles.

A=Staff   B=Guest   C=Manager

A: _____ （你想喝点茅台之类的酒吗？）

B: Is there anything else besides Mao Tai?

A: _____ Yes,（我们中国有八大名酒。）
Would you like to have a try for Wu Liang Ye?

B: Wu Liang Ye from Sichuan Province?

A: Yes, sir. It's very famous in our China.

B: _____（让我尝一尝。）How much is one bottle?

A: Here it is, sir. It's RMB 1500 for one bottle.

B: Oh, it's too expensive. _____（我想投诉你们酒吧的酒水价格比市场价格高出太多。）

A: I'm awfully sorry for that, sir. But I'm sure our drink is authentic.

B: I want to see your manager.

A: Ok, please wait, our manager will be back soon.

C: I'm here. _____（先生，发生了什么事情？）

B: I want to have a bottle of Mao Tai in your bar, but I find the price of drink is too high.

C: I'm awfully sorry for that, sir. I will look into it and give you a reply as soon as possible.
_____（谢谢您关注此事。我真的很感激。）

B: Ok, I'll wait for your answer.

3. Reading the following sentences, and choose the correct answers of settling guest's complaints at the bar.

a. Let the guest to leave hotel.

b. Listen attentively to the hotel guest's complaint.

c. Angry with guests.

d. Identify with the hotel guest.

e. Don't say sorry..

f. Consider the guest's complaint.

g. Delegate a complaint to the appropriate resource.

h. Plot the course towards resourceful action.

4. Choose the best English translation for each sentence.

(1) 先生，我对此非常抱歉，我会马上处理此事。(   )

A. I'm awfully sorry for that, sir. I'll see it right away.

B. I'm awfully sorry for that, sir. I'll see to it right away.

C. I'm awfully sorry for that, sir. I'll arrange it right away.

D. I'm awfully sorry for that, sir. I'll manage it right away.

(2) 请稍等，我们会帮您安排的。(   )

A. Please wait for a moment, we'll help you.　　B. Please wait for moment, we'll handle it.

C. Please wait, we'll arrange for you.　　D. Please wait, we'll arrange you.

(3) 我很抱歉给您带来了诸多不便。(   )

A. I'm sorry to have caused bad things.　　B. I'm sorry to have bad messages to you.

C. I'm sorry to give you big trouble.　　D. I'm sorry to have caused you so much trouble.

(4) 非常抱歉，我们再免费送您一杯雪利酒。(   )

A. I'm terrible sorry, we'll give you another glass of sherry.

B. I'm terrible sorry, we'll give you another glass of sherry for free.

C. I'm sorry, we'll give you another glass of cocktail.

D. I'm sorry, we'll give you another glass of brandy for free.

(5) 我想要投诉你们酒吧的卫生太差。(   )

A. I want to complain about the bad environment of your bar.

B. I want to complain about the bad service of your bar.

C. I want to complain about the poor person of your bar.

D. I want to complain about the poor sanitation of your bar.

5. Read the passage and choose the best answers to the following questions.

Guidelines for Handling Guest Complaints

Dealing with guest complaints is important in meeting guest expectations. Guests are sometimes disappointed or find fault with something or someone at the hotel. The hotel should be especially attentive to guests with complaints and should be especially attentive to guests with complaints and should find timely and satisfactory resolutions to the problems.

Guests complaints fall into four types: mechanical complaints, attitudinal complaints, service-related complaints, and unusual complaints. All guest complaints deserve attention. Hotel management should encourage and settle guest complaints. When handling guest complaints, the employees and management staff should keep the following in mind:

In order to avoid risking potential danger, do not go alone to a guestroom to investigate a problem, for a guest may be quite angry at the moment the complaint arises. If a problem cannot be resolved, admit this to the guest early. Honesty is the best policy when dealing with guest complaints. Some guests complain as part of their nature. Have an approach for dealing with such guests.To be more specific, the following rules will help management staff to handle complaints effectively in a professional manner:

Listen with concern and empathy. Isolate the guest if possible, so that other guests won't overhear. Stay calm, and avoid responding with hostility or defensiveness. Don't argue with the guest. Be aware of the guest's self-esteem. Show a personal interest in the problem. Use the guest's name frequently. Take the complaint seriously. Give the guest your undivided attention. Concentrate on the problem, not on placing blame. Do not insult the guest.

Take notes and write down the key facts. This will save time if someone else must get involved. Besides, guests will tend to slow down when they are speaking faster than you can write. More importantly, the fact that a staff member is concerned enough to write down what they're saying is reassuring to guests. Tell the guest what can be done, and offer choices. Don't promise the impossible, and don't exceed your authority. Set an approximate time for completion of corrective action, be specific, but do not underestimate the amount of time it will take to resolve the problem.

Monitor the progress of the corrective action. Follow up even if someone else resolved the complaint; contact the guest to ensure that the problem has been resolved satisfactorily; report the entire event, the actions taken, and the conclusion of the incident.

(1) What should a staff member do if a complaint cannot be resolved? (　　)

A. Promise the guest it will be settled in the future.

B. Admit it to the guest honestly and early.

C. Give no feedback and let it be.

D. Tell the guest it is being discussed by the management.

(2) What should a staff member do to show the complaint is being taken seriously? (　　)

A. Isolate the guest so that other guests won't overhear.

B. Argue with the guest.

C. Take notes and write down the key facts.

D. All of the above.

(3) After the resolution of the complaint, what should be done according to the passage? (　　)

A. Follow up with the guest.　　　　　　B. Have a talk with the staff involved.

C. Erase the notes completely.　　　　　D. Talk to other guests about it.

(4) Which of the following statements is TRUE according to the passage? (　　)

A. Since some complaints are not reasonable, it is not necessary to take every complaint seriously.

B. Complaints reveal the dissatisfaction of the guest, so the hotel had better discourage complaints.

C. To show the sincerity on the part of the hotel to handle the complaints, the staff members should promise to solve the problem extremely quickly.

D. When dealing with complaints, a staff member should listen attentively, patiently, and politely, and take notes if necessary and if possible.

Challenges and Solutions

1. If the guest is not satisfied with the taste of cocktail at the bar, what will you do?

Solutions:

2. What will you do if your customers complain about your poor service at the bar?

Solutions:

3. If the guest complains that a bottle of brandy is inferior at the bar, what will you do?

Solutions:

4. If the guest wants to speak with your manager and complains about your rude attitude at the bar, what will you do?

Solutions:

5. If the customer complains that a fly is floating in the cup of drink at the bar, what will you do?

Solutions:

6. If the guest complains that the opened wine is kept too long at the bar, what will you do?

Solution:

7. If the guest complains that you break a glass of sherry at the bar, what will you do?

Solutions:

8. If the guest complains that the price of drink is higher than the market price at the bar, what will you do?

Solutions:

M6-33　Knowledge Link

M6-34　Key to Exercises

Chapter 7

Comprehensive Service

Lesson One   Taking Messages

Objectives

➢ To help the students master useful expressions and sentences about taking messages.
➢ To help the students familiar with all kinds of message.
➢ To help the students make some dialogues about taking messages.

Warming Up

1. Look at the following pictures and fill in the blanks according to the corresponding descriptions.

Hotel provides message service while the guests are_____. Message for registered and arriving guests and hotel management must be accepted noted down carefully with all details accurate and delivered promptly. Ensure guests and hotel management can _____ message seasonable.

All guest messages should be entered into the_____ as they are received.

Check that the guest for whom the message is intended is in-house. If the guest is not in-house, check the reservation system for a future booking. A message for a future guest can be made and attached to the reservation in the computer.

Ensure all information is recorded, i.e. _____, _____, the_____ itself and the recipient's name. The system will date and time the message automatically. If a message is taken manually, ensure that the date and time recorded.

To ensure information is accurately recorded, _____ back the details to the caller for verification. Check the guest's room number against the name given to ensure correctly.

Guests who find their message _____ illuminated will call the Guest service center room to receive their message. The message should be read to the guest and entering "Received" in the system should turn off the message light. Guest service center could send letter message to the guestroom on time.

M7-1　Warming Up

Dialogues

Key sentences:

➢ Is there a number where you can be reached?
➢ What would you like the message to say?
➢ Please let me repeat it back to you to make sure the details are correct.
➢ I will repeat it back to you to make sure the details are correct.
➢ We will deliver this message to...

Pre-questions:

1. At what situations guests may need message service?
2. What information need to be noted while taking notes for the guests?

Dialogue 1

Mr. Nobel:	Excuse me.
Concierge:	Yes. What can I do for you?
Mr. Nobel:	I'm here to see Dr. Smith from America.
Concierge:	Do you know when he arrived, sir?
Mr. Nobel:	The day before yesterday. I believe.
Concierge:	Just a moment, please. Let me see. Er... What's his full name?
Mr. Nobel:	Mike Smith from San Francisco.
Concierge:	Oh, here it is. Dr. Mike Smith. May I call to tell him you are here to see him?
Mr. Nobel:	Yes, please.
Concierge:	I'm sorry, sir. Nobody answers the phone. He must have been out.
Mr. Nobel:	Can I leave him a message?

Concierge:	Certainly, sir.
Mr. Nobel:	Could you please tell him that Stephen Nobel invites him to dinner tomorrow evening at Hilton Hotel and will meet him at 6:30 at the gate?
Concierge:	Ok, Mr. Nobel. I'll tell him as soon as I contact him.
Mr. Nobel:	Thank you.

Dialogue 2

Operator:	Good morning, Maple Hotel. Helen speaking. How may I help you?
Guest:	Yes. I'd like to leave a message to a guest staying with you.
Operator:	Certainly. May I ask the guest's name, spelling and room number?
Guest:	His name is Dr. Livingstone. L-I-V-I-N-G-S-T-O-N-E. Room 789.
Operator:	May I take your name and telephone number, please?
Guest:	I am Mr. Stanley, and my phone number is 187-7788-9966.
Operator:	Thank you, Mr. Stanly. What message would you like to leave?
Guest:	I looked for you today. We missed each other at the Victoria Café. Could we meet up tomorrow?
Operator:	Your message reads: "I looked for you today. We missed each other at the Victoria Café. Could we meet up tomorrow?" Is that correct?
Guest:	Yes, that's it.
Operator:	Would you like to give Dr. Livingstone a time for this meeting?
Guest:	Yes, of course. Thank you. Let's say 10:00 a.m.
Operator:	So your message will read: "I looked for you today. We missed each other at the Victoria Café. Could we meet up tomorrow, at 10:00 a.m.?" At the café, Mr. Stanley?
Guest:	Yes, please. When will he get his message?
Operator:	We will leave a printed copy of your message under his door and a light will flash on the phone in his room, so he should get it when he returns to his room.
Guest:	That's great, thank you.
Operator:	My pleasure. Is there anything else I can do for you?
Guest:	No, thank you. You have been a great help. Goodbye.

Vocabulary

meet up 见面	print [prɪnt] *v.* 打印
correct [kə'rekt] *adj.* 正确的	flash [flæʃ] *v.* 闪光

Useful Expressions

1. Would you like to leave a message?
您想要留言吗？

2. May I take a message for you?
我可以给您留言吗？

3. What if someone calls to speak to you?
如果有人打电话找您呢？

M7-2 Practice

Exercises

1. Questions and Answers

(1) Which positions in the hotel will deal with guest message service?

(2) When taking the notes for the guest, what polite expressions can you use?

2. Match the words or expressions in Column A with their Chinese equivalents in Column B.

A	B
(1) date	a. 周年纪念
(2) contact number	b. 旅行
(3) lobby	c. 参观
(4) lounge	d. 约会
(5) trip	e. 展览
(6) sightseeing	f. 生意，事情
(7) anniversary	g. 观光
(8) business	h. 大堂
(9) exhibition	i. 酒廊
(10) visit	j. 联系号码

3. Choose the best English translation for each sentence.

(1) 请问您的房间号是？

A. May I have your room number, please?

B. This is your room number.

C. I should ask him the room number.

D. Room number is an important information, I need to ask.

(2) 请问您的姓名怎么拼写？

A. What's your name?   B. May I know your name?

C. May I know your name spelling?   D. Could you please sign your name here?

(3) 我给您重复一下。

A. I got it.   B. I will check the information with you.

C. Let me say it again.   D. Let me repeat the information for you.

(4) 您想留什么信息呢？

A. What message did you get?   B. What message would you like to leave?

C. What do you want to say?   D. What information do you need?

(5) 您知道他什么时候到吗？

A. What time do you expect to arrive?   B. When will you come here?

C. Do you know the time he arrives?   D. Do you have time?

4. Read the passage and decide if the statements are true (T) or false (F).

In the age of cell phones, telephone etiquette has largely gone by the wayside. Knowing how to take messages is still useful when you're working in an office or taking calls for someone else. Being polite, writing everything down, and delivering the message promptly are key!

1. Answer the phone. The person on the other end asks for your immediate supervisor or co-worker who is not at his/her desk. The first thing you should do is say, "He/she isn't available at the moment. Can I take a message?" Assuming they say yes continue to the next step. If they say no, then please insist they at least allow you to help them. If they refuse politely, ask the person to at least give you their name and company name; be sure to jot down their number off call also let the person know a good time to try back. Just remember to ask if you can do anything else — they might want to call back and leave a message on the answering machine. Be sure to let whomever the call was for who called and when they might try back.

2. Write down everything they say. You may not think what they say is important but the person you are writing the message for might think it is. If needed ask them to repeat information.

3. Say good-bye to the caller.

Exercises:

(1) The key points of taking telephone message are being rude, writing the importance down. (　　)

(2) When you pick up the phone, the first thing is to say "hello". (　　)

(3) "He is not available now." means "He can't answer the phone now". (　　)

(4) If the caller refuses your help, you can hang up the phone directly. (　　)

(5) When taking the notes, you should take everything the caller says. (　　)

Challenges and Solutions

1. How to take a message for the guests?

Solutions:

2. How to let the guest know that there is a message for him/her?

Solutions:

M7-3　Knowledge Link

M7-4　Key to Exercises

Lesson Two　Wake-up Call Service

Objectives

➤ To help the students master useful expressions and sentences about wake-up call service.

> To help the students familiar with all kinds of way about wake-up call service.
> To help the students make some dialogues about wake-up call service.

Warming Up

1. Look at the following pictures and fill in the blanks according to the corresponding descriptions.

_____call is an in-house _____call to a _____ guest at a specific time to _____ him _____, predetermined by the guest. Wake-up call should be done in the morning at_____a.m. It depends on the guest in any time of the day.

It is the duty of _____division to wake up the guest. _____ will make the call.

Wake-up Call Record Sheet

Date 日期	Notifying Person 通知人	Guest Name 客人姓名	Room No. 房间号码	Time for wake-up Call 叫醒时间	Recorded By 记录者	Handled by 叫醒者	Remarks 备注

A wake-up call is very important, it has to be accurate according to request, otherwise people will be late for the_____, _____ or _____ and it will reflect badly on the hotel. The operator need to note the details on the _____.

M7-5　Warming Up

Dialogues

Key sentences:
> What time do you want the call?
> What kind of call would you like, by phone or by knocking at the door?
Pre-questions:
1. How to wake yourself up if you have something to do in the morning?
2. Did you receive any morning-call to wake you up before?

Dialogue 1

Guest:	I need to request a wake-up call for tomorrow morning.
Telephone Operator:	What time do you want the call?
Guest:	I need two calls, one at 7 and another at 7:15.
Telephone Operator:	We can certainly do that. Expect a call from us at 7:00, and then again at 7:15.
Guest:	Actually, can I change the latter wake-up call to 7:30 am?
Telephone Operator:	I can certainly do that. Is there anything else?
Guest:	I can't think of anything. If I do think of something, I'll be sure to call again.
Telephone Operator:	Okay. Good night, sir.

Dialogue 2

Guest:	I've got to get up early tomorrow, so please give me a wake-up call.
Telephone Operator:	Of course. We can give you a call anytime you like.
Guest:	Actually, I need two calls, one at 7 and the other at 7:15.
Telephone Operator:	Your wish is our command. Expect a call at 7, and another one at 7:15.
Guest:	Wait a minute! I don't like 7:15, now that I think about it. Change it to 7:30.
Telephone Operator:	The second call is now changed to 7:30. Is there anything else we can help you with?
Guest:	Nothing that I can think of right now. If something comes up, though, I'll call you.
Telephone Operator:	We're here all night long if you need anything.

Dialogue 3

Guest:	Will you do me a favor, Miss?
Room Attendant:	Certainly, sir.
Guest:	This is my first visit to China. I wonder if your hotel has the morning call service.
Room Attendant:	Yes, sir. Anyone who stays in our hotel can ask for the service. Would you like a morning call?
Guest:	Yes, I must get up earlier tomorrow. I want to go to the Bund to enjoy the morning scenery there. You know this is my first visit to Shanghai. People say there is a marvelous view of a poetic yet bustling life at the Bund just at dawn.
Room Attendant:	That's true. At what time do you want me to call you up, sir?
Guest:	At 6 sharp tomorrow morning，please.
Room Attendant:	What kind of call would you like, by phone or by knocking at the door?
Guest:	By phone. I don't want to disturb my neighbors.
Room Attendant:	Yes, sir. I'll tell the operator to call you up at 6 tomorrow morning. Anything else I can do for you?
Guest:	No. Thanks. Good night.
Room Attendant:	Good night, sir. Sleep well and have a pleasant dream.

Vocabulary

request [rɪ'kwest] *v.* 请求，需求，要求

command [kə'mɑ:nd] *n.* 命令，指挥

expect [ɪk'spekt] *v.* 期待，指望，预料

marvelous ['mɑ:vələs] *adj.* 了不起的，非凡的，令人惊异的

actually ['æktʃuəli] *adv.* 实际上，事实上

poetic [pəʊ'etɪk] *adj.* 诗意的，诗歌的

scenery ['si:n(ə)rɪ] *n.* 风景，景色

bustling ['bʌslɪŋ] *adj.* 熙熙攘攘的

dawn [dɔ:n] *n.* 黎明

Useful Expressions

1. At what time would you like us to call you tomorrow?

您想让我们明天早上什么时候叫醒您？

2. We will wake you up at 5:45 am tomorrow.

我们明早5点45分叫醒您。

3. We offer wake-up call service either by operator, by knocking at your door, or by in-room computer system. Which would you prefer?

我们的叫醒服务可以通过接线员、敲门及客房电脑系统实现。您喜欢哪一种方式？

4. At what time shall we call you?

我们什么时间给您打电话？

5. May I have your room number, please?

请问您的房间号码？

6. Would you like a morning call?

您要叫醒服务吗？

M7-6   Practice

Exercises

1. Questions and Answers

(1) Which positions in the hotel need to deal with the wake-up service?

(2) When a guest asks to be woken at certain time, what information the operator need to record?

2. Match the words or expressions in Column A with their Chinese equivalents in Column B.

A	B
(1) knock	a. 噩梦
(2) ring	b. 记住

(3) alarm   c. 睡懒觉

(4) clock   d. 宿醉

(5) mood   e. 响铃

(6) remember   f. 紧急

(7) nightmare   g. 敲门

(8) sleep late   h. 情绪

(9) hangover   i. 时钟

(10) emergency   j. 警报

3. Choose the best English translation for each sentence.

(1) 我们可以为您提供叫醒服务。

A. We are always at your service.

B. We have wake-up service for you.

C. Wake-up service is not available.

D. Please give me a morning call.

(2) 先生，您想让我几点叫您？

A. When will you come, sir?

B. What time do you want me to call you up, sir?

C. When was the call, sir?

D. What time do you want me to call you back, sir?

(3) 我们的电脑将会为您记录时间。

A. The time is limited if you want to use our computer.

B. Our computer is ok for you to use.

C. Our computer is available for you.

D. D. Our computer will record the time for you.

(4) 早上好，您的叫醒电话，现在是早上6点钟。

A. Good morning. This is your 6 o'clock wake-up call.

B. Good morning. This is the operator speaking.

C. Good morning. Now is 6 o'clock. Do you need wake-up call?

D. Good morning. 6 o'clock is the wake-up call time.

(5) 天气预报说今天有雨。

A. The weather forecast says that it will be stormy today.

B. The weather forecast says that it will be rainy today.

C. The weather forecast says that it will be snowy today.

D. The weather forecast says that it will be cloudy today.

4. Read the passage and decide if the statements are true (T) or false (F).

Wake Up Call Handling Tips

Give full attention to write proper room number, name and time to wake-up guest to avoid any mistake.

Always ensure that guest really wakes up after your call. You can politely ask the guest that if he wants to have a 2nd wake-up call or not.

If no reply is done by the guest while you are calling, or guest just hang up the phone and hardly give any reply then you should call him again.

While calling you should start this way, "Good morning, Mr.X. This is 6 AM in the morning which is your wake-up time. Have a nice day."

After getting your call, a guest may not understand the situation quickly as he just wake up. So give him some time and explain again why you call him.

If after 2nd, guest does not respond at all then send the bell person to knock his door and wake him up.

Exercises:

(1) We don't need to pay full attention when we are recording the guests' information. (   )

(2) We should make sure that guest really wakes up by our call. (   )

(3) If there is no respond by the guest, we should let it go. (   )

(4) We should start with saying "Good morning" of our wake-up call. (   )

(5) If there is still no respond, bell person should knock the room door and wake the guest up.

(   )

Challenges and Solutions

1. How to make morning/wake-up call for the guest?

Solutions:

2. If the guest has no respond for the wake-up call, what should you do?

Solutions:

3. If a guest asked for a morning call but he gave the clerk a wrong room number, what should you do?

Solutions:

4. Is there any other information you can provide to the guests while you making the wake-up call?

Solutions:

M7-7   Knowledge Link

M7-8   Key to Exercises

Lesson Three   Turn Down Service

Objectives

➤ To help the students master useful expressions and sentences about turn down service.

➤ To help the students familiar with all kinds of turn down service.

➤ To help the students make some dialogues about turn down service..

Warming Up

1. Look at the following pictures and fill in the blanks according to the corresponding descriptions.

_____ in hotel industry is a process when hotel staffs prepare guest room warm and inviting for sleeping.

The service is always carried out between _____ and ____ P.M. just before the guests return for the night.

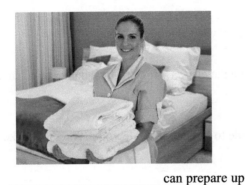

_____ can prepare up to 10 turn-down services per hour.

The conventional practice is to _____ a corner of the blankets to make the bed look inviting and that much more restful.

_____ also either _____ the bedcover nicely at the foot of the bed or put it and the day cushions away in a discreet shelf in the wardrobe.

An item of confectionery such as_____, or mints, fruit, or some other items is sometimes left on the _____ of a pillow or on the bed.

_____ the curtains.

_____ the light.

Some hotels leave the _____ order form or _____ door hanger on the bed.

Tidy the _____ room and _____ room.

M7-9　Warming Up

Dialogues

Key sentences:
> What time do you want the call?
> What kind of call would you like, by phone or by knocking at the door?

Pre-questions:

Whatare the purposes for turn-down service?

Dialogue 1

The room attendant knocks at the door and comes in to do the turn-down service for the guest.

Room Attendant:　Housekeeping. May I come in?

Guest:　　　　　Yes, please.

Room Attendant:　Good evening, sir. May I do the turn-down service for you now?

Guest:　　　　　What do you mean by turn-down service?

Room Attendant:　For turn-down service, I'll switch on certain lights, draw the curtains, make up your bed, empty the waste bin...

Guest:	I've just taken a bath. The bathroom is quite a mess now. The shampoo is spilt. The towels are dirty. The sink needs wiping. And the toilet roll has been finished.
Room Attendant:	No problem, sir. I'll tidy it up.
Guest:	One more thing, the minibar needs refilling.
Room Attendant:	I'll have someone refill it right away.
Guest:	Thank you very much.
Room Attendant:	My pleasure.

Dialogue 2

Room Attendant:	Good evening, madam and sir. May I do the turn down service for you now?
Guest:	Oh, thank you. But you see, we are having some friends over. We're going to have a small party here in the room. Could you come back in three hours?
Room Attendant:	Certainly, madam. I'll let the overnight staff know. They will come then.
Guest:	That's fine. Well, our friends seem to be a little late. Would you tidy up a bit in the bathroom? I've just taken a bath and it is quite a mess now. Besides, please bring us a bottle of just boiled water. We'd treat our guests to typical Chinese tea.
Room Attendant:	Yes, madam. I'll bring in some fresh towels together with the drinking water.
Guest:	Ok.

Having done all on request.

Room Attendant:	It's growing dark. Would you like me to draw the curtains for you, sir and madam?
Guest:	Why not? That would be so cozy.
Room Attendant:	May I turn on the lights for you?
Guest:	Yes, please. I'd like to do some reading while waiting.
Room Attendant:	Yes, sir. Is there anything I can do for you?
Guest:	No more. You're a smart girl indeed. Thank you very much.
Room Attendant:	I'm always at your service. Goodbye, sir and madam, and do have a very pleasant evening.

Dialogue 3

Guest:	Hello, this is Mr. Fox in room 2019.
Receptionist:	Hello! How can I help you?
Guest:	My Daughter will be staying with me tonight, so I need an extra bed in my room.
Receptionist:	OK. We can bring up a fold-out bed for you.
Guest:	Thank you. My daughter is bringing her baby, so I will also need a cot.
Receptionist:	That's no problem.
Guest:	Can you bring some extra blankets as well?
Receptionist:	You have some extra blankets on your wardrobe.
Guest:	Will you bring sheets and bedding for the extra bed?
Receptionist:	Yes, of course.
Guest:	Will there be an extra charge for this?

Receptionist:　No, there will be no extra cost.
Guest:　Good. Thank you.

Vocabulary

mess [mes]　*v.* 弄乱

shampoo [ʃæm'puː]　*n.* 洗发水

spilt [spɪlt]　*v.* 洒出，溢出

sink [sɪŋk]　*n.* 水槽，洗涤槽

wiping ['waɪpɪŋ]　*v.* 擦干

toilet ['tɔɪlɪt] roll　*n.* 卫生纸，卷纸

refill [riː'fɪl]　*v.* 再装满，再充满

overnight [əʊvə'naɪt]　*adj.* 晚上的，通宵的

cozy ['kəʊzɪ]　*adj.* 舒适的，安逸的

fold-out bed　*n.* 折叠床

cot [kɒt]　*n.* 简易床，轻便小床

Useful Expressions

1. May I do the turn-down service for you now?
现在我可以为你做夜床服务吗？

2. I'm sorry to disturb you.
很抱歉打扰您。

3. Please us this card if you need turn-down service.
如需做夜床服务，请使用这张卡片。

4. When would you like me to come back?
您希望我什么时候再来？

5. May I have your room number, please?
请问您的房间号码是多少？

6. Would you like a turn-down service before you go to bed?
睡觉之前您想来个夜床服务吗？

M7-10　Practice

Exercises

1. Questions and Answers

(1) What do we prepare for turn down service?

(2) Do we need to clean the room while turn down service?

2. Match the words or expressions in Column A with their Chinese equivalents in Column B.

A	B
(1) pajama	a. 糖果
(2) slipper	b. 欢迎信
(3) atmosphere	c. 浴巾
(4) flower bunch	d. 睡衣
(5) champagne	e. 拖鞋
(6) bath towel	f. 饼干
(7) candy	g. 气氛
(8) gift card	h. 香槟
(9) cookie	i. 花束
(10) welcome letter	j. 贺卡

3. Choose the best English translation for each sentence.

(1) 乐意效劳。

A. I'm happy to come here.   B. Hope you'll be happy.

C. I'm always at your service.   D. Enjoy your stay.

(2) 您介意我现在收拾房间吗？

A. Would you mind me making up the room now?

B. Would you like to use the room now?

C. Later I'll come to make the room. Is that ok?

D. Would you like me to do the turn down service?

(3) 现在可以为您做夜床服务了吗？

A. May I do the room service for you now?

B. May I do the turn down service for you now?

C. We provide turn down service for every room.

D. Turn down service is available now.

(4) 我可以给您拿一张折叠床过来。

A. I'll bring you a fold-out bed.   B. I'll bring you a small bed.

C. Fold-out bed is out of order, sorry. D. Please send back the fold-out bed.

(5) 没有附加费用。

A. There is no extra charge.   B. Surcharge is needed.

C. Service charge is needed.   C. There is extra charge you need to pay.

4. Read the passage and decide if the statements are true (T) or false (F).

Turndown service:

• The evening boy takes the status report of the floor from the desk.

• Takes the floor key/card and sign for it.

• Take a round of the floor corridor to maintain it clean and tidy. Take out trolley.

• Vacant rooms to be serviced from 6:00 p.m. onward.

• By 10.pm turn down service to be finished of all rooms.

• Departure rooms have to be cleared as per requirements.

Enter the guest room:

• Find out if the guest is in the room.

• Announce yourself before entering the guest room.

• In case the guest is wants you to come back later then, politely as the time for Position the maids cart in front of the guest room.

Turndown the bed:

• Enter the room, empty dustbin and ashtrays.

• Remove the bedcover, fold it and place in the luggage rack drawer.

• Remove pillow from luggage rack and place it on the head of the bed.

• Make 90 angles with the second sheet.

• Quilt and third sheet.

• Spread the foot mat on the side of the bed. [The side where the corner is made] and put slipper on top of foot mat.

- Always give turndown from the telephone side or inner side of the bed.
- For double occupancy, both corner to be made.

Place turndown amenities:
- According to the hotel procedure place the turndown amenities on the bed. (Eg: Flower, Chocolate etc.)
- Place the Breakfast menu knob on the fold.
- Put on the bedside lamp.

Tidy the guest room:
- Look around the room and straighten or tidy anything that is out of order.
- If a room is messy it may require more extensive cleaning.
- Remove any room service tray, dishes and move them to the service pantry.
- Empty the trash cans and replace the wastebasket liners.
- Do a quick vacuum if required.

Tidy the bathroom:
- Neatly fold used towels.
- Wipe the vanity area if required.
- If required replace the bathing towel.
- Clear the dustbin if used.

Create a pleasant atmosphere:
- Turn on the bedside lamps.
- Close the drapes.
- Draw the curtains so that there is no light coming from the corners or center.
- Set the A/C temperature to what was set by the guest.
- Double check everything, lock the room and leave the guest room.
- Update the status report.

Exercises:

(1) Turn down service should finish at 7 o'clock. (　　)

(2) When enter the guest room, we should make sure if the guest is in the room. (　　)

(3) Dust bin and ashtray need to be emptied. (　　)

(4) Bedside lamp or light need to be put on. (　　)

(5) Rock music is very good for creating a pleasant atmosphere. (　　)

Challenges and Solutions

1. What is important about the turn-down service?

Solutions:

2. What are the steps of turn-down service?

Solutions:

3. What we must do if the guests refuse turn-down service?

Solutions:

4. What are all supplies used to make an extra bed?

Solutions:

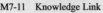
M7-11 Knowledge Link

M7-12 Key to Exercises

Lesson Four Booking Tickets Service

Objectives

➢ To help the students master useful expressions and sentences about booking tickets service.

➢ To help the students familiar with all kinds of way about booking tickets.

➢ To help the students make some dialogues about booking tickets service.

Warming Up

1. Look at the following pictures and fill in the blanks according to the corresponding descriptions.

Ticket-booking in the _____ is a service provided by the hotel to meet the guests' demand of transportation convenience. The tickets mainly include _____, _____, _____, and _____.

_____   _____   _____

M7-13　Warming Up

Dialogues

Key sentences:

➢ What can I do for you?

➢ When will you...?

Pre-questions:

1. Have you ever booked flight ticket before?

2. What will you suggest the guest if all the tickets are fully booked?

Dialogue 1

Clerk:	Good afternoon. What can I do for you?
Guest:	Is there any flight to Beijing on July, 5th?
Clerk:	Let me see. Yes, there are two flights: one is 8 o'clock in the morning, the other is 5 o'clock in the afternoon.
Guest:	I'd like to book the 8 a.m. flight.
Clerk:	Ok. May I have your passport, please?
Guest:	Here you are.
Clerk:	All right. First class or economy class?
Guest:	Economy class.
Clerk:	And a window seat or an aisle seat?
Guest:	A window seat, please. How much is it, please?
Clerk:	$350.

Dialogue 2

Clerk:	Good evening, sir. What can I do for you?
Mr. Black:	Good evening. I'm Jim Black, in room 1703. Is there any flight to New York on December 15th?
Clerk:	Oh, let me see. There are three flights. The planes take off at about 8 a.m., 1 p.m. and 5 p.m..
Mr. Black:	I'll take 1 p.m. plane, then. Would you please book a ticket for me?

Clerk:	Certainly. Would you please fill in this form and show me your passport?
Mr. Black:	All right. Here you are.
Clerk:	How do you want to fly, economy or first class?
Mr. Black:	First class, please.
Clerk:	And a window seat or an aisle seat?
Mr. Black:	A window seat, please. Shall I pay cash now?
Clerk:	Yes, please pay 1000 yuan in advance.
Mr. Black:	Is there any service charge?
Clerk:	Yes, sir. You need to pay an extra charge of 3%.
Mr. Black:	Ok. And when can I get the ticket?
Clerk:	We'll have the ticket sent to you on the morning of December 13th. Would you leave me your phone number?
Mr. Black:	Ok. My telephone number is 18877438865.
Clerk:	All right, sir. Let me check the information with you again. Your name is Jim Black and live in room 1703. You want an economy class flight ticket to New York on December 15th, at 1.p.m. You need to pay 1,030 yuan now.
Mr. Black:	Ok. That's correct. Here is my card.

Dialogue 3

Clerk:	Good morning, sir. How may I help you?
Guest:	I'd like to take my daughter to go to the Disney Land. Would you please help us book the tickets?
Clerk:	Of course, sir. Let me check the information for you. When do you want to go?
Guest:	The day after tomorrow.
Clerk:	Well, sir. How old is your daughter?
Guest:	She is 5 now.
Clerk:	Oh, lovely. How many days do you want to spend there?
Guest:	It's a huge park and my daughter is a fun of the Disney princess. So, I think maybe two days.
Clerk:	Ok. They have a 2-day ticket called Park Hopper Ticket. The price for you is $260, and $248 for your daughter. $508 in total.
Guest:	Well, I'll take it.
Clerk:	May I know your name and your room number, please?
Guest:	My name is Jim Parker, and my room number is 1109.
Clerk:	Ok, Mr. Parker. I've booked the 2-day Hopper Ticket for you and your daughter on line. You can use the tickets within 13 days after you get them. The total price is $508. You don't need to get the ticket by yourself. We'll send the tickets to your room as soon as we get them.
Guest:	That's wonderful. Is there any surcharge?
Clerk:	Yes. The ticket service charge is $20.
Guest:	Ok, that's reasonable.
Clerk:	How would you like to pay, by credit card or in cash?
Guest:	Credit card, please.

Vocabulary

passport ['pɑ:spɔ:t]   *n.* 护照

economy [ɪ'kɒnəmɪ]   *n.* 经济

aisle [aɪl]   *n.* 过道，通道

in advance   *adv.* 提前，预先

charge[tʃɑ:dʒ]   *n.* 收费，费用

Useful Expressions

1. Which day's tickets would you like?

您要哪天的票？

2. Which seats would you like, first class or economy class?

您要什么位子，头等舱还是经济舱？

3. Are the seats together?

座位是要连在一起吗？

4. Which train would you like to take?

您想坐哪次车？

5. A seat or a berth?

您要坐席还是卧铺呢？

6. One way or a round trip ticket?

单程票还是双程票？

7. I'm afraid that flight/train/show is fully booked.

我恐怕那个航班/火车/演出的票已经订完了。

8. There are no seats available on the flight leaving at 16:15.

16点15分起飞的航班，票已经售完。

9. Hard berth tickets are not available now.

硬卧票已售完。

10. How about a soft berth ticket?

软卧怎么样？

M7-14   Practice

Exercises

1. Questions and Answers

(1) What are the reasons about the guests booking tickets from the hotel.

(2) What information should you ask if the guest want to book a travel ticket?

2. Match the words or expressions in Column A with their Chinese equivalents in Column B.

A	B
(1) cancel	a. 靠走廊座位

(2) book	b. 售罄
(3) one-way	c. 旅行社
(4) private room	d. 可利用的，可获得的
(5) aisle seat	e. 单程
(6) seat belt	f. 取消
(7) travel agency	g. 预定
(8) airline	h. 包间
(9) available	i. 安全带
(10) sell out	j. 航空公司

3. Choose the best English translation for each sentence.

(1) 您想看哪天的演出？

A. Whendo you want to see the show?

B. Where is the show played?

C. Which day will you come?

D. What time will you come to the show?

(2) 您想要什么舱位，经济舱还是头等舱？

A. Do you have economy-class seat?

B. Would you like economy-class or the first-class?

C. Which one is cheaper, economy-class seat or the first-class seat?

D. Is the economy-class seat ok for you?

(3) 您需要几张票？

A. How many tickets do you want?　　　　B. How many tickets are available?

C. How much do you need to pay?　　　　D. How would you like to pay?

(4) 票已售完。

A. There is no room for the show.　　　　B. The tickets are not available now.

C. We don't have tickets.　　　　D. We just stopped the tickets booking.

(5) 您在选座方面有什么偏好吗？

A. How do you choose the seat?　　　　B. Do you like the seat?

C. Do you have any preferences about the seat?　　D. Would you like to sit here?

4. Read the passage and decide if the statements are true (T) or false (F).

Seattle Hotel Business Center

With a full range of services, The Westin Seattle's hotel business center has everything guests need to ensure the stay updated and connected while traveling. With access to our Seattle hotel business center's own FedEx Office, guests will be able to conveniently print, fax and ship from our downtown Seattle hotel. Open Monday - Friday from 7:00 AM - 6:00 PM and Saturday and Sunday from 9:00 AM - 2:00 PM, fees at the FedEx Office may apply.

Seattle Hotel Business Center Services:

- 24-hour access with guest room key
- 3 PCs available for use
- Laser printer available for use
- Outlets for headphones and speakers
- Complimentary printing of boarding passes

- House telephone that dials directly to Service Express® and the Customer Support Help Desk

FedEx Office Services:

- Faxing-incoming and outgoing
- Photocopying-black & white, color, transparencies
- High Speed Internet Access and computer workstations
- Laser printing-black & white and color
- Shipping-incoming and outgoing; on-site tracking for packages received; full-service outbound processing of FedEx Express and Ground packages
- Office supplies
- For shipping instructions and a complete list of handling/storage fees, please contact The Westin Seattle's FedEx Office at (206) 441-5116.

Exercises:

(1) Guests can print, fax and ship from the hotel business center. (   )

(2) Guests can enter the business center by their key card. (   )

(3) There are more than 10 computers for use. (   )

(4) Guests can only black photocopy their documents. (   )

(5) FedEx Office is a 24-hour service venue. (   )

Challenges and Solutions

1. If the tickets have been fully booked, what should you do?

Solutions:

2. What you booked the wrong ticket for the guest, what should you do?

Solutions:

3. If your ticket booking system is out of order, what should you do?

Solutions:

M7-15   Knowledge Link

M7-16   Key to Exercises

Lesson Five   Butler Service

Objectives

➤ To help the students master useful expressions and sentences about butler service.

➤ To help the students familiar with all kinds of butler service.

➤ To help the students make some dialogues about butler service.

Warming Up

1. Look at the following pictures and fill in the blanks according to the corresponding descriptions.

"_____" defines as "the principle man servant of a household". This definition remains true even when the butler is employed in a hotel. When the guest checks in and has occupied his suite then this becomes his household, the butler caring for him becomes the "manager" of the suite and in effect of the guest.

The _____ for butler service includes: taking care of guest request, bookings, reservation, problems, complaints, supervising and coordinating every service that receives in suite and ensure guest satisfaction by paying attention to the smallest detail from arrival to departure. Butler services are not required in all hotels. This is considered an amenity at a wide variety of first class resorts.

M7-17　Warming Up

Dialogues

Key sentences:
- ➢ Please let me know if there's anything I can do for you.
- ➢ May I suggest...
- ➢ Would you mind...
- ➢ How many...do you have?
- ➢ I will be careful of...

Pre-questions:

1. What should you do when the guest comes into the business center?

2. What will you suggest the guest if all the tickets are fully booked?

Dialogue 1

Butler:	Good afternoon. Mr. and Mrs. Roy. It's really honoring to have you here. Welcome to our hotel. I'm Tommy, your butler.
Guest:	Good afternoon, Tommy.
Butler:	Your suite is ready. Please follow me, and I will lead you there.
Guest:	That's great. Let's go.
Butler:	Here we are. Let me open the door for you.
Guest:	Thank you.
Butler:	Your suitcase will be here shortly. The bellman is handling them. How do you like this suite?
Guest:	Oh, it looks comfortable and cozy. We like it very much.
Butler:	The rooms are all facing south and commands a good view of the Pearl River.
Guest:	Yes, how lovely it is!
Butler:	It would be stunning in the evening when all the lights on. Don't miss the famous "Night Scene of the Pearl River". You may also take a boat trip along the river at night. It is a must for every tourist to this city.
Guest:	Oh, nice. Thank you for your suggestion.
Butler:	It's a pleasure. Is there anything I can do before I leave?
Guest:	No, thank you very much, Tommy.
Butler:	You're welcome, sir. I'm always at your service. Goodbye, Mr. and Mrs. Roy.

Dialogue 2

Mr. Bloom:	We would like to go for sightseeing tomorrow. Do you have some suggestions?
Butler:	Of course. I'd be more than happy to help. The Status of Liberty is always a good place to start your visit about this city.
Mr. Bloom:	I saw the Status of Liberty on my last visit here. Can you recommend somewhere else?
Butler:	Hmm. What type of interests do you have?
Mr. Bloom:	In my spare time, I really like to view art and go running.
Butler:	Aha! Have you been to Central Park on the Museum of Modern Art?
Mr. Bloom:	No, but I've heard a lot about them.
Butler:	Well, Central Park is wonderful for running. Afterwards, you should head to the Museum to enjoy the art.
Mr. Bloom:	Great! That sounds like a plan. Thanks a lot.
Butler:	I'm sure you'll have a good time there.

Dialogue 3

Butler:	Mr. Robin, what can I do for you?
Guest:	Can you get me a taxi?
Butler:	We offer various types of transportation. Perhaps you'd like to upgrade to a private vehicle?
Guest:	Thanks, but no. A taxi will be just fine.

Butler:	Got it, sir. Where would you like to take the taxi to?
Guest:	My destination is Rockefeller Center.
Butler:	What time do you want to leave the hotel?
Guest:	As soon as possible.
Butler:	I'll call the taxi immediately, Mr. Robin.
Guest:	I'm coming downstairs now.
Butler:	A brand new taxi is pulling up now, Mr. Robin.

Vocabulary

cozy ['kozi]　*adj.* 舒适的，安逸的

command [kə'mænd]　*v.* 命令，指挥

vehicle ['viəkəl]　*n.* 车辆，交通工具

destination [ˌdestɪ'neɪʃ(ə)n]　*n.* 目的地

pull up　停车

Useful Expressions

1. Is this everything, sir?
这是全部东西吗，先生？

2. Here's the closet and there's the bathroom.
这是壁橱。 这是洗澡间。

3. How do you like this room?
您觉得这个房间怎么样？

4. Here is a fax for you.
有您的传真。

5. Pardon me for interrupting.
对不起打扰了。

6. I'm sorry I was so careless.
很抱歉我太粗心了。

7. I'll report it to my manager.
我将向我的经理汇报。

8. Glad to be of service. Please feel free to contact us anytime.
很高兴问您服务。有需要请随时通知我们。

9. I'm sorry I cannot guarantee, but I'll do my best.
对不起，我不能保证，但我一定会尽我全力去做。

10. My pleasure, I'm happy everything was to your satisfaction.
这是我的荣幸。我很高兴一切都能令您满意。

11. Would you like me to call a taxi for you?
您需要我为您叫出租车吗？

M7-18　Practice

Exercises

1. Questions and Answers

(1) What the benefits for butler service?

(2) What qualities does the butler need to fulfill?

2. Match the words or expressions in Column A with their Chinese equivalents in Column B.

A	B
(1) luggage	a. 高雅的

(2) baby sitter   b. 礼节、礼仪

(3) ball   c. 个人卫生

(4) evening gown   d. 满意

(5) etiquette   e. 舞会

(6) shake hands   f. 保姆、儿童看护

(7) decent   g. 晚礼服

(8) elegant   h. 行李

(9) personal hygiene   i. 握手

(10) satisfaction   j. 得体的

3. Choose the best English translation for each sentence.

(1) 您的衣服需要熨烫吗？

A. Does your cloth need to be pressed?   B. Doyou have ironing service?

C. I'd like my clothes pressed.   D. Ironing service is available now.

(2) 您要在哪一天参加舞会？

A. When will you leave?   B. What do you want?

C. Which day would you like to join the ball?   D. Which kind of ticket do you want?

(3) 有直达东京的航班吗？

A. Is there a non-stop flight to Tokyo?   B. I'd like to fly to Tokyo.

C. Do you have one-way ticket to Tokyo?   D. Let's go to Tokyo directly.

(4) 我们愿意为客人提供优质服务。

A. It's our pleasure to serve our guests well.   B. It's out honor to have you here.

C. Great service is our aim.   D. We have great customer service.

(5) 这边请。 这是我们的贵宾室。

A.Come with me please. This is the dining hall.   B. You go first. Our VIP room is over there.

C. This way, please. This is our VIP room.   D. Follow me. Our VIP room is upstairs.

4. Read the passage and decide if the statements are true (T) or false (F).

Butler Service Concept and Practice

"SMS to SMS"

To create warm and limitless hospitality concept on the basis of traditional and modern service approach to delight the guest recommend hotel to others guests and create brand loyalty.

The thinking behind creating world class Butler service is to deliver on our Brand Promise of Limitless Hospitality, i.e.

"An endeavor to fulfill an impossible request

To satisfy a fleeting wish and delight the most discerning Guest"

To provide an international service experience with Indian touch of hospitality which would start from SMS andfinish with SMS.

Butler Service design would consist of seven stages.

Stage 1: Making the reservation

Reservation personal would confirm the guest request two days prior to his arrival sharing services of abutler.

Stage 2: Pre-arrival

1. Butler will follow up for Guest Preference Questionnaire, Guest Profile History & Notes

and if he/she is acelebrity; try to find out information of likes/dislikes from the internet

2. Butler would send an introductory welcome SMS to guest Saying "Namaskar Mr. X! Welcome to Delhi, I amWasim, your Butler, At your Service,waiting in the hotel lobby. Warm regards (name of the hotel.)"

3. Butler would check the room thoroughly in assistance with housekeeping to ensure guest request are taken care of.

4. Butler would coordinate with reservation in regards car pick-up.

5. Butler would check the vehicle amenities and car condition ie music, news paper and fragrance in the car also grooming of a driver as per brand specification.

Stage 3: Guest Arrival

1. Butler would coordinate with the Airport Representative to receive the guest at the arrival gate, and assist the guest in handling baggage.

2. Chauffeur will convey the time of arrival to Butler Cell/DM Cell.

3. Butler to welcome the guest at the Main Porch "Namaskar Mr. X, Welcome to The Lalit New Delhi, I amWasim, At your Service."

4. Butler to direct bell team to handle the luggage.

5. Butler to immediately serve Welcome drink with bottle of water in the lobby upon arrival

6. Butler to ensure guest baggage reaches the room before guest arrives to the room

7. Guest check in formalities would be done in the room by the butler in assistance with front office personal.

8. Butler would make the guest comfortable and will do room familiarization.

9. Butler would arrange for property orientation as per guest convenience "Sir may I arrange property orientation as per your convenience" Also provide information about local tourist attractions andshopping details, if the guest is on a first time leisure trip.

10. Butler would ask for the food and other preferences. "Sir, as per your instruction we have reserveda table for you at Baluchi; our Indian specialty restaurant" .

11. Butler would offer the unpacking of luggage and ask for laundry and shoe care service "Sir, may Iunpack you luggage, and arrange the wardrobe according to your preference. Also would you require laundry service or shoe care service now?"

12. Butler would set up the wardrobe. If guest does not have particular preference please follow wardrobe process SOP

13. Butler would assist the guest in planning the day and entire stay. "Sir, would there be any plans for the day"

14. Butler would check the guest's meal/refreshment requirement and do the needful as per order and instruction by the guest.

15. Should the guest stay in the room and relax, butler would move out of guest room with the guestpermission "Sir, should you need any assistance please call me as per your convenience." Andhand the Butler visiting card

16. Before wishing the guest good night check for Wakeup call or bed tea and morning plans of the guest like YOGA, Swimming, etc.

Stage 4: Guest In house

1. Butler must be the first person entering the room should guest require his services otherwise

butler would meet the guest at the time of breakfast

2. Butler would take care of other service which guest would require like restaurant reservation,laundry, spa etc.

3. Butler would ensure chef of the restaurant meets the guest.

4. Butler would ensure culinary greeting is placed in the room with chef's signature.

5. Butler would follow up the on the housekeeping with regards to room cleanliness and turn down service.

6. Butler would ensure all the amenities are placed on time to time basis.(guest amenities would be changed on daily basis except wine)

7. Butler would ask if guest needs pre dinner cocktails etc. " Sir would you like me to arrange for some cocktails this evening"

8. For the business travelers butler would assist in basic sartorial services and assisting the guest in with regards to meeting and appointment should it happen in the hotel.

9. Butler will act like a medium between guest and hotel operations.

10. Butler would be responsible for room upkeep and cleaning during guest stay in coordination with Housekeeping.

Stage 5: Pre departures

1. Butler would assist guest packing one day prior to their departure from hotel " Sir may I assist you in packing your baggage"

2. Butler would ensure guest feedback is taken and recorded and required action is taken " Sir would you like to share your feedback regarding your stay with us"

3. Butler would coordinate with guest as well as with GM as per guest convenience, butler to arrange for a souvenir which would be handed over by GM/RM/FOM to guest.

4. Butler will check the exact time of guest departure and would arrange the transfer accordingly.

Stage 6: Departures

1. Butler would ensure proper bill settlement is done in the room itself with the assistance of a Front office personal.

2. Butler would coordinate with bell desk in regard to the language transfer and loading.

3. Butler would check the room thoroughly to ensure no baggage or article is left behind.

4. Butler will escort the guest till main porch and bid farewell "thank you for staying at The LaLiT New Delhi and giving us the pleasure of serving you. Have a safe journey"

Stage 7: Follow up

1. Butler will send SMS saying "Thank you for choosing The LaLiT , it was pleasure to serve you with regards (butler name)and (hotel name")

2. On the next day of guest departure a thank you mail would be send to the guest by the GM also requesting them to leave a feedback on e-survey.

3. Butler would create guest record system in computer as per the standard format.

Exercises:

(1) It is unnecessary to do any preparation before guest comes. (   )

(2) Butler would coordinate with the Airport Representative to receive the guest at the arrival gate, and assist the guest in handling baggage. (   )

(3) Butler has no responsibility to set up the wardrobe. (　　)

(4) Butler should help the guest plan their stay in the hotel. (　　)

(5) Butler need to make sure the guest departure time before guest living. (　　)

Challenges and Solutions

1. How to call the taxi for the guest?

Solutions:

2. How to prepare the wedding anniversary to the guest?

Solutions:

3. What need to be prepared before the guest check in as the butler?

Solutions:

4. How to give tourist advice to the guest?

Solutions:

M7-19　Knowledge Link

M7-20　Key to Exercises

Lesson Six　Handling Complaints

Objectives

➢ To help the students master useful expressions and sentences about complaints in hotel.

➢ To help the students familiar with the common complaints in the hotel service aspects.

➢ To help the students analyze the reasons of complaints and handle complaints in the hotel service aspects.

Preamble

To:manager@hotelone.com

Subject: Registering my protest against below par services

Respected Sir,

I am writing this email to file my complaint against the unprofessional attitude of your staff. I am a regular visitor of Hotel One and during my last visit on Sunday, October 11, 2016 I was very disappointed by the standard of your service.

I booked room number 251 well in advance and then got confirmation before leaving but when I reached they told me there is no reservation against my name. Though, I got a room but then the service was so substandard that I had to leave early in the morning.

This is so unprofessional and I was not expecting this from an organization like yours. I hope you will look into this matter and resolve this situation. You can contact me on 962-194-174.

I will wait for your response.

Sincerely,

Matt Keyworth

Dialogues

Key sentences:

➢ What's the problem with...?

➢ I'm sorry, sir. ...will come and check it right away.

➢ I'll send for a/an ... for you.

➢ Any comments and suggests are always welcome.

➢ I assure you it will never happen again.

Pre-questions:

1. What complaints are always happening about hotel service?

2. How should we deal with the angry guest?

Dialogue 1

Guest:	When I first arrived I was assured that a bottle of Chivas Regis would always be in the mini-bar. Well I'm here now and the bottle isn't. what kind of hotel are you running here anyway!
Staff:	I sincerely apologize for the oversight, sir. We have been exceedingly busy today because of the convention. I'll have a complimentary bottle delivered immediately. Please accept it with our compliments.
Guest:	Well, I should hope it would be complimentary. Thank you. Good bye.

Dialogue 2

Guest:	I had reserved a tennis court, but it has been taken over by someone else.
Staff:	Yes, sir. I understand. But we have a policy that if a party is more than 15 minutes late for a starting time, we schedule the courts for other waiting guests. I'm so sorry for the inconvenience. Would you like to reschedule?
Guest:	I requested the eggs over hard, these are over easy.
Staff:	Sorry about that, sir. Let me make you some more right away.

Dialogue 3

Guest:	This tea is sweetened, and I specifically wanted unsweetened tea.
Waiter:	I am sorry, ma'am. I'll bring an unsweetened tea immediately. Please excuse the mistake.
Guest:	No problem, things happen.
Waiter:	Here's your tea, ma'am. Let me know if I can be of further assistance. Enjoy the rest of your meal.
Guest:	Thank you.

Vocabulary

assure [ə'ʃɔ:] *v.* 保证，确保

oversight ['əuvəsaɪt] *n.* 疏忽

exceed [ɪk'si:d]   *v.* 超过，胜过

convention [kən'venʃ(ə)n]   *n.* 大会，会议

complimentary [kɒmplɪ'ment(ə)rɪ]   *adj.* 赠送的，免费赠送

compliment ['kɒmplɪm(ə)nt]   *n.* 致意，心意，恭维

policy ['pɒləsɪ]   *n.* 政策

schedule ['skedʒʊl/'ʃedju:l]   *v.* 安排，计划

Useful Expressions

1. Would you mind giving me some details? If I could just have your name, room number, what time you called and who you spoke to exactly.

您介意告诉我更多信息吗?您能告诉我您的名字和房间号，以及是什么时候给客房部打电话，和谁通话的呢？

2. I'll speak to housekeeping straight away. Apologies for the inconvenience, I would like to offer you free voucher for two nights stay on your next visit. You can use it any time you like.

我会马上和客房部沟通。我确保不会再发生这样的事情了。为了弥补给您造成的不便，我想给您提供未来2晚的免费入住。我把这个券给您，您可以随时使用。

3. I'd like to apologize on behalf of our hotel.

我想代表我们酒店表达我最深的歉意。

4. I'm sorry，sir. Please excuse her. We are very busy today.

对不起，先生，请您原谅她，我们今天实在太忙了。

5. I am sorry，sir. We are short of hands today. Would you please have a drink first?

先生对不起，我们今天人手少，您是不是先喝点什么？

6. We might overlooked some points.

我们可能忽略一些细小的地方。

7. We do apologize for the inconvenience.

我们为给您带来不便深表歉意。

8. There could have been some mistake. I do apologize.

可能是出了什么差错，实在对不起。

9. Our manager is not in town. Shall I get our assistant manager for you?

我们的经理不在本地。我帮您叫助理经理来好吗？

10. To express our regret for all the trouble，we offer you a 10% discount/complimentary flowers.

我们给您带来这么多麻烦，为了表示歉意，特为您提供9折/免费花篮。

11. This is really the least we can do for you.

我们能为您做的实在太有限了。

Exercises

1. Match each word or phrase in the column on the left with its meaning in the column on the right

(1) manager   a. to go to an event such as a meeting or a class.

(2) understaffed   b. to have something in your hand, hands, or arms.

(3) policy   c. to make it possible for someone to have or do something.

(4) attend   d. someone whose job is to manage part or all of a company or other

organization.

(5) hold   e. not having enough workers, or fewer workers than usual.

(6) request   f. a way of doing something that has been officially agreed.

(7) instruction   g. a polite or formal demand for something.

(8) arrange   h. a statement telling someone what they must do.

(9) attitude   i. something done.

(10) action   j. the opinions and feelings that you usually have about something.

2. Complete the following dialogue according to the Chinese in brackets and read it in roles.

A=Staff   B=Guest

A: Good evening, sir. Did you ring for service? What can I do for you?

B: Good evening. The light in my room is too dim. _____（您能给我换个亮一点的吗？）

A: Certainly, sir. I'll be back right away.

(A few minutes later, the housekeeper replaces the light bulb)

A: How is the light now?

B: It's much better now. Thank you.

A: You're welcome. _____（还有什么我能为您做的吗？）

B: Oh, yes, the room is too cold for me. Can you turn off the air conditioner?

A: Certainly, sir. But the air conditioner is already off.

B: Maybe I've caught a cold. I think I need to take some medicine.

A: _____（我帮您倒杯水好吗）？

B: Thanks a lot.

A: _____（不用谢）.

3. Choose the best English translation for each sentence.

(1) 我们会设法安排的。

A. We'll take care of it.   B. We'll take it.   C. We'll manage it.   D. We'll handle it.

(2) 我保证这种事情不会再发生了。

A. Iassure you it won't happen again.   B. I'm sure you'll be fine.

C. I'm sure you'll find out the result.   D. I'm assure it will happen again.

(3) 这是饭店的规定。

A. It's the method of the hotel.   B. It's the policy of the hotel.

C. You're not allowed to do in our hotel.   D. This is the way of the hotel.

(4) 我马上处理这件事。

A. I'llattend to it at once.   B. I'll go there as soon as possible.

C. I'll do it right now.   D. I'll help you.

(5) 我理解您的感受。

A. I got it.   B. Oh, I see.

C. Iunderstand how you feel.   D. I know your meaning.

4. Read the passage and answer the following questions.

How to Deal with Complaints

Hotel staff, like people working in other service businesses, are bound to receive complaints and criticisms as well as compliments and commendations. Some of the complaints and criticisms are well justified and very constructive. They are perfect reminders of the areas of hotel service that still leave something to be desired. Other complaints are just the result of fastidious and difficult personalities. People who make complaints and criticism can be friendly and reasonable; they can also be rude and argument with the guest is the most undesirable thin that can happen to a staff member and the hotel.

In handling complaints, the hotel staff should always be polite and helpful. He/She should always must not interrupt the guest unless necessary. It is also advisable for him/her to jot down what the guest has said. He/ She should then make a short apology and express his/her understanding of the guest's situation or sympathize with the guest. Only when he/she puts himself/herself in the guest's shoes can he/she look at the problem from the other person's perspective. And only when the staff member can look at the guest's problem in guest's way can he/she be ready to sympathize with the guest. After that the staff member should take actions quickly to remove the complaint, either by making polite, patient and detailed explanations, or making shift, effective corrections and remedies, or reporting the complaint to a superior. But whatever he/she intends to do he must keep the guest informed of the measures or actions he plans to take and when he/she will carry them out.

It is not easy to always be nice to the guest, especially when the guest is unfriendly and rude, even abusive. But the success of any business in the hospitality industry depends on people-pleasers. With good training and a lot of practical experience with guests everyone can master the art of being nice to guests. Just keep one thing in mind: that is, a dissatisfied guest means a loss of potential future business while a pleased guest leaves the hotel with a warm memory of the hospitality he has enjoyed and inclination to repeat his visit to the hotel.

Questions

1. Why do we say hotel staff receive not only compliments and commendations?
2. Is it reasonable for hotel staff to argue with an unfriendly guest?
3. What kind of attitude should service givers take when a customer complaint?

Challenges and Solutions

1. If the guest's behavior is against the hotel policy, what should you do?
Solutions:
2. What will you do if the guest lost his valuable goods in the room?
Solutions:
3. If the guest mistook something but he insists to complain our hotel staff, what will you do?
Solutions:
4. If the guest is very rude, what will you do?
Solutions:

M7-21 Knowledge Link

M7-22 Key to Exercises

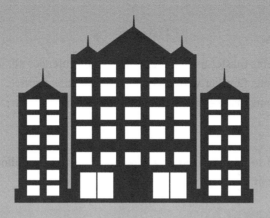

Chapter 8

Other Services

Lesson One   Meeting Service

Objectives

➢ To help the students master useful expressions and sentences about meeting service.
➢ To help the students familiar with procedures of meeting service.
➢ To help the students make some dialogues about meeting service.

Warming Up

1. Many items need to be prepared in a meeting. Look at the following pictures and write down the correct names of items by the corresponding description.

_____ is an optical device that projects an image (or moving images) onto a surface, commonly a projection screen.

_____ is a device used to control a remote operation.

_____ is an an electronic machine that can store, organize and find information, do calculations and control other machines.

_____ is a machine that makes paper copies of documents and other visual images quickly and cheaply.

_____ is a small book or binder of paper pages, often ruled, used for purposes such as recording notes or memoranda, writing, drawing or scrapbooking.

_____ is a board put on a table as a means of displaying one's identity.

_____ is a instrument for recording images.

_____ is a device used to hold sheets of paper together, usually made of steel wire bent to a looped shape.

M8-1　Warming Up

Dialogues

Key sentences:

➢ Would you please find a room for our trade fair?
➢ It's 100 dollars per hour.
➢ How long will you be using the conference room?
➢ For how long would you need it?
➢ The translation service is at cost, plus a twenty percent service charge.

Pre-questions:

1. Do you know about a meeting or seminar?
2. Do you know how to serve guests in the meeting?
3. Do you know how to arrange catering for a meeting?

Dialogue 1

Stuff:	Good afternoon, madam. What can I do for you?
Guest:	Good afternoon. I would just like to check the meal times for the next week seminer.
Stuff:	Well. Breakfast buffet will be served in the main dining room from 7 till 10 as usual. Do you have special requirements there?
Guest:	Yes. We do have rather a lot of Americans and Englishmen attending the seminer, so I think it would be a good idea to serve Aamerican breakfast and British breakfast, in addition to Chinese breakfast.
Stuff:	Very good, sir. Lunch is at 12:00. Do you want to have the buffet lunch on Monday and Tuesday?
Guest:	Not really. Can we have the normal waiter service on Tuesday?
Stuff:	Yes. And how about the teatime? Would you like coffee to be served in the lecture room?
Guest:	No. I'd like to have something else for a change. I think Chinese jasmine tea will be OK.

Stuff:	Yes, I'm sure we can arrange that.
Guest:	Thank you very much.
Stuff:	My pleasure, sir.

Dialogue 2

Stuff:	Good morning, Business center. May I help you?
Guest:	Would you please find a room for our trade fair?
Stuff:	How many people do you have?
Guest:	Well, about fifty.
Stuff:	We have such conference rooms. It is 200 dollars per hour.
Guest:	OK. Please help me to arrange one. We will use it at 9:00 am.

Dialogue 3

Business center tuff:	Good afternoon, sir. What can I do for you?
Guest:	Do you a printer? I need to print some materials.
Business center tuff:	Yes, we have.
Guest:	How much is it for one copy?
Business center tuff	One yuan for one copy. How many copies do you need?
Guest:	I need 30 copies.
Cafe Attendant:	OK. Here you are. That will be 30 yuan.
Guest:	Can I put that on my hotel bill?
Cafe Attendant:	Yes, of course.

Vocabulary

projector [prə'dʒektə(r)]　n. 投影仪
remote control　遥控
computer [kəm'pju:tə(r)]　n. 电脑
printer ['prɪntə(r)]　n. 复印机；打印机
name board　名牌
paper clip　n. 曲别针
bottled water　n. 瓶装水
white board　n. 白板

tea bag　n. 茶袋
instant coffee　n. 速溶咖啡
microphone ['maɪkrəfəʊn]　n. 话筒；麦克风
loudspeaker[,laʊd'spi:kə(r)]　n. 音箱
laptop ['læptɒp]　n. 笔记本电脑
schedule['ʃedju:l]　n. 时刻表；进度表
agenda [ə'dʒendə]　n. 日程；议程

Useful Expressions

1. Good morning, business center. May I help you?
早上好，商务中心，有什么可以帮助您的？

2. Would you please find a room for our trade fair?
可否为我们的洽谈会找一个开会的屋子？

3. How many people do you have?
一共有多少人？

4. We have such conference rooms.
我们有这样的会议室。

5. It's 100 dollars per hour.
每小时100美金。

6. How long will you be using the conference room?

会议室您需要用多长时间？

7. For how long would you need it?

您需要多长时间？

8. The tramslation service is at cost, plus a twenty percent service charge.

翻译服务是收费的，外加百分之二十的服务费。

9. Do you have special requirements there?

您有特殊的要求吗？

10. How many copies do you need?

您需要多少份？

11. Can I put that on my hotel bill?

我可以记在账上吗？

M8-2　Practice

Exercises

1. Questions and Answers

(1) Have you ever attended a meeting before?

(2) Could you list five devices in a meeting room?

(3) What's projctor?

2. Match the words or expressions in Column A with their Chinese equivalents in Column B.

A	B
(1) Camera	a. 复印机
(2) Cookie	b. 照相机
(3) Name board	c. 投影仪
(4) Projector	d. 曲别针
(5) Tea bag	e. 遥控
(6) Printer	f. 袋茶
(7) Computer	g. 电脑
(8) bottled water	h. 曲奇
(9) Remote control	i. 名牌
(10) Paper clip	j. 瓶装水

3. Choose the best English translation for each sentence.

(1) 可以给我们找一个开会的屋子吗？

A. Can you open the door?　　B. Could you please find a meeting room for us?

C. Can you?　　　　　　　　　D. What is your room number?

(2) 你们一共多少人？

A. How many people do you have?　　B. What does she do?

C. How old are you? D. What is the time?

(3) 我们有这样的会议室。

A. We have 3 restaurants. B. We had a meeting yesterday.

C. I want a cup of tea. D. We have such conference room.

(4) 会议室你们打算用多久？

A. How long will you be using the conference room?

B. How long will it takes from Beijing to Shanghai?

C. How much is it?

D. How often do you do exercise?

(5) 您需要印多少份？

A. It is free? B. Do you want to have a cope?

C. Do you have a printer? D. How many copies do you have?

4. Read the passage and decide if the statements are true (T) or false (F).

A well run meeting can be used to effectively train employees, close an important sale, set business goals and keep major projects on the right track. A successful meeting starts well before everyone is gathered in a conference room. The person running the meeting needs to make arrangements, gather materials, send out invitations and coordinate the activities. Participants need to be prepared to handle any required tasks, provide feedback, make presentations or brainstorm ideas. Doing the groundwork ahead of time will keep the meeting running smoothly and help you meet your goals.

Exercises:

(1) A good meeting can be used to train employees. (   )

(2) Business goals can't be set in a meeting. (   )

(3) A successful meeting starts well after everyone is gathered in a conference room. (   )

(4) People who run the meeting should arrange the meeting. (   )

(5) Participants don't need to be ready for tasks. (   )

Challenges and Solutions

1. What is a meeting?

Solutions:

2. How many kinds of meeting do you know?

Solutions:

3. What meeting room facilities do you know?

Solutions:

4. Have you ever took part in a meeting?

Solutions:

5. If the guests want to rent a meeting room for one day, what will you do?

Solutions:

6. If the guest wants you to copy some materials, what will you do?

Solution:

7. If the guests want to have a break, what should prepare for them?

Solutions:

8. If the guests want bottled water, what shall you do?
Solutions:

M8-3　Knowledge Link　　　　　　M8-4　Key to Exercises

Lesson Two　Exhibition Service

Objectives

➢ To help the students master useful expressions and sentences about exhibition services.
➢ To help the students familiar with all kinds of exhibitions.
➢ To help the students make some dialogues about exhibition services.

Warming Up

1. Many iems can be used in a exhibition. Look at the following pictures and write down the correct names of each item by the corresponding description.

_____ are cards bearing business information about a company or individual. They are shared during formal introductions as a convenience and a memory aid.

_____ is a board-shaped material used to by display information about products in exhibitions.

_____ is a badge or sticker worn on the outermost clothing as a means of displaying the wearer's name for others to view.

_____ is a small, portable personal computer.

_____ is an object with a round folding frame of long straight pieces of metal covered with material, that you use to protect yourself from the rain or from hot sun.

_____ is an informative paper document (often also used for advertising) that can be folded into a template, pamphlet or leaflet.

_____ is drinking water packaged in PET Bottle or GlassWater Bottles.

_____ is a block of electrical sockets that attaches to the end of a flexible cable, allowing multiple electrical devices to be powered from a single electrical socket.

M8-5　Warming Up

Dialogues

Key sentences:
- ➤ Have you ever had a trade show before?
- ➤ Would you like to look at our brochure?
- ➤ I will give you an introduction.
- ➤ Would you like to try it?
- ➤ We can mail you some samples.

Pre-questions:

1. Do you know what is a exhibition?

2. Do you know the basic expressions in a exhibition?

3. Do you know how to discuss an exhibition?

Dialogue 1

A:　Is it your first time to set up for a trade show, Alan?

B:　Yes.

A:　We should try and make our booth stand out.

B: That's right. Maybe we can do something with this boring wall.

A: We can nail up a sign board above the wall, and paint our company's name on it.

B: Good idea!

A: And put our products here.

B: OK, let's do now.

Dialogue 2

A: Do you think we still need to participate in the Berlin exhibition this September?

B: Yes, why not?

A: Don't you know that our budget on exhibition will be cut heavily because of the financial crisis?

B: Yes, I know. But this exhibition is the most important one in this industry. It has great fame.

A: Well, it's also the most expensive one.

B: But we always get discount on the price of the booth from the organizer.

A: Well, I agree we should make every penny count. I will reconsider my decision.

Dialogue 3

A: I am going to attend your trade show this year. Could you send me the floor plan of your exhibition?

B: Sure. And for your reference, I'll also send you the price list of the booths.

A: OK, thanks. I'm interested in your booth No.8 which is at the entrance of the hall.

B: Yes, it's one of our most popular booths.

A: Do you think I can get a discount?

B: I'm afraid not.

A: Well, I really hate to bargain with you, but it will exceed our budget.

B: Sorry, maybe you can choose another one.

Vocabulary

name card   *n.* 名片

exhibition [ˌeksɪˈbɪʃn]   *n.* 展览；陈列

display board   *n.* 展板

sample [ˈsɑːmpl]   *n.* 样品；样本

model [ˈmɒdl]   *n.* 模型；模特

umbrella [ʌmˈbrelə]   *n.* 伞

brochure [ˈbrəʊʃə]   *n.* 小册子；手册

plug board   *n.* 插座；插线板

Luxury [ˈlʌkʃəri]   *n.* 奢侈品；*adj.* 奢侈的

art [ɑːt]   *n.* 艺术；艺术作品

porcelain [ˈpɔːsəlɪn]   *n.* 陶瓷

furniture [ˈfɜːnɪtʃə(r)]   *n.* 家具

automobile [ˈɔːtəməbiːl]   *n.* 汽车

jewelry [ˈdʒuːəlrɪ]   *n.* 珠宝

beverage [ˈbevərɪdʒ]   *n.* 饮品

electronic product   电子产品

Useful Expressions

1. Have you ever had a trade show before?
您以前参加过展会吗？

2. What have you got?
您这里都有什么？

3. Would you like to look at our brochure?
您想看一下我们的宣传彩页吗？

4. Do you need a bottle of water?
您需要喝水吗？

5. I will show you something in detail.
我可以给您展示一些细节。

6. I will give you an introduction.
我会给您做一个讲解。

7. Would you like to try it?

要不要体验一下？

8. We can mail you some samples.

我们可以给您寄一些样品。

9. Is it your first time to set up for a trade show?

您是第一次参加展会吗？

10. This exhibition is the most important one in this industry.

这个展会是该领域最重要的一个。

11. Could you send me the floor plan of your exhibition?

能否给我看看展会发布局图？

12. Do you think I can get a discount?

我可以享受到折扣吗？

M8-6　Practice

Exercises

1. Questions and Answers

(1) Have you ever attended a exhibition before?

(2) Could you list five kinds of exhibitions?

(3) What's name card?

2. Match the words or expressions in Column A with their Chinese equivalents in Column B.

A	B
(1) Plug board	a. 名片
(2) Antique	b. 插线板
(3) Furniture	c. 展板
(4) Umbrella	d. 油画
(5) Name card	e. 笔记本电脑
(6) Lap top	f. 家具
(7) Brochure	g. 伞
(8) Oil painting	h. 珠宝
(9) Jewelry	i. 宣传彩页
(10) Display board	j. 古董

3. Choose the best English translation for each sentence.

(1) 您想不想看看我们的宣传彩页？

A. Would you like to look at our brochure?　　B. Can you show me the way?

C. Are you interested?　　D. Maybe you have have a try.

(2) 您想喝瓶水吗？

A. I need some hot water.　　B. I am thirsty now.

C. Are you hungry?　　D. Do you need a bottle of water?

(3) 我会为您展示一些细节。

A. I will show you some details.　　B. I wil take it.

C. I really like it.　　D. It is so nice.

(4) 你想试一下吗?

A. Can I try it on?　　　　　　　　B. Have you ever seen it before?

C. Do you like it?　　　　　　　　　D. Would you like to try it?

(5) 这是您第一次参加展会吗?

A. Is it your first time to attend an exhibition?　B. Have you ever been there before?

C. Do you like this movie?　　　　　　　　　　D. Have we ever seen each other before?

4. Read the passage and decide if the statements are true (T) or false (F).

The Beijing Exhibition Center was established in 1954 as a comprehensive exhibition venue in Beijing, China. Built in the Sino-Soviet architectural style that was popular in the 1950s, the Beijing Exhibition Center contains three large exhibition halls as well as museums.

It has a theater hall with 1,000 seats, playing a wide range of shows including Chinese plays, Western and Chinese operas and ballets, musicals and rock concerts.

Exercises:

(1) The Beijing Exhibition Center was established in 1960s. (　　)

(2) The building combines both China and Soviet Union style. (　　)

(3) Sino-Soviet architectural style wasn't popular in the 1950s.(　　)

(4) There are museums in Beijing Exhibition Center. (　　)

(5) In the theater, you can enjoy ballets. (　　)

Challenges and Solutions

1. What is exhibition?

Solutions:

2. How many exhibitions do you know?

Solutions:

3. Have you ever took part in an exhibition?

Solutions:

4. If the guest can not find the way in an exhibition, what will you do?

Solutions:

5. If the guest wants to copy some materials, what will you do?

Solutions:

6. If the guest wants to use internet, what will you do?

Solution:

7. If the floor is dirty, what will you do?

Solutions:

8. If the exhibition room is hot, what will you do?

Solutions:

M8-7　Knowledge Link

M8-8　Key to Exercises

Lesson Three   Recreation Service

Objectives

➢ To help the students master useful expressions and sentences about recreation service.
➢ To help the students familiar with all kinds of recreation facilities.
➢ To help the students make some dialogues about recreation service.

Warming Up

1. There are many kinds of recreation facilities in a hotel. Look at the following pictures and write down the correct names of them by the corresponding description.

_____ is a structure designed to hold water to enable swimming or other leisure activities.

_____ is a sport or leisure activity in which a player rolls or throws a bowling ball towards a target.

_____ a building where theatrical performances or motion-picture shows can be presented.

_____ is a type of entertainment in which a machine plays only the music of popular songs so that people can sing the words themselves.

_____ is a very large room used for dancing on formal occasions.

_____ is a place that you can play different kinds of video games.

_____ is a place that you can enjoy movies.

_____ is a room or hall with equipment for doing physical exercise, for example in a school.

M8-9　Warming Up

Dialogues

Key sentences:

➤ We are very proud of your health club.

➤ What facilities do you have?

➤ Would you like to try our gym?

➤ Do you have any recreational facilities in the hotel?

➤ What other night-life activities do you have?

Pre-questions:

1. Do you know about recreation department in a hotel?

2. Do you know how to introduce the recreation facilities and activities to the guest?

3. Do you know how to recommend recreation facilities and activities to guests?

Dialogue 1

Guest:　　　　　Is there any place for exercise?

Staff:	Yes, we have a health club on the fourth floor.
Guest:	What do you have there?
Stuff:	We provide ample facilities like weight-lifting, chest-expanding, and there is a swimming pool. What's more, we have a sauna bath with a massage service there, too.
Guest:	It sounds good! Is it free for hotel guest?
Staff:	Yes. Please show your room key when you go there.
Guest:	Thank you very much indeed.
Staff:	You are welcome.

Dialogue 2

Hairdresser:	Good evening, madam. Would you like your hair done?
Guest:	Yes. I'd like my hair shampooes and set.
Hairdresser:	That the seat, please.
Guest:	Well, I'd like my head and face massaged, too.
Hairdresser:	All right, madam. Please have a look. Is this the style you want?
Guest:	Yes, it looks great. Thank you.

Dialogue 3

Recreation clerk:	Good evening, sir. May I help you?
Guest:	What time will you close?
Recreation clerk:	We are open till 12:00 pm.
Guest:	How much do you charge for an hour?
Recreation clerk:	50 dollars per hour. Would you like to have a try?
Guest:	OK.
Recreation clerk:	Thank you, sir. How would you like to pay, in cash or credit card?
Guest:	Credit card. Here is my room key.
Recreation clerk:	Thank you. We will keep your room key here. You can get it back after playing. Slippers and personal shoes are not allowed in the bowling room. Special bowling shoes are available here. Would you please tell me your size?
Guest:	Yes, size 38.
Recreation clerk:	Here are the shoes. Lane 10, please.

Vocabulary

bowling ['bəʊlɪŋ]　*n.* 保龄球

pool [pu:l]　*n.* 游泳池

theatre ['θɪətə]　*n.* 剧院

karaoke [ˌkæri'əuki]　*n.* 卡拉OK

ballroom ['bɔ:lru:m]　*n.* 舞厅

cinema ['sɪnəmə]　*n.* 电影院

gym [dʒɪm]　*n.* 体育场；体育馆；健身房

chess [tʃes]　*n.* 棋类

badminton [bædmɪntən]　*n.* 羽毛球

table tennis　*n.* 乒乓球

billiards ['bɪliədz]　*n.* 台球

tennis ['tenɪs]　*n.* 网球

archery ['ɑ:tʃəri]　*n.* 射箭

yoga ['jəugə]　*n.* 瑜伽

golf [gɒlf]　*n.* 高尔夫球

jogging ['dʒɒgɪŋ]　*n.* 慢跑

boxing ['bɒksɪŋ]　*n.* 拳击运动

Useful Expressions

1. We are very proud of your health club.
我们对于您的健康俱乐部感到十分自豪。

2. What facilities do you have?
那里都有什么设备？

3. The hotel has a lot of outdoor recreation facilities to offer.
酒店提供很多娱乐设备。

4. Would you like to try our gym?
想不想试一下我们的健身房？

5. Do you have any recreational facilities in the hotel?
酒店有娱乐设施吗？

6. How much is it for one game?
玩一次多少钱？

7. What other night-life activities do you have?
有没有夜生活？

8. Is there any place for exercises?
有锻炼身体的地方吗？

9. What do you have there?
您那里有什么？

10. Is it free for hotel guest?
对于酒店的客人免费吗？

11. Would you like your hair done?
您想理发吗？

12. Is this the style you want?
这是您想要的风格吗？

13. What time will you close?
您几点关门？

M8-10 Practice

Exercises

1. Questions and Answers

(1) What kind of recreational activities do you know?

(2) Could you list five famous recreational activities?

(3) What's yoga?

2. Match the words or expressions in Column A with their Chinese equivalents in Column B.

A	B
(1) Billiard	a. 游泳池
(2) Golf	b. 游戏厅
(3) Video game center	c. 台球
(4) Karaoke	d. 高尔夫球
(5) Badminton	e. 保龄球
(6) Pool	f. 舞会
(7) Ballroom	g. 瑜伽
(8) Archery	h. 卡拉OK
(9) Bowling	i. 羽毛球
(10) Yoga	j. 射箭

3. Choose the best English translation for each sentence.

(1) 你们那里有什么设备？

A. What facilities do you have?　　　　B. What is the matter?

C. What can you see?　　　　　　　　D. Do you have a laptop?

(2) 想不想试一下我们的体育馆？

A. Are you interested?　　　　　　　B. Can you show me the way to the gym?

C. Where is the gyme?　　　　　　　D. Would you like to try our gym?

(3) 玩一次多少钱？

A. How much is it?　　　　　　　　　B. How much is it for one game?

C. How much do you have in your pocket?　D. What is your salary expectation?

(4) 有可以健身的地方吗？

A. Is there any place for exercise?　　B. Do you want to take an exercise?

C. There is a gym.　　　　　　　　　D. Where can I swim?

(5) 您那里都有什么？

A. What do you have there?　　　　　B. Do you have it?

C. Where is it?　　　　　　　　　　D. What can we do?

4. Read the passage and decide if the statements are true (T) or false (F).

Yoga's history has many places of obscurity and uncertainty due to its oral transmission of sacred texts and the secretive nature of its teachings. The early writings on yoga were transcribed on fragile palm leaves that were easily damaged, destroyed or lost. The development of yoga can be traced back to over 5,000 years ago, but some researchers think that yoga may be up to 10,000 years old old. Yoga's long rich history can be divided into four main periods of innovation, practice and development.

Exercises:

(1) The history of yoga is very clear.(　　)

(2) The sacred texts are transmitted by books.(　　)

(3) Early writings of Yoga were written on palm leaves. (　　)

(4) The palm leaves are fragile. (　　)

(5) The history of Yoga is very long. (　　)

Challenges and Solutions

1. What is Yoga?

Solutions:

2. What recreational forms do you know?

Solutions:

3. What facilities can we find in a gym?

Solutions:

4. Can you swim?

Solutions:

5. If the guest wants to Karaoke, where shall he go?

Solutions:

6. If the guest is not satisfied with the service, what will you do?

Solution:

7. If guest want to do some sports to lose weight, what kind of sport will you recommend?
Solutions:

M8-11   Knowledge Link

M8-12   Key to Exercises

Lesson Four   Shopping Service

Objectives

➢ To help the students master useful expressions and sentences about shopping service.
➢ To help the students familiar with all kinds of shops and goods.
➢ To help the students make some dialogues about shopping service.

Warming Up

1. There are many kinds of goods. Look at the following pictures and write down the correct names of goods by the corresponding description.

_____ is pieces of jewellery or decorative objects that contain precious stones.

_____ is a type of small clock that you wear on your wrist, or (in the past) carried in your pocket.

_____ are the things that you wear, such as shirts, jackets, dresses and trousers.

_____ is a substance made into a small stick, used for colouring the lips.

_____ is a small meal or amount of food, usually eaten in a hurry.

_____ is an alcoholic drink made from the juice of grapes that has been left to ferment.

_____ is a container made of paper or plastic, that opens at the top, used especially in shops/stores.

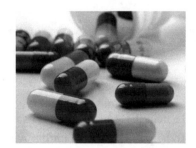

_____ is a substance, especially a liquid that you drink or swallow in order to cure an illness.

M8-13　Warming Up

Dialogues

Key sentences:
- ➤ Is there anyone serving you?
- ➤ I'd like to do some shopping.
- ➤ Please feel free to look around, and do call me if you need anything.
- ➤ Would you please look at this?
- ➤ What size do you want?

Pre-questions:

1. Do you know about coffee?

2. Do you know how to serve guests in the coffee shop?

3. Do you know how to recommend coffee to guests?

Dialogue 1

Salesman:	What can I do for you, sir?
Guest:	I am traveling in China and I'd like to find something before I leave, but may I have a look first?

Salesman:	Of course, take your time.
Guest:	You have a big store. There are so many antiques and Chinese paintings here. Are they genuine?
Salesman:	No. Not all of them. We have both genuine and artifical products. All our reproductions are clearly marked and priced. They are sold at a fair price.
Guest:	May I see that old jade horse? How much is it?
Salesman:	It is 100 dollars.
Guest:	OK, I will take it.

Dialogue 2

Shop assistant:	Is there anything I can do for you?
Guest:	I want to buy some souvenirs, something typical Chinese. What do you suggest?
Shop assistant:	Would you please com over here? I would like to show you the special articles.
Guest:	They are beautiful. Are they expensive?
Shop assistant:	Not really. These bracelets are only 50 Yuan a pair, and the earrings are 45 Yuan a pair.
Guest:	Are they? I'll choose a pair of bracelets and two pairs of earrings. How much do they come to?
Shop assistant:	It's 140 Yuan.

Dialogue 3

Salesman:	Good afternoon, madam. What can I do for you?
Guest:	I am looking for a Chinese traditional cheongsam for myself.
Salesman:	What color do you like? How about the blue one? It is made of pure Chinese silk and also it is hand made.
Guest:	Well, it looks very nice. May I try it?
Salesman:	Yes, madam. What size do you wear?
Guest:	Medium.
Salesman:	Here you are. The fitting room is over there.
(After a while)	
Guest:	Well, I like it very much. How much is it?
Salesman:	It is 3200 Yuan.
Guest:	It is a little expensive. Can you give me any discount?
Salesman:	Sorry madam. This is the best price I can give.
Guest:	OK, I will take it.
Salesman:	OK. Thank you.

Vocabulary

recreation [ˌrekri'eɪʃn]   *n.* 娱乐；消遣
acceptable [ək'septəbl]   *adj.* 可以接受的
packing ['pækɪŋ]   *n.* 包装；打包
postage ['pəʊstɪdʒ]   *n.* 邮费；邮资
souvenir [suːvə'nɪə(r)]   *n.* 纪念品

handmade [rost]   *adj.* 手工制作的
pure [pjʊə(r)]   *adj.* 纯的
cheongsam [tʃɒŋ'sæm]   *n.* 旗袍
bracelet ['breɪslət]   *n.* 手镯
earring ['ɪərɪŋ]   *n.* 耳环

design [dɪ'zaɪn]   *n.* 设计
dressing room   *n.* 试衣间
cotton ['kɒtn]   *n.* 棉

fashion ['fæʃn]   *n.* 时尚
jewelry['dʒuːəlrɪ]   *n.* 珠宝
convenient [kən'viːniənt]   *adj.* 方便的

Useful Expressions

1. What can I do for you?
有什么可以为您效劳的？

2. Is there anyone serving you?
有人在服务您吗？

3. I'd like to do some shopping.
我想买点东西。

4. Ours is well-reputed and our wares are always dependable.
我们的信誉是良好的，商品质量您可以放心。

5. Please feel free to look around, and do call me if you need anything.
请您随意看看吧，如果有问题可以来找我。

6. I would be glad to show you around and explain some of the items.
我很乐意陪您转转，并且给您详细介绍一下一些物品。

7. Would you please look at this?
可以看看这个吗？

8. What size do you want?
您想要多大的？

9. I will take it.
我买了。

10. Is there anything I can do for you?
有什么可以为您效劳的？

11. Would you please come over here?
您可以过来一下吗？

12. Are they expensive?
这些贵吗？

13. May I try it?
我可以试一下吗？

14. What color do you like?
您喜欢什么颜色的？

15. The fitting room is over there.
试衣间在那里。

M8-14   Practice

Exercises

1. Questions and Answers

(1) Do you like going shopping?

(2) What do you usually buy when you go shopping?

(3) What luxury brands do you know?

2. Match the words or expressions in Column A with their Chinese equivalents in Column B.

A	B
(1) Snack	a. 手表
(2) Watch	b. 小吃
(3) Chanel	c. 药品
(4) handbag	d. 西服

(5) Prada   e. 葡萄酒

(6) Medicine   f. 唇膏

(7) Suit   g. 手提包

(8) Versace   h. 香奈儿

(9) Wine   i. 范思哲

(10) lipstick   j. 普拉达

3. Choose the best English translation for each sentence.

(1) 有人在服务您吗？

A. Is there anyone serving you?   B. What can I do for you?

C. Do you like Chinese food?   D. Can I help you?

(2) 我想买点东西。

A. Do you want to buy something?   B. I'd like to do some shopping.

C. I want to by a glass of milk.   D. I want to Paris.

(3) 您可不可以看一下这个？

A. Would you please look at this?   B. Which one do you like?

C. Do you like it?   D. Can you hear it?

(4) 您想要多大号的？

A. What's the size of it?   B. What is the color of it?

C. Do you want it?   D. What size do you want?

(5) 这些贵吗？

A. What's the price?   B. How many do you want?

C. Do you really like it?   D. Are they expensive?

4. Read the passage and decide if the statements are true (T) or false (F).

Most large cruise ships have several shops, usually placed together in an onboard "mall" area. On a typical ship, you'll find a boutique that sells handbags and cruise-y clothing (with and without the cruise line's logo), T-shirts, books, items for kids and souvenirs; a high-end jewelry store that also sells watches; and another store that sells duty-free items, such as perfume, cigarettes, chocolate, alcohol and makeup. Some ships have even more specialized designer boutiques. Celebrity Cruises, for example, has a standalone Michael Kors boutique and also carries name brands like Kate Spade, Cole Haan, Trina Turk and Hugo Boss on some ships.

Exercises:

(1) On cruise ships, we can find shops.(　　)

(2) Mall area is place that people mainly have their meals there.(　　)

(3) We can buy handbags in boutiques.(　　)

(4) Jewelry store doesn't sell watches. (　　)

(5) On Celebrity Cruises, there are no specialized designer boutiques. (　　)

Challenges and Solutions

1. Do you like going shopping?

Solutions:

2. If you go shopping, where do you usually go?

Solutions:

3. What is duty-free shop?

Solutions:

4. If you want to buy a handbag, which brand will you choose?

Solutions:

5. Can you list five brands of watch?

Solutions:

6. If the guest to buy some souvenir, what will you recommend?

Solution:

7. If the guest have no RMB, what will you do to help him?

Solutions:

8. If the guest needs a translator, what will you do?

Solutions:

M8-15   Knowledge Link   M8-16   Key to Exercises

Lesson Five   Special Service

Objectives

➤ To help the students master useful expressions and sentences about special service.

➤ To help the students familiar with all kinds of special services.

➤ To help the students make some dialogues about special service.

Warming Up

1. There are many items related to special services. Look at the following pictures and write down the correct names of these items by the corresponding description.

_____ is a secure lockable box used for securing valuable objects against theft and/or damage from fire.

_____ is a small plastic card that you can use to buy goods and services and pay for them later.

_____ is a machine that sends and receives documents in an electronic form along telephone wires and then prints them.

_____ a metal container with water or chemicals inside for putting out small fires.

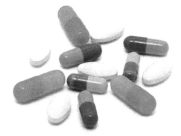

_____ is a substance, especially a liquid that you drink or swallow in order to cure an illness.

_____ is a strip of cloth used for tying around a part of the body that has been hurt in order to protect or support it.

M8-17　Warning Up

Dialogues

Key sentences:

➢ How are you feeling now?
➢ Have you had something to eat?
➢ Do you feel seasick?
➢ What has happened?
➢ Do you need some medicine?

Pre-questions:

1. Have you ever encountered any emergencies before?
2. What should we do in the face of emergencies?
3. Do you know how to calm the guests down when there is an emergency?

Dialogue 1

Tourist:　　　Can you help my friend please? It's an emergency. He was just hit by a car.

Local:　　　　I'll call an ambulance. Let him lie down there. I know some first aid.

Tourist:	Is there a hospital nearby?
Local:	Yes, there is a large emergency department not far from here. The ambulance is on its way. What happened?
Tourist:	It was a hit-and-run. We were just crossing the road when a car crashed into him and drove straight off.
Local:	Take your sweater off and we can wrap it around his arm. Do you know what blood type your friend is?
Tourist:	Yes, he is O positive. Do you think our travel insurance will cover the hospital visit.
Local:	I'm not sure but we need to get your friend to a doctor straight away. I can hear the siren. The ambulance is around the corner now.

Dialogue 2

Tourist:	I need to report a theft. I was just robbed.
Police:	OK. Tell me what happened and what was stolen.
Tourist:	I was on West Street when a man ripped my handbag from my shoulder and ran off.
Police:	What was in your handbag?
Tourist:	My wallet with my credit cards, my phone, a small digital camera and my passport.
Police:	You have to cancel your credit cards immediately and you will need to get in touch with the Chinese Embassy to get a replacement passport.
Tourist:	Can I use your phone?
Police:	Of course. Did you get a look at the thief? Can you describe him to me? Were there any witnesses?
Tourist:	This is the phone number of a witness you can contact. She saw it happen. It all happened so quickly. I hardly had time to react.

Dialogue 3

Mark:	Hi honey, I'm home.
Jane:	Where have you been? It's almost 6 o'clock. I was beginning to get nervous.
Mark:	I was involved in a traffic accident today.
Jane:	Were you, Mark? Are you okay now?
Mark:	Yes, I'm fine, thank God. But I have to admit I was really shaking in my boots at the time.
Jane:	What happened?
Mark:	Well, I thought that the usual way I got back to the hotel was too long, and I was pretty exhausted at that point, so I decided to hail a cab.
Jane:	So what?
Mark:	We had been driving for about 3 minutes when we reached a cross-roads. We had a green light, so we proceeded through, when out of nowhere, a public bus came careen into the intersection from the other street. The cabbie was alert, so he swerved to avoid the bus, but in doing so he was forced into the bicycle lane. We almost hit a lady on her bike!

Jane:	You did? And was she badly hurt?
Mark:	Fortunately, no one was hurt, and the only damage to the car was a dented front bumper.
Jane:	Mark, it sounds terrifying! Did the police come?
Mark:	Yes, there was an officer at the intersection. He saw the whole thing. Boy! He gave the bus driver a tongue-lashing! He let us go after we wrote out a brief report. There shouldn't be any problem.
Jane:	Well, I'm glad you're safe.
Mark:	Amen, I'm glad everyone is OK.

Vocabulary

ambulance ['æmbjələns] *n.* 救护车

complaint [kəm'pleɪnt] *n.* 抱怨；投诉

first aid 急救

emergency [i'mɜ:dʒənsi] *adj.* 紧急的

department [dɪ'pɑ:tmənt] *n.* 部门；系

sweater ['swetə(r)] *n.* 毛衣

blood [blʌd] *n.* 血液

insurance [ɪn'ʃʊərəns] *n.* 保险

handbag ['hændbæg] *n.* 手提包

digital ['dɪdʒɪtl] *adj.* 数码

passport ['pɑ:spɔ:t] *n.* 护照

Embassy ['embəsi] *n.* 大使馆

Useful Expressions

1. How are you feeling now?

您现在感觉如何？

2. Have you had something to eat?

您吃东西了吗？

3. Are you all right?

您还好吗？

4. Do you feel seasick?

您晕船吗？

5. What has happened?

发生了什么？

6. Do you need some medicine?

您需要吃药吗？

7. You'd better drink some hot water.

您最好喝点热水。

8. You need to take good care of yourself.

你需要照顾好自己。

9. Can you help my friend please?

您可以帮助我朋友吗？

10.Is there a hospital nearby?

附近有医院吗？

11.I know some first aid.

我懂一些急救知识。

12. Do you know what blood type your friend is?

你知道你朋友的血型吗？

13.What was in your handbag?

您手提包里有什么？

14.Are you okay now?

您现在还好吗？

M8-18　Practice

Exercises

1. Questions and Answers

(1) What other services do you know?

(2) Have you ever met any emergencies?

(3) What's fire extinguisher?

2. Match the words or expressions in Column A with their Chinese equivalents in Column B.

A	B
(1) Fire exthinguisher	a. 保险箱
(2) Bandage	b. 信用卡
(3) Safe	c. 传真
(4) printer	d. 灭火器
(5) Medicine	e. 绷带
(6) Fax	f. 护照
(7) Suitcase	g. 地图
(8) Credit card	h. 行李箱
(9) Map	i. 药品
(10) Passport	j. 打印机

3. Choose the best English translation for each sentence.

(1) 你现在感觉如何？

A. Are you OK?   B. Are you happy?

C. How are you feeling now?   D. Are you sick?

(2) 你肚子疼吗？

A. Have you had stomachache?   B. Are you sick?

C. What's wrong with you?   D. How are you feeling now?

(3) 发生了什么？

A. What happened?   B. Are you all right?

C. Have you had stomachache?   D. You need to drink some hot water.

(4) 你应该保重身体。

A. You need to take good care of yourself.   B. You need to watch out.

C. May you be healthy.   D. You should go to see the doctor?

(5) 附近有医院吗？

A. Is there a hospital nearby?   B. Where is the hospital?

C. Where are you now?   D. Can you show me the way?

4. Read the passage and decide if the statements are true (T) or false (F).

Every year in the United States, about 2,000 people lose their lives in residential fires. In a fire, smoke and deadly gases tend to spread farther and faster than heat. That's one reason why most fire victims die from inhalation of smoke and toxic gases, not from burns. A majority of fatal fires happen when families are asleep because occupants are unaware of the fire until there is not adequate time to escape. A smoke alarm stands guard around the clock, and when it first senses smoke, it sounds a shrill alarm. This often allows a family the precious, but limited, time needed to escape.

Exercises:

(1) Many people are killed by fires every year. (   )

(2) In fire, heat spreads faster than fire and smoke. (   )

(3) Most fire victims die from burns.(   )

(4) Fires easily happen when families are asleep. (   )

(5) A smoke alarm is very important for every family to prevent fire. (   )

Challenges and Solutions

1. What is a fire exthinguisher?

Solutions:

2. How many types of fire extinguisher do you know?

Solutions:

3. Have you ever been taught how to use the fire-fighting devices?

Solutions:

4. If a fire happen in the hotel, what will you do?

Solutions:

5. If the guest feel stomachache, what will you do?

Solutions:

6. If the guest loses his purse, what will you do?

Solution:

7. If a guest can't find the way back to hotel, what will you do?

Solutions:

8. If the guest has a car accident, what will you do?

Solutions:

M8-19   Knowledge Link   M8-20   Key to Exercises

Lesson Six   Handling Complaints

Objectives

➢ To help the students master useful expressions and sentences about complaints in the shop or place of entertainment.

➢ To help the students familiar with the common complaints in the shop or place of entertainment.

➢ To help the students analyze the reasons of complaints and handle complaints in the shop or place of entertainment.

Preamble

TuesdayJanuary23, 2018

Dear Sir,

I am writing this letter to bring your attention that I am not satisfied with the shopping experience on January 10,2018. I want to let you know that I was very upset with your staff's performance. They used to deal with me quite inefficiently and did not show their interest which they must show when dealing with regular customers.

I have been a regular client of your business but now I am completely disappointed. I expect quality services from you and request you to address this issue with immediate attention. I expect full comprehension and look forward to your replies within shortest time.

Sincerely yours,

(Signature) James King

Dialogues

Key sentences:

> ➤ Are you satisfied with the gym?
> ➤ Do you want to change to another court?

Pre-questions:

1. What are the common complaints in the shop or place of entertainment?

2. How to deal with complaints?

3. If the guest become angry, what will you do?

Dialogue 1

Attendant:	Housekeeping, may I help you?
Guest:	Yes, I'm missing a skirt. I send it in the laundry three days ago, but my laundry was returned without it.
Attendant:	May I have your room number, please?
Guest:	1105.
Attendant:	1105. let me check our delivery records. Just a moment, please. Hello, I'm sorry to have kept you waiting . We made a mistake delivering the laundry. We'll send it up to your room at once. We're very sorry for the inconvenience.
Guest:	It's really of nothing.

Dialogue 2

A: I want to make a complaint.

B: I'm sorry to hear that. What's the problem?

A: I wanted to use your gym this morning before breakfast but it was closed.

B: Yes, it opens at 9 a.m.

A: That's too late. When it open I went in and it was disappointing.

B: How was that, sir?

A: Most of the machines were broken and the equipment that did work was shabby and dirty.

B: I'm sorry about that, sir.

A: It's also smelly. It was disgusting and messy. You should do something about it.

B: I do apologize. I will get someone to fix the machines and clean up straight away.

A: Thank you.

Dialogue 3

Attendant: Good afternoon, sir. May I help you?

Guest: Yes, I have a complaint to make.

Attendant: I'm sorry to hear that. What exactly was the problem?

Guest: I have been waiting in my cabin for more than half an hour, but one piece of my baggage has not been sent up yet. What's the matter?

Attendant: Oh, I'm awfully sorry about that. May I have your name and cabin number, please?

Guest: James King. Room 936.

Attendant: Thank you, Mr. King. Would you give me some features of your baggage?

Guest: Sure. It's just an ordinary medium-sized brown suitcase.

Attendant: Is your name tag attached to it?

Guest: Of course.

Attendant: I'm afraid that your suitcase must have been delivered to a wrong cabin. Let me ask the porter to look for it and send it to your room as soon as possible.

Vocabulary

skirt ['skɜːt]　*n.* 裙子

disappointing [ˌdɪsə'pɔɪntɪŋ]　*adj.* 令人失望的

delivery [dɪ'lɪvəri]　*n.* 投递

laundry ['lɔːndri]　*n.* 洗衣店

equipment [ɪ'kwɪpmənt]　*n.* 设备；器材

shabby [shabby]　*adj.* 破旧的

baggage ['bægɪdʒ]　*n.* 行李

Useful Expressions

1. I'm awfully sorry for that, sir. I'll see to it right away.

先生，对此我非常抱歉，我会马上处理此事。

2. I'm sorry to have caused you so much trouble, but I'll manage to solve it tight away.

我很抱歉给您带来了很多不便，我会想办法尽快解决问题。

3. I understand how you feel and we'll try to do our best to help you.

我理解你的心情。我会尽我们最大的努力来帮助您。

4. No problem sir, we will manage it.

没问题先生，我们会解决的。

5. I received a complaint in written form.

我收到一份书面投诉。

6. Housekeeping department received a complaint.

客房部收到了一项投诉。

7. I would like to find a complaint of the poor service of your hotel.

我想要投诉贵酒店的服务质量差。

8. Please allow me to make an apology.

请允许我向您道歉。

9. How could you resolve this complaint?

你想怎么解决这起投诉？

10. We should make an apology first.

我们应该先道歉。

Exercises

1. Match each word or phrase in the column on the left with its meaning in the column on the right.

(1) emergency	a. a collection of things for public display.
(2) danger	b.an instrument that project an enlarged image onto the screen.
(3) Ambulance	c.a sudden unforeseen crisis.
(4) crucial	d. space or equipment necessary for doing something.
(5) facility	e. something designed to serve certain functions.
(6) rude	f. a condition of being harmed.
(7) clinic	g.lacking of good manners.
(8) exhibition	h. a kind of vehicle used to transfer patients in danger.
(9) brochure	i. a medical establishment.
(10) projector	j. of great importance.

2. Complete the following dialogue according to the Chinese in brackets and read it in roles.

Front office attendant: Good morning sir. How can I help you?

Guest:＿＿＿＿＿＿＿＿＿＿＿＿＿＿＿＿＿＿（我房间里的迷你冰箱出了些问题。）

Front office attendant: What exactly is the problem, sir?

Guest: well, you see, the mini-bar is fully stocked, but a couple of the bottles have been filled with something rather than alcohol.

Front office attendant: I think I know what the problem is, sir. Your alcohol bottles have been empties and filled with tap water.

Guest:＿＿＿＿＿＿＿＿＿＿＿＿＿＿＿＿（恐怕是这样的。）

Front office attendant: I am terribly sorry, sir. This happens sometimes. A previous passenger must have pours out the contents and filled the bottles with something less costly.

Guest: And he has left me with the problem.

Front office attendant: Don't worry about it. It's not a problem at all. _____
（我马上派客房服务员去处理此事。您的名字和房间号是什么？）

Guest: I'm James King in E402.

Front office attendant: Please let me apologize for this, Mr. King.

Guest: It's all right. I just wanted to straighten this all out before I pay my bill.

Front office attendant: I see. If you should have any more complaints, please do not hesitate to let us know.

Guest: Don't worry, I will.

Front office attendant: Thank you for informing us about the mini-bar.

3. Choose the correct steps for settling guest's complaints in the shop or place of entertainment.

A. If the problem is not handled and you are going to get off duty, hand it over to the next duty.

B.If the problem can not be solve, as supervisor for help.

C. Ask someone who is in charge of this issue to solve the problem.

D. Say sorry again.

E. Make an apology to the guest.

F. Inquire the problem.

G. When the problem is settled, report it guests and record the handling process.

H. Promise to solve the problem.

4. Choose the best English translation for each sentence.

(1)我想投诉你们的服务。（　　）

A. I need your help.　　　　　　　　　B. I want to pay the bill.

C. I want to complain about the food.　　D. I want to complain about your service.

(2)商品的质量太差。（　　）

A. The quality of good is too bad.　　　B. I want to have some sample.

C. I want to go shopping.　　　　　　　D. Where is the shopping mall?

(3)我们应该先道歉。（　　）

A. You are wrong.　　　　　　　　　　B. I do apologize.

C. I am so sorry.　　　　　　　　　　　D. We should make an apology at first.

(4)我们收到投诉了。（　　）

A. Have you got it?　　　　　　　　　　B. I will call you later.

C. We have received complaints.　　　　D. I have received your email.

(5)这个部门处理各种回馈。（　　）

A. Please be careful.

B. I am responsible for this issue.

C. This division can take care of all the feedback.

D. I am working in this department.

5. Read the passage and choose the best answers to the following questions.

Six Steps to Dealing with Customer Complaints

At some point, everyone in business has to deal with an upset customer. The challenge is to handle the situation in a way that leaves the customer thinking you operate a great company. If you're lucky, you can even encourage him or her to serve as a passionate advocate for your brand.

When it comes down to it, many customers don't even bother to complain. They simply leave and buy from your competitors. Research suggests that up to 80 percent of customers who leave were, in fact, "satisfied" with the original company. Obviously, customer satisfaction is not enough. Businesses nowadays need to positively delight customers if they want to earn their loyalty.

It may seem counter-intuitive, but a business owner's ability to effectively deal with customer complaints provides a great opportunity to turn dissatisfied customers into active promoters of the business. Here are some customer-oriented tips I've learned while working in the business coaching business:

Listen carefully to what the customer has to say, and let them finish. Don't get defensive. The customer is not attacking you personally; he or she has a problem and is upset. Repeat back what you are hearing to show that you have listened.

Ask questions in a caring and concerned manner.

The more information you can get from the customer, the better you will understand his or her perspective. I've learned it's easier to ask questions than to jump to conclusions.

Put yourself in their shoes.

As a business owner, your goal is to solve the problem, not argue. The customer needs to feel like you're on his or her side and that you empathize with the situation.

Apologize without blaming.

When a customer senses that you are sincerely sorry, it usually diffuses the situation. Don't blame another person or department. Just say, "I'm sorry about that."

Ask the customer, "What would be an acceptable solution to you?"

Whether or not the customer knows what a good solution would be, I've found it's best to propose one or more solutions to alleviate his or her pain. Become a partner with the customer in solving the problem.

Solve the problem, or find someone who can solve it— quickly!

Research indicates that customers prefer the person they are speaking with to instantly solve their problem. When complaints are moved up the chain of command, they become more expensive to handle and only add to the customer's frustration.

There is no getting around customer complaints, regardless of your industry. However, by employing these steps and taking the time to review the issue with the customer, you can turn challenges into something constructive.

(1) What is the challenge that people face when dealing with upset customer? (   )

A. Dealing with complaints.

B. Facing upset consumers.

C. Making the customer think that you operate a great company.

D. Running a great company.

(2) Why don't customers bother to complain?(   )

A. Because they are busy.   B. Because they buy from other companies.

C. Because they are satisfied.   D. Because they are unhappy.

(3) If you want to earn loyalty from costumers, what shall you do? (   )

A. Make costumers happy.   B. Handle complaints timely.

C. Blame guests.   D. Ask them to go to other companies.

(4) Why do we need to solve the problem quickly? (　　)

A. Because if the problem is not solved quickly, someone will solve it.

B. Because the complaint is moved up to the chain of command.

C. Because consumers are frustrated.

D. Because it is easier to handle when we solve the problems quickly.

Challenges and Solutions

1. If the guest is not satisfied with the taste of cocktail, what will you do?

Solutions:

2. What will you do if your customers complain about your poor service?

Solutions:

3. If the guest complains that a bottle of brandy is inferior in your hotel, what will you do?

Solutions:

4. If the guest wants to speak with your manager and complains about your rude attitude, what will you do?

Solutions:

5. If the customer complains that a fly is floating in the cup of drink, what will you do?

Solutions:

6. If the guest complains that the opened wine is kept too long in your hotel, what will you do?

Solution:

7. If the guest complains that you break a glass of sherry, what will you do?

Solutions:

8. If the guest complains that the price of drink is higher than the market price in your hotel, what will you do?

Solutions:

M8-21　Knowledge Link　　　　M8-22　Key to Exercises

Appendix

Elementary Vocabulary for Hotel Staff in Hotels

Hotel Departments

general manager's office 总经理办公室

executive division 行政部

public relation department 公共关系部

purchasing department 采购部

rooms division 房务部

laundry room 洗衣房

security department 保安部

engineering department 工程部

West food restaurant 西餐厅

room service 送餐服务部

staff restaurant/canteen 员工餐厅

multifunctional hall 多功能厅

Dancing/ball hall 舞厅

sauna room 桑拿浴房

Vip room 贵宾接待室

cashier counter 收银台

beauty parlor 美容厅

massage parlor 按摩房

human resources division 人力资源部

sales and marketing department 市场营销部

finance division 财务部

Front office 前厅部

Reception desk 接待处

housekeeping department 管家部

public area 保洁部

entertainment & recreation department 康乐部

food & beverage department 餐饮部

Chinese food restaurant 中餐厅

banquet reservation 宴会预定部

cafe 咖啡厅

bar 酒吧

gym 健身房

business center 商务中心

training department 培训部

clinic 医务室

internet bar 网吧

Position

chairman of the board 董事长

executive director 执行董事

Administration Director 行政总监

adviser 顾问

executive secretary 行政秘书

clerk 文员

chief receptionist 接待主管

receptionist 接待员

executive housekeeper 行政管家

senior supervisor 客房高级主管

floor supervisor 楼层主管

floor captain 楼层领班

PA supervisor PA 主管

public area 保洁员

room attendant 客房服务员

bell captain 礼宾部领班

bellman/bellboy 礼宾员

door man /door girl 门童 / 女门童

mechanic 技工

ironer 平烫工

flatwork ironer 大烫工

hand ironer presser 小烫工

dry-cleaner 干洗工

washer extractor 水洗工

dishwasher 洗碗工

linen attendant 布草收发员

laundryman　男洗衣工

laundrywoman　女洗衣工

seamstress　女缝工、女裁缝

hostess　迎宾员 / 咨客

head　主管

coffee shop supervisor　咖啡厅主管

captain　领班

foreman　管事部领班

operation supervisor　运行主管

operation captain　运行领班

pantry captain　备餐间领班

chief engineer　工程总监

engineering manager　工程部经理

storekeeper　仓管员

lift operator　电梯工

room maintenance section head　客房维修主管

repairing supervisor　维修主管

boiler man　锅炉工

carpenter　木工

electrician　电工

air-conditioning mechanic　空调技工

network administrator　网络维护员

EDP supervisor　电脑部主管

purchasing manager　采购部经理

purchasing agent　采购员

barber　理发师

beautician　美容师

beauty salon attendant　美容服务员

manicurist　指甲修剪师

masseur　男按摩师

masseuse　女按摩师

recreation supervisor　娱乐主管

entertainment captain　康体领班

lifeguard　救生员

supervisor　主管

department head　所有部门总监 / 经理

coach　教练

chief　主管

general manager　总经理

deputy general manager　副总经理

general manager assistant　总经理助理

human resources manager　人力资源部经理

training manager　培训部经理

personnel supervisor　人事主管

casual laborer　临时工

front office manager　前厅经理

director of rooms division　房务总监

front office manager　前厅经理

housekeeping department manager　客房经理

assistant manager　大堂副理

laundry manager　洗衣房经理

beverage manager　酒水部经理

booking clerk　预定服务员

business center clerk　商务中心文员

chief operator　接线生主管

operator/telephone operator　话务员；总机

shop supervisor　商场部主管

shop assistant　商场营业员

director of food &beverage　餐饮总监

food &beverage manager　餐饮部经理

Western restaurant supervisor　西餐厅主管

Chinese restaurant supervisor　中餐厅主管

vegetable washer　洗菜工

banqueting manager　宴会部经理

waiter　男服务员

waitress　女服务员

head bartender　酒吧主管

executive chef　行政总厨

sous-chef Chinese kitchen　中餐厨师长

sous-chef Western kitchen　西餐厨师长

room service captain　送餐领班

chief Baker　西饼房主管

assembler　配菜厨师

chef　厨师

dim sum maker　点心师

pantry man　备餐员

food runner　传菜员

apprentice cook　见习厨师

amah　厨房杂工

bar boy　酒吧男侍应

barmaid　酒吧女侍应

bartender　酒吧服务员

tap man　调酒员

tea ceremony keeper　茶艺师

handyman 勤杂工
apprentice 学徒
sales manager 销售经理
VIP manager 贵宾部经理
PR manager 公关部经理
accounting manager 财务部经理
accountant 会计师
chief cashier 总出纳
cashier 收款员、出纳员
auditor 查帐员、审计员

entertainment & recreation manager
    康乐部经理
front office cashier 前台收银员
recreation captain 娱乐领班
security manager 保安部经理
fire control supervisor 消防主管
security guard 保安员
doctor 医生
secretary 秘书

Greeting

good morning 早上好
good afternoon 下午好
good evening 晚上好
good night 晚安
how do you do 你好
how are you 你好吗
nice to meet you 很高兴见到你
see you/good bye 再见
see you later 待会儿见
not at all 一点也不
Excuse me 打扰一下
hope you'll enjoy your staying here
希望您住店愉快
I do appreciate your help 我真是感谢您
apologies 道歉
I'm sorry, it's my fault 对不起，这是我的错
I'm sorry，I don't understand
对不起，我没明白您的意思
I'm sorry to hear that 听到这件事我很抱歉
may I help you 我能帮您吗
what can I do for you 我能为你做什么
Is that all right 这样可以吗
of course 当然
of course not 当然不
I'll get it at once 我马上把它取回来
give me your hands 帮一下忙
after you 您先走
anything else 还有别的吗
may I have your name 能告诉我您的名字吗
what's your name 你叫什么名字

don't worry 别担心
Take it easy 放心好了
leave the message 留口讯
pass the message 转达意思
line is busy 线路很忙
follow me 跟我来
take the elevator/lift 乘电梯
good luck 祝您好运
keep well 祝您健康
enjoy your stay 祝您快乐
sleep well 您睡个好觉
take care 保重
very well 非常好
It doesn't matter 没关系
that's nothing 没什么
sir 先生
madam 女士
lady 小姐
gentleman 先生
welcome to our hotel 欢迎光临我们酒店
welcome to stay in hotel 欢迎入住酒店
thank you very much 非常感谢
thanks a lot 多谢
you are welcome 不客气
It's my pleasure 这是我的荣幸
It's very kind of you 您太客气了
welcome to have your meals here
欢迎您来这里用餐
thank you for your praise 感谢您的夸奖
I apologize for this 我为此道歉

sorry to disturb/interrupt you
对不起打扰了

I apologize for what I've said just now
我为我刚才所说的话道歉

that's all right　没关系

let's forget it　算了吧

anything I can do for you　有什么我可以帮您

I'm at your service　很乐意为您效劳

I afraid not　恐怕不行

I don't think so　我不这样认为

just a moment　请稍等

that's no problem　没问题

may I come in　我可以进来吗

where are you going　您要去哪里

would you like to sit here　坐这里可以吗

here you are　给您

mind your step　请走好

please be careful　请当心

hold on　别挂断

hold the line　别挂断

pardon　再说一遍

turn left/right　向左 / 右拐

go straight　直行

up/down stair　上、下楼梯

have a good time　祝您快乐

have a nice day　祝您愉快

have a nice trip　祝您旅途愉快

hope to see you again　希望能再次见到您

don't mention it　别提了

never mind　别放在心上

happy birthday　生日快乐

Front Office Department Vocabulary

information desk　问讯处

hotel register　酒店登记簿

counter　柜台

lounge　休息室

escalator　自动楼梯

lobby　大厅

lobby lounge　大堂吧

executive lounge　行政酒廊

newsstand　受报处

postal service　邮局服务处

cellar　地窖

broom closet　杂物室

wall plate　壁上挂盘

Chinese painting　国画

charge　收费

check in　登记入住

check out　退房

late check out　延迟退房

voucher　证件

identification card/ID card　身份证

passport　护照

procedure　手续；程序

procedure fee/handling charge　手续费

change money　换钱

conversion rate　换算率

traveler's cheque　旅行支票

note　纸币

cash　现金

sign　签字；署名

signature　签名

book/reserve　预定

make a reservation　做预定

ground floor/first floor　一层

reasonable　合理的

bank draft　汇票

credit card　信用卡

accept　接受

agent　代理

concierge　礼宾部

typewriter　打字机

typing paper　打字纸

carbon paper　复写纸

stapler　订书机

stationery　文具用品

letter paper　信笺

envelope　信封

note book　记事本

memo pad　便条薄

log book　交班薄
paper clip　曲别针
safety-pin　安全别针
copier　复印机
photocopying　影印机
printing/printer　打印 / 打印机
telecommunication　电信
hard disk　硬盘
soft disk　软盘
business/visit card　名片
scotch tape　透明胶
conference room　会议室
secretarial service　秘书服务
translation　翻译
brochure/booklet　小册子
equipment rental　设备出租
slide　幻灯片
overhead projector　投影仪
binding　装订
newspaper rod　报纸夹
internet　互联网
website　网站
daily sales report　营业日报表
rate of room occupancy　住房率
remotion memorizer　移动存储器
room reservation forecast　订房预测（分析）
room reservation report　订房报告表
extension number　分机号
telephone　电话
hold the line　勿挂线
area code　区号
country code　国家代码
collect call　对方付款
put through　转电话
local call /city call　市话
hang up　挂线
long distance call　长途电话
wake up call/morning call　叫醒服务
turn-down service　夜床服务
telephone directory　电话簿
can't hear somebody　听不见
can't get through　打不通

inland telegram　国内电报
switchboard　交换台
central exchange　电话总局
The connection is bad　听不清
house phone　内部电话
special line　专线
dial a number　拨号码
hold the line　别挂电话
can't put somebody through　接不通
ordinary telegram　普通电话
receiver　听筒
telephone number　电话号码
replace the phone　挂上电话
Line, please　请接外线
The line is busy (engaged)　占线
call somebody up　打电话给某人
jet lag　飞行时差反
special rate　特价
early arrival　提前入住
full house　满房
void　空房
estimated time of arrival　预抵时间
pets　宠物
bell service desk　礼宾部
stay over　过夜
hotel brochure　酒店宣传册
banquet　宴会
meeting　会议
luggage / baggage　行李
room key　房卡
upgrade　升级入住
debit　借
free transportation　免费交通
package rate　包价
inspected　检查
city ledger　酒店挂帐
extension cord　接线板
airport pick up service　接机服务
for sale　待售
group rate　团队价
electricity　电
group　团队

additional　额外的

no vacancy　无空房

confirmation number　确认号

opposite　反的，背面

no charge　免费

television　电视机

house use　自用房

pay out　退款

travel agency　旅行社

parcel service　打包服务

preference　优先选择

receipt　收据

free of charge　免费

parcel/packet　包裹

IDD(international direct dialing)　国际直拨

regular/repeat/return guest
常客 / 重新入住客人 / 回头客

vacant/clean　空的 / 干净的

occupied/dirty　住客的 / 脏的

confirmation　确认

convention　会议

flight planner　航班计划

rollaway/extra bed　加床

air conditioning　空调

heated pool　加热池

lost & found　失物招领

car park　停车场

over booking　超预订

block reservation　保留预订

adapter　适配器

shuttle bus　豪华大巴

separate bill　分单

handing charge　手续费

express mail/DHL/EMS　特快专递

paper Clip　纸夹

folder　文件夹

letterhead　信签纸

questionnaire　意见表

mail rates　邮寄价目表

lounge-chair　休闲沙发

stereo/music　立体声 / 音乐

private & confidential　私人密件

express Service　快递服务

urgent　紧急的

estimated time of departure　预离店时间

advance deposit guarantee　预交担保押金

long term/long staying guest　长包房客人

E-mail　电子邮件

low season　淡季

please make up　请即打扫房

CO(check-out room)　退房

O(Occupied)　住客房

reception desk　接待处

registration form　登记表

cashier　收银处

fill in/out　填写

dining room/hall　餐厅

basement　地下室

cloak room　行李房；存衣处

boutique　精品商场

suit　套装

tie　领导

mend　修补

attendant　服务员

desk clerk　值班服务员

rent　租金

bill　账单

management　管理、经验

price　价格

commission　佣金

market price　市价

price list　价目表

coin　硬币

exchange rate　汇率

bank draft　汇票

check/cheque　支票

interest　利息

tip　小费

reservation desk　预定处

cancel（cancellation）　取消

postpone　延期

pay　付款

luggage label　行李标签

record　记录

forecast 预报

expected 预计

arrival 到达

departure 离开

carrier 交通工具

method of payment 付款方式

status 情况

treatment 待遇

guarantee 保证

room rate 房价

special rate 特价

rack rate 对外价

net rate 净价

surcharge 服务费

prepaid 预付

government tax 政府税

advance deposit 押金

amendment 更改

pick up 接机

cooperate 合作

transportation 运输

remark 备注

black list 黑名单

no-smoking floor 非吸烟区

discount 折扣

nationality 国籍

permanent address 永久地址

valid 有效的

house use 内部使用

day use 半天租房

contract rate 合同价

room status 房态

room assignment 房间分配

rooming list 分房清单

safety deposit box 保险箱

skipper 逃账者

zip code 邮编

Address 地址

minimum charge 最低消费

rate sheets/tariff 价目表

night audit 夜核

high risk 欠账多的客人

COMP (complimentary) 免费

P.I.A (pay in cash) 已预付

on duty 值班

off duty 下班

bell service 行李服务

luggage store-room 行李寄存处

trunk dock 行李装卸处

baggage cart 行李车

label/tab 行李标签

hotel sticker 酒店标签

small baggage (luggage) 小行李

brief case 公事包

traveling bag 旅行袋

hand bag; grip sack 手提包

package 包裹

small trunk 小箱子

suit-case 手提箱

cosmetic case/toilet case 梳妆小提箱

suit bag 衣服袋

carton 纸盒

cardboard box 硬纸盒（箱）

shoulder bag 背囊（旅行背袋）

personal articles 自用物品

contraband 违禁物品

unaccompanied luggage 不随行物品

NO BUMPING/NO SHOOT 切勿投掷

NO NOT DROP 切勿坠落

NO NOT CRUSH 切勿压挤

USE NO HOOKS 勿用手钩

FRAGILE 易碎物品

CAUTION 小心

HANDLE WITH CARE 小心轻放

GLASS(WITH CARE) 小心玻璃

LIQUID 液体物品

INFLAMMABLE ERISHABLE 易燃物品

CORROSIVES 易腐物品

EXPLOSIVES 爆炸物品

strap already broken （束）带已断

POISON 毒品

KEEP DRY 勿受潮

KEEP UPRIGHT 勿倒置

DON'T TURN UPSIDE DOWN 切勿倒倾

break to pieces　敲碎

crush　压碎

smash　击碎

already strapped　已捆扎

rope already broken　绳已断

already baled　已打包

ordinary mail　平信

express telegram　加快电报

special dispatch　专电

registered fee　挂号邮资

postcard　明信片

accompanied/personal luggage　随身行李

exchange voucher　代金券

gross　总的

guest account　宾客帐户

corporate rate　协议价

expected arrival list　预抵客名单

guaranteed reservation　确保的预订

guaranteed no show　担保预订未到

double occupancy　重复入住

foreign exchange　外汇

adjacent room　临近房间

baby cot /crib　婴儿床

front of the house　客区

meeting package　会议包价

expected departure list　预离店名单

paid-out　付出的费用

rush room　赶房

time difference　时差

group leader　领队

DDD(domestic direct dialing)　国内直拨

guest history record　客史记录

welcome letter　欢迎信

reception logbook　前台交班本

average rate per guest　平均房价

guest ledger　客账

authorization code　授权号

petty cash　零用现金

extended　延长的

envelope　信封

transportation service　接送服务

complimentary　免费赠送

gloves　手套

cap　帽子

weather forecast　天气预报

fax　传真

mail / Post　邮件

message　信息

voice Mail　语音留言

newspaper　报纸

store room　储物间

flyer　传单

morning report　日报表

raise/lower the flag　升旗 / 降旗

group check in/out　团队抵 / 离店

scale　秤

post man　邮递员

no show　预订未到

stamp　邮票

letter　信件

log book　交班本

fax machine　传真机

high season　旺季

VC(Vacant room) 空房

DND (Do Not Disturb)　请勿打扰

OOO(Out of Order)　待修房

long stay　长住房

Housekeeping Department Vocabulary

room number　房间号码

room card　房卡

suite　套房

luxury suite　豪华套房

presidential suite　总统套房

business suite　商务套房

single room　单人间

double room　双人间（大床房）

standard room　标间（双床房）

three-bed room　三人间

deluxe king-size room　豪华大床房

sitting-room/living-room　起居室 ; 客厅

curtain　窗帘

clothes—hanger　衣架

pillow　枕头

pillow case　枕套

quilt　被子

cotton terry blanket　毛巾被

blanket　毛毯

sofa bed　沙发床

hard mattress　硬床垫

soft mattress　软床垫

laundry list　洗衣单

laundry bag　洗衣袋

sewing kit　针线包

towel　毛巾

towel rail/towel rack　毛巾架

shampoo　洗发水

conditioner　护发素

toothbrush　牙刷

toothpaste　牙膏

soap　香皂

tissues　面巾纸

toilet paper　卫生纸

comb　梳子

thermometer　温度计

washbasin　洗漱盆

bath tub　浴缸

stool　凳子

bench　条凳

sofa/settee　长沙发

sectional sofa　拼合沙发

bath towel　浴巾

face towel　小方巾

bath mat　地巾

shower cap　浴帽

bath robe　浴袍

hairdryer　吹风机

tap　水龙头

tea table　茶几

Tea trolley　活动茶几

night table/stand　床头柜

safety door hook　安全门

bed－head　床头

electric kettle　电热水壶

chips　薯片

slippers　拖鞋

folder　文具盒

writing paper　信纸

envelope　信封

wardrobe　衣柜

data line　数据线

peep hole　门镜猫眼

cloth hanger　衣架

lamp shade　灯杆

quilt cover　被罩

no smoking card　请勿吸烟卡

bed skirting　床裙

fax form　传真纸

scissors　剪刀

shoe basket　鞋筐

door stopper　门堵

ceiling　天花板

toilet bowl/pot　马桶

toilet water tank cover　马桶水箱盖

toilet board　马桶坐板

toilet seat　马桶盖

alarm clock　闹钟

wall picture　挂画

ball pen　圆珠笔

shoe shine mitt/paper　擦鞋布

razor /shaver　剃须刀

candy bottle　糖果盅

safety chain　安全链

bathroom scale　体重秤

tray　托盘

telephone　电话

mini bar mini　冰箱

cotton ball　棉球

shower head　喷头

tissue paper box　面布纸盒

note pad　变迁

carpet　便签

door handle　门把手

sanitary bag　卫生袋

water closet　抽水马桶

sponge　海绵

plug　插头

evening gown　睡袍

soap　香皂

soap dish　皂托

nail file　指甲锉

bath foam　沐浴露

socket　插座

two-pin socket　两相插座

temperature adjuster　温度调节器

mosquito incense　蚊香

electric kettle　电热水壶

rubber gloves　防护手套

shoe paper　擦鞋纸

tie　领带

perfume　香水

hair dryer/ 吹风筒

wall plate　壁上挂盘

Chinese painting　国画

writing desk　写字台

closet/wardrobe　壁橱

chest of drawer　五斗橱

screen　屏风

bedclothes　床上用品

switch　开关

bed room　卧室

twin beds　单人床

king size bed　双人床

bedside lamp　床头灯

sheer curtain　纱帘

vanity/dressing table　梳妆台

bed cover/bedspread　床罩

sheet　床单

drawer　抽屉

bedding　被褥

smoking set　烟具

light bulb　电灯泡

breakfast card　早餐卡

ashtray　烟灰缸

matches　火柴

tea　茶

coffee　咖啡

shoes board　鞋拔子

toilet/lavatory/washroom　卫生间

iron　熨斗

electric iron　电熨斗

ironing board　熨衣板

floor lamp　落地灯

table light　台灯

adapter　插头

extension code　接线板

transformer　变压器

chair　椅子

folding chair　折叠椅

swivel chair　转椅

wicker chair　藤椅

armchair　扶手椅

easy chair　安乐椅

windowsill　窗台

rocking chair　摇椅

trolley　工作车

mineral water　矿泉水

door knob　门把手

switch board　控制板

safety box　保险箱

bedside table　床头柜

door bell　门铃

door knob/door handle　门把

door knocker　门环

lock　锁

TV remote control　电视遥控器

rubbish bin　垃圾桶

flash light　手电筒

key hole　取电器

wall lamp　壁灯

air － conditioner　空调

refrigerator　冰箱

plant　植物

rubber mat　防滑垫

hook/peg　挂衣钩

hat rack　帽架

vase　花瓶

shower cap　浴帽

shower curtains　浴帘

wash Basin　面盆

bed pad　白拍

bed head board　床头板

shopping bag　购物袋

key insert　取电器

lock　门锁

sill　窗台

vase　花瓶

plunger　橡皮塞子

Shower curtain and rod　淋浴帘和架子

pot　冷水壶

soap dish　皂碟

clothes brush　衣刷

towel rail　毛巾架

wall paper　墙纸

arm chair　扶手椅

cup　茶杯

mug　口杯

mirror　镜子

bookcase　书橱

bookshelf　书架

radiator　暖气片

central heating　暖气

cushion　垫子

wall lamp　壁灯

electric fan　电扇

cushion　垫子

waste-paper basket　废纸篓

Venetian blind　百叶窗帘

shutters　百叶窗

running water　自来水

shower nozzle　喷头

shower/shower bath　淋浴

dressing table　梳妆台

balcony　阳台

bathmat　浴室防滑垫

ceiling　天花板

shower head　淋浴喷头

door mat　门前的擦鞋棕垫

wet vacuums　吸水机

rotary floor scrubber　吸水机

thermos　热水瓶

stain　污迹

uniform　制服

remove control　遥控器

restroom　卫生间

Food and Beverage Department Vocabulary

bowl　碗

chopsticks　筷子

spoon　汤匙；调羹

fork　叉子

napkin　餐巾

cork　软木塞

screw/bottle opener　开瓶器

corkscrew　螺丝开瓶器

wine opener　开瓶刀

appetizer　开胃菜

soup　汤

main course/entree　主菜

dessert　甜点

beverage/drink　酒水

juice　果汁

champagne flute　窄口香槟杯

champagne saucer　宽口香槟杯

red/white wine glass　红 / 白葡萄酒杯

old fashioned / rocks　古典杯

beer mug　扎啤杯

beer tumbler　啤酒杯

hi-Ball　饮料杯

Ice tongs　冰夹

cocktail strainer　过滤器

stirrer　调酒棒

straw　吸管

candle stand　烛台

chafing dish　热炉

oil & vinegar stand　油醋架

water pitcher　水壶

cutlery　刀具

glassware　杯具

cook　厨师

gin　金酒

tequila 龙舌兰

vodka 伏特加

rum 朗姆酒

cocktail 鸡尾酒

brandy 白兰地

whisky 威士忌

Spirit/liquor 烈酒

champagne 香槟酒

wine 葡萄酒

sugar 糖

cubic sugar 方糖

rock sugar 冰糖

ice cube 冰块

vermouth 苦艾酒

aniseed 大茴香酒

port 砵酒

sherry 雪莉酒

milk 牛奶

whole milk 全脂奶

spices 调味料

green tea 绿茶

Non-carbonated 非碳酸饮料

carbonated 碳酸饮料

water 水

soda water 苏打水；汽水

mineral water 矿泉水

purified water 纯净水

soft drink 不含酒精的饮料

cocoa 可可

Coca cola 可口可乐

Marinda 美年达

Sprite 雪碧

vegetables 蔬菜

lettuce 生菜

broccoli 西兰花

cauliflower 菜花

watercress 西洋菜

choisum 菜心

mushroom 蘑菇

carrot 红萝卜

turnip 白萝卜

radish 小白萝卜

asparagus 芦笋

bamboo shoot 竹笋

celery 西芹

spinach 菠菜

cucumber 黄瓜

eggplant 茄子

pumpkin 南瓜

lotus root 莲藕

potato 土豆

green Bean 绿豆角

green Pea 青豆

beans spouts 豆芽

bean curd 豆腐

chili 红辣椒

green Pepper 青椒

ginger 姜

garlic 蒜

leek 蒜苗

fruits 水果

apple 苹果

pear 梨

plum 李子

banana 香蕉

peach 桃

strawberry 草莓

cherry 樱桃

grape 葡萄

almond 杏仁

figs 无花果

kiwi 奇异果

watermelon 西瓜

honeydew melon 哈密瓜

persimmon 柿子

orange 橙子

mandarin orange 桔子

tangerine 柑橘

pomelo 柚子

pistachio 开心果

cashew nut 腰果

hazelnut 榛果

juniper 杜松子

avocado 牛油果

mango 芒果

olive 橄榄

lime 酸橙

lemon 柠檬

dragon fruit 火龙果

papaya 木瓜

durian 榴莲

rambutan 红毛丹

cumquat 小金桔

pomegranate 石榴

loquat 枇杷

mangosteen 山竹

guava 番石榴

carambola 杨桃

lemonade 柠檬水

meats 肉类

mutton 羊肉

vhicken 鸡肉

fuck 鸭肉

goose liver 鹅肝酱

vhicken Breast 鸡胸

vhicken Leg 鸡腿

vhicken Wing 鸡翅

turkey 火鸡

potatoes 土豆类

hash brown potato 土豆饼

mashed potato 土豆泥

baked potato 烤土豆

croquette potato 炸薯茸条

gratin potato 焗芝士

condiments 调味品

tabasco 辣椒水

mustard 芥末

ketchup 蕃茄酱

mayonnaise 蛋黄酱

maggi sauce 美极鲜酱油

soya sauce 酱油

vinegar 醋

red wine vinegar 红酒醋

salt 盐

pepper 胡椒

monosodium glutamate 味精

olive oil 橄榄油

brown sugar 黄糖

white sugar 白糖

peanut butter 花生酱

tartar sauce 蛋黄沙司

gravy sauce 肉汁

black pepper sauce 黑椒汁

mushroom sauce 蘑菇汁

onion sauce 洋葱汁

red wine sauce 红酒汁

sour cream 酸奶油

mint sauce 薄荷汁

horseradish 辣根汁

oyster sauce 蚝油汁

braised 烩／炖／焖

taste 味觉

oily 油的

bitter 苦的

hot 烫的

tender 嫩的

fat 肥的

greasy 油腻的

lean 瘦的

lightly 清淡的

rich 醇厚的

spicy 辣的

sour 酸的

sweet 甜的

salty 咸的

raw 生的

rare 二分熟

medium rare 三四分熟

medium 半熟

medium well 七八分熟

well-done 全熟

over-done 做得很老

pasta 面类

spaghetti 意细面条

penne 空心面

linguine 扁面条

fettuccine 扁平细面条

fusilli 螺丝面

cannelloni　肉馅卷

tagliatelle　干面条

rotelle　车轮粉

favioli　小方饺

farfalle　蝴蝶饺

lasagne　烤宽面条

ragatoni　波纹贝壳通心粉

bean thread noodle　米粉

rice vermicelli　米线

rice noodle　河粉

glass vermicelli　粉丝

egg noodle　鸡蛋面

won ton wrapper　馄饨皮

rice paper　米纸

soba　日式荞麦面

udon　日式乌冬面

cheese　芝士（干酪）

edam　荷兰干酪

emmental　瑞士多孔干酪

provolone　意大利熏干酪

mozzarella　意大利奶酪

ricotta　意大利乳清奶酪

feta　希腊羊奶干酪

mascarpone　意大利奶油乳酪

blue cheese　蓝纹奶酪

brie　法国咸味干乳酪

camembert　法国浓味软乳酪

parmesan　巴马干酪

gruyere　瑞士干奶酪

cheddar　英国切达干酪

roquefort　法国羊乳干酪

flatware　餐具

steak knife　牛扒刀

dinner knife　主刀

dinner fork　主叉

dinner spoon　主匙

salad knife　沙律刀

salad fork　沙律叉

dessert spoon　甜品匙

soup spoon　汤匙

bouillon spoon　汤匙

tea spoon　茶匙

ice tea spoon　长匙

demi-tasse spoon　小咖啡匙

butter knife　黄油刀

fish knife　鱼刀

fish fork　鱼叉

oyster fork　牡蛎叉

snail tong　田螺夹

snail fork　田螺叉

cheese knife　芝士刀

dim sum　点心

soybean milk　豆浆

rice gruel　稀饭

porridge　粥

deep-fried dough stick　油条

sesame seed pastry　芝麻饼

steamed stuffed bun　肉包

dumpling　水饺

pickle　泡菜

steamed carp　清蒸鲤鱼

sweet and sour croaker　糖醋黄花鱼

stewed turtle　清炖甲鱼

stir-fried eel with brown sauce　干烧黄鳝

sweet and sour pork chops　糖醋排骨

fried crisp pork　脆皮锅酥肉

plain sauté shrimps　清炒滑虾仁

chicken cubes with chili peppers　辣子鸡丁

pork shreds with fish seasoning　鱼香肉丝

smoked crisp fish　烟熏酥鱼

special spicy chicken　怪味鸡

noodles Sichuan style　担担面

fried rice YangZhou style　扬州炒饭

fried soybean scum roll　炸响铃

dongpo pork　东坡肉

hangzhou roast chicken　杭州烤鸡

cold duck web　拌鸭掌

three-delicious-in gredient soup　三鲜汤

sichuan chicken cube-lets　宫保鸡丁

roast chicken　烧鸡

chicken chops　白斩鸡

chicken in casserole　沙锅鸡

shrimps fritters　炸虾球

fried rice with shrimps　虾仁炒饭

shrimp fritter 面拖虾

crab meat with egg 芙蓉蟹肉

fried crab meat 炒蟹肉

broccoli with crab meat 蟹肉芥兰

wine preserved crab 醉蟹

mushrooms with crab meat 蟹扒鲜菇

sweet corn with crab meat 蟹肉粟米

plate 底盘

dish 碟子

butter plate 黄油碟

knife 刀

cooktail fork 开胃叉；海鲜叉

salt shaker 盐瓶

pepper shaker 胡椒瓶

measure for liquor 量酒器

bus boy 传菜员

menu carid 菜单

table card 餐牌

butter and bread separator 黄油和面包刀

glass 玻璃杯

cup 耳杯

highball 海波杯

goblet 高脚水杯

mug 马克杯

mixing glass 调酒杯

ballon glass 大红酒杯

coupette / margarita 玛格利特杯

Irish coffee glass 爱尔兰咖啡杯

decanter 沉淀杯

juice glass 果汁杯

shaker 摇酒器

wine cooler stand 酒桶架

ice bucket 冰桶

wine cooler 冰酒桶

punch bowl 香槟桶

bread basket 面包蓝

wine Basket 红酒蓝

holloware 器皿类

tableware 餐具

cooker 厨具

table 餐桌

electric blender 电动搅拌机

bar spoon 吧匙

jigger 量酒杯

tray 托盘

coaster 杯垫

toothpick 牙签

cognac 干邑白兰地酒

beer 啤酒

coffee 咖啡

latte 拿铁

mocha 摩卡

Americano 美式咖啡

cappuccino 卡布奇诺

flat white/white coffee 白咖啡（牛奶咖啡）

black coffee 黑咖啡（不加牛奶的）

con panna 康宝莱

macchiato 玛奇朵

Viennese 维也纳咖啡

espresso 意式浓缩咖啡

instant coffee 速溶咖啡

tea 茶

jasmine tea 茉莉花茶

black tea 红茶

scented tea 花果茶

Tie Guanyin 铁观音

Oolong tea 乌龙茶

strong tea 浓茶

weak tea 淡茶

Lipton Teas 立顿茶

Pepsi-Cola 百事可乐

7-UP 七喜

Fanta 芬达

shallot 葱

onion 洋葱

artichoke 朝鲜蓟

water Spinach 空心菜

enoki 金针菇

green Kale 芥兰

beet Root 甜菜根

sweet Corn 玉米

baby Corn 小玉米

savoy Cabbage 卷心菜

chinese Cabbage 大白菜

herbs　香草

parsley　西芹

coriander　香菜

lemon Grass　柠檬草

tarragon　龙蒿叶

basil　紫苏

thyme　百里香

horseradish　辣根

rosemary　迷迭香

sage　鼠尾草

savory　香薄荷

anise　大茴香

star Anise　八角

tamarind　罗望子

cumin　孜然

spring onion　葱

chive　韭菜

cinnamon　肉桂

five spice power　五香粉

nutmeg　肉豆蔻

poppy seed　罂粟籽

saffron　藏红花粉

seafood　海鲜

fish　鱼

snapper　鲷鱼

mackerel　马鲛鱼

herring　青鱼

trout　鳟鱼

pike　梭子鱼

carp　鲤鱼

eel　鳝鱼

snail　蜗牛

snake　蛇

scallop　带子

grouper　石斑鱼

perch　鲈鱼

sea bass　黑鲈

tuna fish　金枪鱼

halibut　比目鱼

sardine　沙丁鱼

sole fish　左口鱼

caviare　鱼子酱

abalone　鲍鱼

shark's fin　鱼翅

lobster　龙虾

salmon　三文鱼

sashimi　生鱼片

shrimp　虾仁

clam　文蛤

prawn　虾

oyster　生蚝

cod fish　鳕鱼

mussel　青口

pork　猪肉

kidney　腰子

pork Knuckle　咸猪手

pork loin　猪柳

pork hoof　猪蹄

beef　牛肉

veal　小牛肉

lamb chop　羊排

sausage　香肠

ham　火腿

bacon　烟肉

rabbit　兔

pigeon　鸽子

venison　鹿肉

carpaccio　生牛肉片

ox-tongue　牛舌

ox-tail　牛尾

quail egg　鹌鹑蛋

schnitzel　炸肉排

pork tripe　猪肚

pork intestine　猪大肠

chili sauce　辣椒汁

whipped cream　泡沫奶油

butter　黄油

margarine　人造黄油

jam　果酱

preserve　果酱

marmalade　橘子酱

lemon butter sauce　柠檬黄油汁

honey　蜂蜜

cookery　烹饪

steamed　蒸

boiled　煮

scrambled　炒蛋

fried　油炸的

deep-fried　炸

barbecued　烤烧

grilled　扒

stewed　炖

smoked　烟熏

dry-sauteed　干煸

pan-fried　煎

sauteed　炒

baked　烘烤

stuffed　填充

roast　烤

salted　盐腌的

mixed　混合的

assorted　什锦的

cutting method　切割方式

sliced　切片

diced　切丁

shredded　切丝

boneless　去骨的

minced　切碎的

bakery　面包类

shite toast　白吐司

whole wheat Toast　全麦吐司

muffin　小松饼

soft Roll　软包

hard Roll　硬包

doughnut　甜麦圈

french bread　法包

rye bread　裸麦包

cake　蛋糕类

mousse　慕斯；奶油冻

pie　派

pudding　布丁

parfait　芭菲冻糕

strudel　卷

cheese cake　烤芝士蛋糕

tiramisu　意大利芝士蛋糕

buffet　自助餐

A la carte　零点

doily paper　花纸垫

tissue paper　餐巾纸

note paper　便笺纸

match　火柴

lighter　打火机

cigarette　香烟

cigar　雪茄

news paper　报纸

magazine　杂志

podium　讲台

baby chair　婴儿椅

parking ticket　停车票

bill　账单类

check folder　账单夹

pay Cash　付现金

vip Card　贵宾卡

discount card　打折卡

sign Bill　签单

charge to room　挂房账

one Check　一张单

separate check　分单

chinaware　瓷器类

dinner plate　主盘

salad plate　沙拉盘

dessert plate　甜品盘

B.B plate　面包盘

oval plate　椭圆盘

egg cup　蛋盅

creamer　奶盅

sauce boat　汁斗

coffee pot　咖啡壶

tea pot　茶壶

sugar bowl　糖盅

coffee cup　咖啡杯

tea cup　茶杯

soup cup　汤杯

soup cup underliner　汤杯底碟

cereal bowl　麦片碗

carving knife　切肉刀

carving fork　切肉叉

salad tong　沙拉夹

dessert tong　甜品夹

serving fork　服务叉

serving spoon　服务匙

soup ladle　汤勺

cake server　饼铲

sauce ladle　汁勺

lemon squeezer　柠檬夹

wooden pepper mill　木胡椒瓶

wonton　馄饨

dessert　甜点

sandwich　三明治

noodles　面条

longevity noodles　长寿面条

noodle soup　汤面

fried eggs　煎蛋

boiled eggs　水煮蛋

poultry　家禽

sea slugs with brown sauce　红烧海参

sea slugs with chicken cream　鸡绒海参

sea slugs with crisp rice　海参锅巴

mixed sea slugs　什锦海参

shrimp eggs & sea slugs　虾子海参

fried prawns with brown sauce　红烧明虾

prawn cutlets　炸明虾

broiled Prawns with chili sauce　烧明虾

prawns with spiced salt　椒盐明虾

fried prawns sections　煎明虾段

broiled lobster with chili sauce　干烧龙虾

grilled lobster　铁扒龙虾

broiled lobster　烤龙虾

bisque of lobster　龙虾浓汤

fried shrimps with cashew nuts　腰果虾仁

fried shrimps with bamboo shoots　笋炒虾仁

fried shrimps with green peas　青豆虾仁

fried shrimps with tomato sauce　茄汁虾仁

shrimps saute　清炒虾仁

shrimps with bean curd　虾仁豆腐

shrimp balls with tomato sauce　茄汁虾球

fried shrimps with crisp rice　锅巴虾仁

fried shrimps with bean-leaf　豆苗虾仁

salted shrimps　盐焗虾

phoenix tail prawns　凰尾虾

sauteed shrimps　油爆虾

fresh shrimps with fermented soya beans
豆豉虾仁

fried shrimps omelet　虾仁炒蛋

prawn balls & broccoli　玉兰虾球

fried shrimp & pig kidney　炒虾腰

fried shrimp balls　炒虾球

Bar Vocabulary

wine list　酒水单

night club　夜总会

distillation　蒸馏

fermentation　发酵

bar cashier　酒吧收银员

order wine　点酒

ingredient　原料；材料

concoction　调制

bisquit　百事吉

hennessy　轩尼诗

courvoisier　拿破仑

martell　马爹利

remy martell　人头马

scotch whiskey　苏格兰威士忌

Irish whiskey　爱尔兰威士忌

canadian whiskey　加拿大威士忌

bourbon whiskey　波本威士忌

American whiskey　美国威士忌

red wine　红葡萄酒

white wine　白葡萄酒

rose wine　玫瑰葡萄酒

carlsberg　嘉士伯（丹麦）

heineken　喜力（荷兰）

guinness　键力士（爱尔兰）

coors　库斯（美国）

pabst blue ribbon　蓝带（美国）

budweiser　百威（美国）

suntory　三得利（日本）

tiger　虎牌（新加坡）

tsingtao　青岛（中国）

good tastes 高品质

crisp 酸爽

earthy 土香

easy 易入口

flowery 花香

fresh 鲜酸

fruity 水果味

honey 蜜糖味

oaky 橡木味

wine steward 酒水服务员

with-dinner drink 佐餐酒

chilled 冰镇的

can 听；罐

sommelier 斟酒服务员

pay the bill 买单；结账

appetite 食欲

garnish 装饰

VS(very special) 2 年以上的干邑

VSOP（very superior old pale）

4 年以上的干邑

XO（extra old） 5 年以上的干邑

Extra A 6 年以上的干邑

Brut 低糖的香槟酒（小于 15 克糖 / 升）

Sec 中等甜度的香槟酒（17-35 克糖 / 升）

Demi-sec 半干 / 半甜香槟酒（33-55 克糖 / 升）

Doux 甜香槟（大于 50 克糖 / 升）

extra dry 特干的酒

dry 干的酒

medium dry 半干的酒

sweet 甜的酒

singapore sling 新加坡司令

gin & tonic 金汤力

Irish coffee 爱尔兰咖啡

blue hawaii 蓝色夏威夷

cube Libre 自由古巴

blue diablo 蓝色妖姬

tequila sunrise 特基拉日出；龙舌兰日出

margarita 玛格丽特

bloody mary 血腥玛丽

screw driver 渐入佳境

bad tastes 低品质

yeasty 起泡沫的

vinegary 酸溜溜的

acidic 过酸的

corky 霉塞味

rough 粗糙

cloudy 浑浊的

hollow 中虚

empty 中空

Recreation and Entertainment Department Vocabulary

beauty salon /hair dresser 美容美发沙龙

Recreation center 康乐部

gym center 健身中心

sauna and massage center 桑拿和按摩中心

facility 设施

massage 按摩

foot massage 足浴

healthcare massage 保健按摩

weight reduction 减肥

tuina 推拿

acupuncture 针灸

traditional Chinese massage 中式按摩

hot stone therapy 热石疗法

pedicure 修脚

manicure 修手

cupping /jar therapy 火罐

scraping /guasha treatment 刮痧

bowling 保龄球

rugby 英式橄榄球

table tennis 乒乓球

play football 踢足球

play basketball 打篮球

play billiards 打台球

play volleyball 打排球

go jogging 慢跑

go to bars 去酒吧

listen to music 听音乐

playing DVD 看 DVD

singing Karaoke 唱歌

playing cards 玩扑克

lifting dumbbell　举哑铃

show　节目

upright bike　立式自行车

recumbent bike　卧式自行车

seated leg curl　腿曲伸

reversed deck　蝴蝶机

leg extension　腿伸展

treadmill　跑步机

strength equipment　无氧器械

push/pull　推 / 拉

foot care/massage　足疗

neck care　肩颈

aerobics rooms　健美操室

earphone　耳机

cross trainer　旋转机

stepper　台阶机

facial care　美容

skin care　护肤

facial cleanser　洗面奶

makeup remover　卸妆

whitening　美白

facial mask/masque　面膜

eye mask　眼膜

(deep) pore cleanser　去黑头

exfoliating scrub　去死皮

go dancing　跳舞

go boating　划船

go fishing　钓鱼

go camping　宿营

go hunting　打猎

go skating　滑冰

go skiing　滑雪

do boxing　拳击

play cards　打扑克

play tennis　打网球

play golf　打高尔夫球

play badminton　打羽毛球

on-sale　减价销售

bargain　廉价品

watch movie　看电影

science fiction　科幻小说

western　西部片

romance　爱情片

horror　恐怖片

war　战争片

action　动作片

musical　音乐剧

comedy　喜剧

newspaper　报纸

magazine　杂志

price list　价目表

sauna room　干蒸房

throwaway　宣传册

sneaker　运动鞋

cardio equipment　有氧器械

swimming pool　游泳池

stretch mat　健身毯

relaxation lounge　休息大厅

treatment room　按摩室

golf practice　高尔夫练习

locker key　更衣柜钥匙

wellness ball　健身球

Other Vocabulary

visa　签证

exit visa　出境签证

transit visa　过境签证

travel permit　居留签证

health certificate　健康证书

entry visa　入境签证

gift shop　礼品店

Spring　春天

Summer　夏天

Autumn　秋天

Winter　冬天

Monday　星期一

Tuesday　星期二

Wednesday　星期三

Thursday　星期四

Friday　星期五

Saturday　星期六

Sunday　星期天

Valentine's day　情人节

Easter　复活节

Thanksgiving day　感恩节

Christmas eve　平安夜

Christmas　圣诞节

April fool's day　愚人节

Father's day　父亲节

Mother's day　母亲节

see a doctor　就诊；看医生

make an appointment　预约

have a cold　感冒

have a headache　头疼

have a cough　咳嗽

have a diarrhea　腹泻

have a runny nose　流鼻涕

have a fever　发烧

have a stomachache　胃疼

have insomnia　失眠

sleeping pill　安眠药

city tour　市内游

quarantine station　检疫站

quarantine　检疫

C.I.A(cash in advance) 大使馆

embassy　大使馆

consulate　领事馆

souvenir　纪念品

January　一月

February　二月

March　三月

April　四月

May　五月

June　六月

July　七月

August　八月

September　九月

October　十月

November　十一月

December　十二月

Spring festival　春节

The lantern festival　元宵节

New year's day　元旦

Tomb-sweeping day　清明节

Labour day/May day　劳动节

Mid-autumn day　中秋节

National day　国庆节

patient 病人

sneezing　打喷嚏

faint/dizzy　头晕

toothache　牙疼

vomit　呕吐

blood pressure　血压

appendicitis　阑尾炎

anxiety　焦虑

infection　传染；感染

take the medicine　喝药

allergic　过敏

References

[1] 赵丽. 新编饭店实用英语听说教程 [M]. 北京：清华大学出版社，2009.

[2] 钱嘉颖，吴云. 酒店英语 [M]. 上海：上海交通大学出版社，2011.

[3] 舒飞燕，王纪玉，杨燕. 酒店实用英语 [M]. 吉林：吉林大学出版社，2017.

[4] 朱华. 酒店英语（视听版）[M]. 北京：北京大学出版社，2014.

[5] 金丽. 邮轮服务英语 [M]. 大连：大连海事大学出版社，2016.

[6] 杨杰. 邮轮实用英语 [M]. 北京：对外经济贸易大学出版社，2010.

[7] 董树国. 葡萄酒事典 [M]. 北京：化学工业出版社，2014.

[8] 傅生生. 酒水服务与酒吧管理 [M]. 辽宁：东北财经大学出版社，2014.

[9] 潘桂君. 酒店服务英语 [M]. 北京：中国商业出版社，2014.

[10] 姜文宏. 饭店服务英语 [M]. 北京：高等教育出版社，2015.

[11] 丁国声. 酒店英语 [M]. 上海：上海交通大学出版社，2012.

[12] 黄雅丹，邵笑宇. 万用生活英语 [M]. 大连：大连理工大学出版社，2012.

[13] 杨石云. 酒店英语 [M]. 西安：西北工业大学出版社，2013.

[14] 艾丽丽. 宾馆餐饮英语急用话题 124 个 [M]. 北京：中国宇航出版社，2007.

[15] 王正元. 迎宾英语 [M]. 北京：知识出版社，2002.

[16] 韩敏. 酒店服务英语 [M]. 北京：中国铁道出版社，2013.

[17] 陈晶晶. 餐饮英语口语脱口而出 [M]. 北京：机械工业出版社，2011.

[18] 司爱侠，陈红美. 饭店酒店管理英语实用教程 [M]. 天津：南开大学出版社，2008.

[19] 陈的非，刘朝晖. 饭店实用英语 [M]. 北京：机械工业出版社，2008.

[20] 王青，沈建龙. 酒店英语实训教程 [M]. 北京：中国人民大学出版社，2016.

[21] 王丽华. 酒店情景英语 [M]. 北京：中国旅游出版社，2016.